Being Chinese

Being Chinese

Voices from the Diaspora

Wei Djao

The University of Arizona Press

Tucson

The University of Arizona Press
© 2003 The Arizona Board of Regents
First printing
All rights reserved
♾ This book is printed on acid-free, archival-quality paper.
Manufactured in the United States of America

08   07   06   05   04   03   6   5   4   3   2   1

Library of Congress Cataloging-in-Publication Data
Djao, Wei, 1943–
Being Chinese : voices from the diaspora / Wei Djao.
p. cm.
Includes bibliographical references and index.
ISBN 0-8165-2302-9 (Paper : alk. paper)
1. Chinese — Foreign countries. I. Title.
DS732.D45 2003
305.895′1–dc21

2003001361

British Library Cataloguing-in-Publication Data
A catalogue record for this book is available from the British Library.

In loving memory of
my parents, Yen Shu-Jen and Djao Sing-Ming,
and
my parents-in-law, Rosy Wing and Steven Sun-Hon Chan

Contents

I | The Chinese Diaspora

II | Voices from the Diaspora

III Being Chinese in the Diaspora

Figures

Preface

On the last day of a very pleasant stay in Yogyakarta, central Java, several years ago, our tour guide took us to her office to confirm our international flight out of Indonesia the next day. On the way, she mentioned that the agency owner, Mrs. Kala M., would probably be at prayer, because it was just about noon then. As we made sure that travel arrangements for the next day were all in order, Kala finished praying and came out to greet us. After an exchange of pleasantries and after she had learned that my family and I were Chinese from North America, she simply said that she could not speak Chinese well. That was the first hint at her Chinese ancestry; her employee, our tour guide, had no inkling about this until then. Our guide only knew that her boss was a devout Muslim from Sumatra who happened to have a lighter skin color.

In the course of our conversation, Kala revealed that her family, originally from Fujian Province, had been in Bangka, Sumatra, Indonesia, for about seven generations. According to her, there were so many Chinese in Bangka in the past that whole villages were Chinese-speaking. Her father's grandmother was a *Hakka* (a subethnic group of the Han; see chapter 22). Kala's father could speak Chinese, but she could say only a few words. She declined to say them in front of us, claiming that it was village speech. She married a Javanese. Both she and her husband studied in the Netherlands and could speak Dutch fluently. In fact they still speak Dutch to each other sometimes. One of Kala's sisters married a full-blooded Chinese from Bangka, and they now live in Jakarta. Her father at one time told her that once the blood of a merchant was in you, you would always be a merchant. Kala knew that the merchant's blood was in her.

This rather unexpected encounter with Kala stirred up my curiosity. I was unable to ascertain whether she was *peranakan* (offspring of Chinese and native Indonesian marriage) or Muslim Chinese. That was not quite as intriguing as how it came about that someone so thoroughly acculturated in another way of life still retained an awareness of her Chinese ancestry. Obviously, it was a self-perception that she did not broadcast to the world every day; nonetheless, it was genuine and a source of self-respect.

That curiosity lingered, and the only way I could satisfy it was to ask people of Chinese ancestry living in non-Chinese societies how they were Chinese. To understand that question and its answers, it would be necessary to hear them describe how they live. This was how I started on this journey that took me to various countries and — this is the best part of my quest — the far more enchanting inner landscapes of the hearts of those who graciously answered my questions.

As I listened to my interviewees, their descriptions of life experiences and their sense of being Chinese struck familiar chords in my own mind. My father was born in Nanchang, Jiangxi Province, China. My mother, my siblings, and I were all born in Shanghai. Our family moved to Hong Kong in the 1950s, and then immigrated to Canada in the 1960s under circumstances very different from those of earlier Chinese settlers in North America. By the 1970s I realized that no matter what my birthplace, education, or other accidents of life were, I had crossed the invisible line from being Chinese to being Chinese overseas, that is, an ethnic Chinese living in a non-Chinese society. I never liked the term "ethnic Chinese" and still bristle at it. But I came to embrace the legacy of endurance and bravery left behind by the early Chinese immigrants who often lived the life of the bachelor community, and worked in the mines, railway construction, laundries, plantations, grocery stores, restaurants, and in other occupations too menial for the dominant groups of various societies. My biological ancestors did not do these things, but my ancestors in the new land did, and I was proud of them. Moreover, since my daughter is a fourth-generation Chinese Canadian, this is her heritage in the full meaning of the word. It is fitting, therefore, that a collective tribute is paid to all the ancestors of the Chinese diaspora in the words of their descendants. They are descendants in both the literal and figurative senses because many, many Chinese migrants to different parts of the world in the period 1842–1949 died without issue.

The narrators really create the book. Without them this book could not have been written. My heartfelt gratitude goes to each one of them. The opinions and views given in the narratives are those of the people I interviewed. My interpretation and analysis are in part 3. It must be emphasized that the narrators and I do not necessarily agree with each other's ideas or conceptual frameworks. All the same, it was an immense pleasure and an inestimable honor for me to listen to their experiences and thoughts as they opened their hearts and minds to me.

There were other Chinese overseas whom I interviewed but whose life stories are not included in this book. I am deeply grateful to them too because each one of them enriched my understanding of the phenomenon of the Chinese diaspora.

Altogether writing this book has been a delightful experience. However, I am sure my spouse, Tony Chan, and daughter, Lian, might have wondered at times what madness possessed me to be chasing interviews in the far corners of the world. They were with me when the taxi driver got lost in the bewildering traffic of Jakarta. They trooped along halfway across London on the hottest August day on record in forty years. They drove me in search of Chemainus up Vancouver Island when all the water of the Pacific Ocean seemed to be dumped on us. They drank endless cups of tea in Singapore while I tried to interview yet one more person. It is therefore very much a family project and, on their part, truly one of patience and dedication.

I would like to thank North Seattle Community College for granting me a sabbatical leave during the spring 2000 quarter. It was spent in revising the curriculum of two courses: Pacific Asia and the Global Society. Some of the material I found then is incorporated into chapter 1 "Leaving China: A Brief History of Emigration" and chapter 23 "Being Chinese Overseas."

Many other people have given immeasurable assistance. I thank my many colleagues and friends who assisted me in my research, read

various iterations of the manuscript, and offered invaluable sugges-
tions: Jerome Chen, Edith Wollin, Adrienne Chan, Steve Wong, Mar-
cia Barton, Rose Wu Liang, Doreen Indra, Hayne Wai, Bobby Siu,
Rochelle de la Cruz, and Dia Mamatis.

I am grateful to the University of Arizona Press and Dr. Christine
Szuter, Director, for their interest and support. Dr. Yvonne Reineke's
helpful guidance is particularly appreciated. Nancy Arora, Anne
Keyl, Melanie Mallon, Gilda Guerry-Aguilar, and their staff provided
the best professional editorial services possible. I would also like to
express my appreciation for the constructive criticisms provided by
the two reviewers selected by the publisher.

My sister Irene Chu wrote the Chinese calligraphy of the book
title for which I am both proud and grateful.

Finally, my loving thanks to Tony and Lian for being with me
always.

Introduction

The Chinese Overseas

Cellist Yo-Yo Ma, martial arts stars Michelle Yeoh and the late Bruce Lee, former president of Singapore Lee Kuan Yew, architect I.M. Pei, business tycoons Lien Sioe Liong (Sudono Salim) and Mochtar Riady (Li Wenzheng), Hollywood actor Anna May Wong, orchestra conductor Helen Quack, and entrepreneur Aw Boon Haw (Hu Wenhu) of Tiger Balm fame all have one thing in common. They are part of the Chinese diaspora. Yet besides these famous people, the world knows little about large numbers of Chinese outside of China. Estimated at nearly 37 million in 1990, they are scattered over 136 countries (Poston, Mao, and Yu 1994).

In this book twenty-two Chinese living and working outside of China tell us something about their lives and what it means to be Chinese. They are the people of the Chinese diaspora whose ancestors came from China. They were born and raised, or have lived most of their lives, outside of China. They are the *huayi,* the descendants of Chinese, referred to as the "Chinese overseas" in this book. This book is not about the famous people. It is about ordinary men and women doing ordinary things. For this very reason it is fascinating. The life stories told in this book are centered on two questions:

- How do the Chinese overseas live?
- How are they Chinese?

This book lets the Chinese overseas speak for themselves. In their own voices, men and women of Chinese ancestry describe their experiences living in Australia, Canada, Cuba, Germany, India, Indonesia, Malaysia, Mexico, the Netherlands, New Zealand, Peru, the Philippines, Singapore, the United Kingdom, the United States, and Zimbabwe. Many who tell their stories have roots, several generations deep, in their countries of residence. They let the reader take a look from the inside: How do the Chinese overseas in different countries feel, think, and act? And how do they see themselves as Chinese in the world?

In a sense, this is a personal book. It delves into the feelings of being Chinese. It bares the yearnings, disappointments, despair, aspirations, and triumph buried in the inner recesses of the hearts of the Chinese overseas. Yet these qualities are also the "stuff" that makes up the universal human condition. The Chinese overseas express in some distinctive patterns what they have in common with all humanity. What emerges is a picture of the Chinese overseas who are unequivocally different from and yet, at times, subtly or astonishingly similar to the people in China.

Several narrators in the book are of mixed ancestry; a few do not even look Chinese. But appearance is deceiving. As shown in the book, being Chinese is a state of mind and a feeling. The sentiment is at times vigorous, at other times fragile, and quite often deeply sustaining to those who feel it. Such a feeling is not jingoistic nationalism, for it transcends political allegiance, as many in the book will be only too ready to emphasize. They are not pro–People's Republic of China or pro–Republic of China in Taiwan. The feeling is one of identification with a place, a history, some elements of Chinese culture, a few motivating and guiding principles, or simply an awareness of whence they came. Their identity of being Chinese, and the elements of Chinese culture they have inherited and spread around the world, make up the global heritage that they in turn give to the world. Such a heritage needs to be recorded and cherished. That is the purpose of this book.

This book has three parts. Part 1 sets out a brief history of Chinese emigration.

Part 2 is the heart of the book. People of Chinese ancestry—from Asia, Africa, the Americas, Europe, and Oceania—in different walks of life tell their life stories and explain what it is like being Chinese. Each narrative is vivid and personal, revealing to the reader their experiences, thoughts, and feelings. There is no claim that these twenty-two individuals represent or speak for all the Chinese overseas. What they present is life in the diaspora as experienced by them, for the reader to savor and enjoy.

Part 3 is a discussion of the two questions posed in this project: How do the Chinese overseas live, and how are they Chinese? Findings of this study challenge the common view about Chinese identity in the diaspora.

It should be noted that China is a multiethnic society consisting of fifty-six nationalities (ethnic categories) today. The largest ethnic category is the Han, who make up over 93 percent of China's population. The narrators all have Han ancestry.

I use the Pinyin system of romanization for names of people and places in this book. The only exceptions are a few terms unique to some dialects, in which case they are romanized according to the local dialect pronunciation.

The Research Process

The narratives in this book are based on interviews conducted over a period of three and a half years. The narrators were selected because they were willing to talk about their lives and to explain how they were Chinese. The objective criteria in the selection process were 1) each narrator must either have been born outside of China, or have lived overseas most of his or her life; and 2) each narrator must have ancestors who migrated from China between 1842 and 1949. Consideration was also given to the narrators' geographical locations in the Chinese diaspora. All the continents where the Chinese immigrated are included. However, it is regrettable that people from many places with a long and rich history of Chinese immigration could not all be included.

The selection of narrators was not random as it should have been if it were a survey. Hence, there is no attempt to generalize from a small group to all the Chinese overseas living around the world. This is a case study in which a small number of Chinese overseas from different parts of the world describe how they live, how they feel about being Chinese, and how, in some instances, these ideas and sentiments have come about.

The goal of a case study is not to make statistical generalizations, as from a sample to a population or universe. Rather it is to expand theoretical statements: to elaborate on the relationships between factors (for example, ethnicity and identity), and to elucidate the structure or formation process of that relationship. In other words, the case study as a research method seeks to produce "analytical generalizations" (Yin 1984:21). The observations presented in this book will help elucidate some aspects of how a people in diaspora live and how they see themselves. These observations may also clarify the relationships between existence and consciousness that have always intrigued social scientists.

The two basic research questions of the study—How do the Chinese overseas live, and how are they Chinese?—were put to each interviewee. A set of previously prepared questions and statements was used to explain the research questions or to probe specific topics. Generally the narrators simply told their life stories and described their views and feelings about being Chinese. It is important to note that each interviewee was asked two questions, but the answer, more often than not, was one. Many narrators talked about how they lived and how they were Chinese in the same breath. They described how they were Chinese by describing how they lived. Or vice versa. I seemed to be separating real-life experiences into categories that might not have made sense at all to the interviewees who were answering the questions.

The narratives varied greatly in length because some narrators were better storytellers or more forthcoming about the details of their lives. Others, even with probing questions, had less recall of details. Some of the interviewees had a lot to say about being Chinese. Obviously aspects of being Chinese and living in non-Chinese societies were something that they had often thought about, or perhaps talked about with others previously. My invitation to them to answer some questions was simply the lifting of a floodgate. They had much to share. It is for these reasons, I believe, that the narratives vary in terms of the depth of feelings.

I conducted all the interviews in Chinese (Mandarin or Guang-zhou dialect) or in English. I recorded them on audiotapes. I transcribed the recorded interviews and rendered them into narratives with stylistic editing. Neither additional facts nor interpretations were inserted into the narratives. Any necessary explanation or clarification is given in parentheses following the term in question, or in a note.

As this book is not a history of the Chinese diaspora, it does not attempt to present the histories of the Chinese overseas in various immigrant societies. Such books already exist (see Zhu 1956; Chen 1991; Zhu 1994; Pan 1998; and others about individual societies). This book, therefore, cannot offer any analysis of differences among the immigrant societies.

I

The Chinese Diaspora

1 Leaving China

A Brief History of Emigration

Evidence of Early Emigration

The Chinese have had a history of going abroad for thousands of years. The earliest mention of China's neighbors overseas is in the *Book of Poetry*, the world's earliest anthology of poems. The most ancient poem in the collection is a hymn, entitled "The Rise of Shang," that was composed probably in the year 1713 BCE. It glorifies the ancestors of the Shang rulers. One of them, Xiang Tu, is celebrated in the hymn as a martial leader of renown such that vassals "from overseas" would obey him (*Book of Poetry* 1993:750; see the appendix for a list of China's dynasties). This suggests contact with people in faraway places.

The Shang dynasty was at its peak during the reign of King Wuding (1328–1263 BCE). Many large oracle bones of his time were excavated from the Shang tombs in the present-day north-central Henan Province. The oracle bones are of particular importance in the history of Chinese civilization because they are the earliest records of the Chinese writing system. During the Shang period, oracle bones were tools of divination. Questions about the future, such as the predictions of weather and hunting or military expeditions, were inscribed on tortoise shells or shoulder bones of cattle. The shells of the giant tortoise of King Wuding's time came from around the Malay Peninsula. From the Shang royal tombs were also bones of other animals: elephants from India, tapir from tropical Malaysia, bears from the Wusuli River at the border between northeastern China and Russia, and wolf from Northern Asia. Moreover, buried in the Shang tombs were pieces of jade, which came from the present-day Xinjiang Uyghur Autonomous Region in China's northwest, and sea shells, which came from China's seas to the east and were used as currency at that time. These findings show that even three or four thousand years ago people were traveling long distances. If visitors would bring things from afar, it would also be likely that Chinese would be going to these places (Zhu 1956:1–2).

Even Kong Fuzi (meaning Master Kong, 551–479 BCE, popularly known in the West[1] by the latinized name of Confucius), a teacher and a philosopher who has shaped Chinese culture for the last 2,500 years, seemed to be enticed by the prospect of going abroad at one time. Kong Fuzi did not hesitate to include the poor among his students. His teachings were later recorded by his followers in the *Confucian Analects*. It describes how the master, weary that his teaching was not heeded by the rulers of the fragmented Zhou dynasty (circa 1122–256 BCE), one time said that since his principles could not be put into practice, he would like to ride on a raft and go overseas (*Confucian Analects* 5:7). This suggests that in Kong Fuzi's lifetime there were already people who went abroad, thus making it a plausible option for him. The *Confucian Analects* certainly provides the earliest recorded aspiration of emigration from China. Parenthetically, while some people in China may feel disdain toward the Chinese overseas for being less culturally Chinese, the master whose teaching is at the foundation of Chinese culture for the last 2,500 years did not find living abroad such an unworthy idea!

China was unified by the first emperor, Qin Shihuang, in 221 BCE. The first recorded emigration by the Chinese was under his auspices. The book *Shiji (Historical Records)* by Sima Qian (circa 145 BCE) describes two voyages led by Xu Fu. Xu sailed eastward with several thousand boys and girls in order to find the herb of immortality for the emperor. According to Chinese folklore and official histories of a later dynasty, the place Xu Fu and his followers reached was Japan. Japanese historians are generally of the view that a first wave of Chinese immigrants arrived in Japan before the Qin period and another wave during the Qin (Zhu 1994:37). Sea voyages would be possible, but a more likely route would be through the Korean peninsula. Emigration to Korea and Japan during the Qin dynasty (221–207 BCE) was an escape route from the harsh rule of the first emperor, Qin Shihuang.

After the overthrow of the Qin dynasty and a short period of conflicts among warring parties, China was again unified, this time by the founder of the Western Han dynasty in 202 BCE. From that time on, China's contact with foreign countries was continuous, varying only in direction, scope, and intensity. There were three geographical directions in which such contact developed. The first was eastward toward Korea and Japan, as mentioned already. The second was the famous Silk Road in the northwest through today's Xinjiang into what was then known as the Western Regions, that is, central Asia and parts of the Middle East. The third was the sea route to the south and southwest. In the *Han Shu,* the official history of the Western Han period, written during the Eastern Han by Ban Gu (32–92 CE) and completed by his sister Ban Zhao (45–114 or 51–120 CE) (Lee 1994), the section on geography delineates a route from northern Vietnam (which was part of the Han empire then), through Thailand and Myanmar, to India. This maritime route was attempted and established because travel from China to India over land was thwarted by the ethnic groups in China's southwest Yunnan Province (Zhu 1994:41–43). The ships relied on sails, hugging the coastline for the most part. Sailing on the open seas with more sophisticated navigational technology would begin in the Tang dynasty (618–907 CE).

Reasons for Leaving China

For two thousand years, from the time of the Western Han dynasty to the middle of the Qing, the last imperial dynasty (202 BCE to 1800 CE), contact with foreign societies was for the most part initiated by China. The reasons for traveling and even settling in the three directions mentioned above can be grouped into three categories: political, economic, and, to a lesser degree, religious.

Political Reasons

In the political category were the many diplomatic delegations to distant places throughout Chinese history. These were goodwill missions, exploring neighboring places and forging friendships with gifts. Rulers of these countries would be invited to reciprocate a visit to the Chinese capital, also bearing gifts. This was the famous tribute system.

As the Han dynasty (202 BCE to 220 CE) was beset with invasions by the nomadic tribes from the north, it was urgent for the diplomatic exploration to establish military alliances with countries similarly threatened. The famous Zhang Qian led two such trips, in 139–126 BCE and 119 BCE, to the Kushan Empire in contemporary Afghanistan. His expeditions opened up the Silk Road, which began from the present-day city of Xian in the east all the way to Rome in the west. The Roman patrician families desired the soft silk fabrics from China and paid for it with gold. In order to safeguard the corridor in the Chinese territory for the silk trade, garrisons were installed as far west as the Pamir Mountains. Ban Chao (32–102 CE), the twin of Ban Gu and brother of Ban Zhao, for example, was stationed in the Pamirs for thirty-one years. Some merchants and officials no doubt settled along the Silk Road.

The most stupendous diplomatic expeditions were undertaken in the Ming dynasty (1368–1644 CE) under the leadership of the eunuch admiral Zheng He. Between 1405 and 1433 CE, he led seven voyages, sailing to virtually all countries in Southeast Asia (the Philippines, Vietnam, Brunei, Java, Sumatra, Cambodia, Malaysia, and Thailand) and South Asia (Bangladesh, Sri Lanka, India, and Maldives). His largest ship was 125 meters (over 400 feet) long, equipped with watertight compartments, a compass, and a balanced rudder. The fleet of each voyage carried thousands of men, but there was no military conquest of any country. China did not set out to be a great colonial power, although it had the capability. The longest voyage took Zheng He to Hormuz in the Persian Gulf; Mecca in Arabia; Aden on the Red Sea; and Mogadishu, Malindi, and Mombasa in eastern Africa. All this preceded the voyages of Christopher Columbus and Vasco da Gama by over fifty years.

It is not clear whether any of his sailors stayed in the ports of call. In 1935, an Italian anthropologist went to study the Bajuni islanders in East Africa and found a subclan of the Famao called Washanga. They claimed to be descended from some shipwrecked Chinese sailors (Levathes 1994:199–201). If the folklore was true, the Washanga ancestors came earlier than Zheng He, because large quantities of Chinese pottery dating back to between the eighth and the fourteenth centuries CE have been found at the village of the Washanga. During Zheng He's visit, the king of Malindi in East Africa sent a pair of giraffe to the Ming emperor, and one of them died en route. The details of this gift were recorded by the Chinese in their history. Curiously enough, these details were also part of the folklore passed through generations of Washanga down to the twentieth century (Levathes 1994:200).

Another political reason for going abroad was for political refuge. The fanciful aspiration of Kong Fuzi could fall into this category. Actually, many did flee China for political reasons, as in the case of emigrants to Korea and Japan in the Qin dynasty. Once the sea routes gained ascendancy during the Tang dynasty, rebels and exiles fled to Vietnam, Sumatra, Thailand, Laos, the Philippines, and other parts of present-day Southeast Asia. Chen (1991:6) listed five major escapades from the late ninth to the mid-nineteenth centuries by participants in unsuccessful insurrections or resistance movements.

In the political category were other kinds of "involuntary" emigrants. Soldiers on military campaigns who were taken prisoner or were too ill to leave became settlers. This happened, for example, when the Mongol conquerors under Kublai Khan unsuccessfully invaded Vietnam in 1288 CE and Java in 1293 CE (Chen 1991:6–7).

Religious Reasons

The religious reasons for traveling abroad resulted in some of the best-documented intercultural exchange between China and its neighbors. Buddhism was introduced into China toward the end of the Western Han dynasty, and the Buddhist religion was well established in China by the end of the Eastern Han. Its legacy could still be seen in the Buddhist grotto art along the Silk Road, the oldest dating back to the second century CE. Monks from India came to teach in China, and Chinese men and women went to India to learn the scriptures from the source. One monk, Fa Xian, in the fifth century CE wrote a book about his fourteen-year journey covering India, Pakistan, Nepal, Sri Lanka, and over twenty other countries, entitled *A Record of the Buddhist Countries*. This book is the earliest detailed account of China and its neighbors by land and by sea (Bai 1982:186).

More Buddhists went to India in the Tang dynasty; the most famous was the monk Xuan Zhuang, also known as Tripitaka. After his return, he translated seventy-five Buddhist books into 1,335 chapters. Assisted by his disciple Bian Ji he wrote the *Records of Western Travels* in which he described in detail the geography, social customs, and religions of many states in southwest and central Asia. This travel account was later fictionalized and dramatized, creating the endearing character of the Monkey King.

Cultural contact with Japan reached its peak in the Tang dynasty when Japan sent to China as many as eighteen delegations, the largest having six hundred members (Zhu 1994:64). Chinese Buddhists also traveled to Japan to teach.

Aside from some Buddhists going to India, Korea, and Japan, to learn or to teach, especially in the Tang and Song dynasties, the Chinese did not establish religious communities in other lands. On the other hand, Chinese of different faiths undoubtedly made pilgrimages. For example, the famous admiral of the Ming dynasty, Zheng He of the seven ocean voyages, was a Muslim, hence the visit to Mecca.

Economic Reasons

Economic reasons accounted for most of the traveling abroad by the Chinese. According to official dynastic histories, from the Tang to the mid-Ming dynasties, roughly from 700 to 1550 CE, the Chinese traders traveled not only east to Korea and Japan, and west along the Silk Road, but also greatly expanded their commerce throughout Southeast Asia, extending toward the Indian subcontinent, the Persian Gulf, the Arabian Sea, and the East Africa coast (Zhu 1994:89–90).

The Tang dynasty, a golden period in Chinese history, is known, among other things, for the prolific literary outpour by thousands of poets. The best known and possibly the most beloved poetic genius through the ages is Li Bai (701–762 CE). He was born near the modern city of Tokmak in Kyrgystan a century after his family moved to the then Tang frontier in the Western Regions, and he spoke the local Turkic language as a child. When the precocious child was five years old, his father relocated the big family back to China and settled in the present day Sichuan Province (Sun 1982:21). Li Bai's unique cultural background influenced his lyrics and outlook on life.

The Silk Road was a busy thoroughfare in the Tang dynasty. It was recorded that the Chinese merchants and handicraft workers, like Li Bai's family, lived among the local populations in over three hundred small cities all over the Western Regions. Their numbers were estimated to be in the tens of thousands (Zhu 1956:15). It was on the Silk Road that the important Chinese invention of papermaking was spread through the Islamic world of central and west Asia, and then North Africa into Europe (Chinese Academy of Sciences 1986:176–83). By a similar route the Chinese printing techniques were transmitted to Europe (China Science and Technology Museum Preparatory Committee and the Ontario Science Centre 1982).

A new development in the Tang dynasty was the rise of maritime trade. Expanded in the later dynasties, it would have lasting economic and migratory significance. China exported by sea large quantities of silk, porcelain, tea, lead, zinc, lacquer ware, and bronze ware. In return, China imported incense and various medicinal ingredients from Africa; horses and pearls from Arabia; crystals and glassware from Egypt and India; cotton from India; and spices, pearls, and medicinal herbs from Southeast Asia (Zhu 1994:66–67). Sometimes the Chinese ships would carry cargo not originating in China, such as camphor, sandalwood, elephants, horses, and spices. They would transport goods between points in Southeast Asia, India, and west Asia (Zhu 1956:29). Thus peoples from distant lands intermingled, exchanging useful and luxury goods.

Persian, Arab, Jewish, and Indian merchants came to China by the Silk Road and by sea. They formed their own communities in the Tang capital of Changan (modern Xian) and the Northern Song capital of Kaifeng, and in all the major coastal cities, such as Yangzhou, Ningbo, Hangzhou, Quanzhou, Fuzhou, Xiamen and Guangzhou

(Fan 1965:782–85). Just as merchants from west and south Asia came to China, Chinese traders also traveled by sea around the Indian Ocean (for example, to Cochin), to west Asia (Baghdad and Damascus), and even to East Africa (the Washanga claim mentioned above) in ancient times. At least some settled in the foreign places.

Archaeological excavations throughout Southeast Asia and Chinese records show that the most extensive reciprocal contact was between China and that entire region. Some journeys were part of the official tribute system, which paved the way for private trade between the Chinese and the Southeast Asians, and also Chinese settlement in Southeast Asia. Eventually all of Southeast Asia and parts of south Asia, where so many Chinese merchants, artisans, sailors, and workers played such a significant economic role, came to be known in Chinese as *Nanyang,* the South Seas. The travelers to Nanyang were from the provinces of Fujian, Guangdong (including Hainan Island), and, to a lesser degree, southern Zhejiang. Some of those who were engaged in long-distance commerce settled abroad, having brought their families with them or marrying local people to form families. It would be in Nanyang that a new category of Chinese, the Chinese overseas, would emerge.[2]

Nanyang: Maritime Trade and Chinese Overseas

The maritime trade was vitally important to the Song dynasty (960–1279 CE), which was beset with invaders who established kingdoms in Chinese territories in the west, northwest, and northeast. In the Song period, therefore, the Silk Road through the northwest corridor was in enemy hands. In 1127, the northeastern Jin kingdom conquered the northern half of China, and the Song court moved its capital from Kaifeng to Hangzhou. With that move, the southern provinces became the mainstay of China's economy, which they continue to hold to this day, and the maritime routes became even more important to its economy.

In the Song dynasty, so much of the government revenue was dependent on overseas trade that the Song government monopolized it. It established a ministry in charge of maritime trade, allowing only the national or local governments to be engaged in it. At the same time it prohibited any merchant to conduct overseas trade on a private basis. The Song imperial edict of 976 was the first ban on the Chinese traveling by sea. It served as a model for the bans in the Ming and Qing dynasties, although the later bans were based more on political reasons. The Song ban, however, did not prevent ingenious Chinese or Javanese traders from pretending to be high officials paying tribute while in fact conducting private trade. As with the later prohibitions, the Song ban was poorly enforced, if at all. The merchants, sailors, and artisans continued to ship goods to and from Nanyang, especially throughout the present-day Indonesian archipelago, with or without official sanction or knowledge (Zhu 1994:65–66).

In the Song dynasty, all kinds of crafts improved in quality and craftsmen in productivity, a development linked to the increase in domestic and international trade. Commerce within China increased to such a level that the use of paper money made its appearance (Bai 1982). The phenomenal growth in trade along the sea route was also due to major technological advances that took place in the Tang and Song dynasties.

Even in the short-lived Sui dynasty (581–618 CE), which preceded the Tang, the largest warship had five levels and could carry eight hundred soldiers (Zhu 1994:72). By the Tang time, the Arab Suleiman recorded that the Chinese ships were too large to dock in Durdur and had to moor at Siraf near the mouth of the Persian Gulf. Ships made by the Chinese had watertight compartments so that when one area was damaged, the rest of the ship would not be affected (Zhu 1956:16–22). The Chinese ocean-going ships were so sturdy and dependable that by the eighth century, most Arabs traveled in them (Zhu 1994:72). By the Song time, a system of balanced rudders was in general use in China. Chinese shipbuilders and navigators had sails of various shapes and very early on mastered the technique of sailing against the wind by taking a zigzag course and coordinating the sails with the leeboard and stern rudders. Ocean-going ships had sails twice as wide as those for inland waters but one-third shorter. This was to lower the point of wind impact, because gale force at sea could be strong, and the ship would be in danger of capsizing (Zhou 1986).

Another technological development that aided navigation and,

therefore, international trade was the use of the magnetic compass on
the open sea. As far back as the Warring States period of the Zhou
dynasty (475–221 BCE), the Chinese knew about the magnetic property of lodestone to point to the south. The magnetic stone was used
in guiding directions. The use of the compass in maritime travels was
first recorded in the year 1119 CE by a certain Zhu Yu in Guangzhou.
The first recorded use of the compass on an official delegation was in
1123 (Northern Song period) on a voyage to Korea (Zhu 1956:22–
23). The Europeans most likely learned about the Chinese compass
from the Arabs a whole century later (Zhu 1994:74).

During the Yuan dynasty (1271-1368 CE), the Silk Road was
within the Mongol empire and was again used as a communication
link between China and the Western Regions. However, the maritime
trade routes continued to be used, especially for private trade, and
became increasingly important to the Chinese economy. The famed
Venetian Marco Polo allegedly came to Beijing on the Silk Road and,
after a stay of several decades in China, returned to Italy by sea. When
the Yuan was replaced by the Ming dynasty founded by a Han Chinese Zhu Yuanzhang, the Silk Road was lost to China because the
Mongols still had control of it. So China's foreign trade during the
Ming dynasty was virtually all by sea. The awesome voyages of Admiral Zheng He, described earlier, began in the fourth decade of the
Ming dynasty. When the Spaniards took control of the Philippines in
1571, there was already in Manila a thriving community of Chinese
and Southeast Asian merchants with a network of trading links
among China, Vietnam, Japan, Indonesia, Thailand, and other places
(Hall 1988).

The Coming of European Powers to Asia

China's trade with other nations, whether official or private, was
always initiated by one of the trading partners. No intervening third-
party nations were involved. Also, the private Chinese who traveled
abroad were mostly merchants. From the late fifteenth century on,
Europeans powers, led by the Portuguese, began to seize territories,
often fighting among themselves, throughout the Indian subcontinent

and Southeast Asia. Spain formally colonized the Philippines. The Dutch East Indies Company, based in Java, competed with the Portuguese and Spanish traders. The British East India Company, based in India, competed with the Dutch for the dominant position in Asia. Both the British and Dutch trading companies were private enterprises with shareholders, but they were given charter for trade monopoly by their respective governments and were endowed with legal, administrative, and military powers to act as colonial governments. It was not until 1795 that Britain got the upper hand by taking over the Dutch East Indies. In 1824 Britain and the Netherlands reached an agreement. Using the Malacca Strait as the dividing line, territories to its north, encompassing the whole Malay peninsula and Singapore, became British possessions, while islands to the south of the strait, the whole of present-day Indonesia, became Dutch colonies (Zhu 1994:104).

Thus the European trading companies and their governments became the intervening third party, affecting the number and categories of Chinese leaving for Nanyang. Meanwhile the Ming dynasty in China was replaced in 1644 by the Qing, established by a foreign ethnic group from the northeast, the Manchu. The Qing government Edict of 1672 prohibited the Chinese from traveling overseas because the Manchu rulers feared that the Han Chinese resisters would launch a military expedition from Taiwan or Nanyang to overthrow their regime.

Despite the ban, Chinese merchants continued to ship porcelain, tea, silk, and other products to the European trading companies in Nanyang. Much of the cargo would then be reshipped to Europe or other colonies. The famous Manila galleon was a striking example of this reshipment activity. Begun in 1573, this trade, in which predominantly Chinese products were carried from Manila to Acapulco, Mexico, in exchange for silver from South America, was to last for 250 years (Hall 1988). According to Leonard Blusse's research into the value of Chinese trade to Batavia (Jakarta today), it was mainly the Chinese goods and people that made the city of Batavia the hub of international commerce for two hundred years (quoted in Chen 1991:96).

While some Chinese merchants supplied luxury goods to the European traders in Nanyang, others imported cloth, water buffalo, flour, and a variety of articles for everyday use to the local populations all over Nanyang. Thus much local commerce, from import to distribution and retail, was in the hands of Chinese merchants.

The Europeans, as the intervening third party in Nanyang commerce, also required artisans and skilled workers. Thus a second type of Chinese migrants besides the merchants — carpenters, shipbuilders, weavers, masons, tailors, barbers, bakers, candle makers, bricklayers, metal workers, and all kinds of craftsman — traveled to Nanyang in increasing numbers.

A third group of Chinese emigrants would be the unskilled workers. They were required to do the heavy manual work for the Europeans in construction, transportation, mining, and plantations. Many worked in the fields, growing Chinese vegetables and fruits, or tending the fisheries. In the Philippines, for example, they largely developed the area around Laguna Bay near Manila. Through them the potato, a product of the Andes, was introduced into China.

The attitudes of the European officials in Nanyang toward the Chinese immigrants were a mixture of contradictions. While the colonizers needed the Chinese immigrants, some officials were unhappy about the lucrative local trade in the hands of the Chinese and felt that they were making too much money or too many of them were coming. Another cause of tension between the authorities and the Chinese immigrants were the coercive measures taken by the colonial officials to press Chinese workers into slavery. The Chinese were forced to build fortresses, toil on plantations, or work on ships in times of war. The harsh treatment of the Chinese resulted in insubordination and even uprisings in the Dutch East Indies and the Philippines. Some Chinese joined the native populations in rebelling against the colonial authorities. Thus the Chinese were banned from entering certain territories at various times. Tensions also resulted in massive violence against the Chinese. Between 1593 and 1763 six major incidents of looting and killing of Chinese took place in the Philippines. The massacres in 1602 and 1639 were particularly horrifying, with over twenty thousand Chinese killed in each case. In the Dutch East

Indies, racial violence in October 1740 resulted in the burning of Chinatown in Batavia for three days. Over four thousand Chinese, including women and children, perished (Chen 1991).

This pattern of Chinese migration was repeated in other parts of Nanyang: Vietnam, Laos, and Cambodia colonized by France, and Malaya and Burma by Britain. Nevertheless, from the sixteenth century to the mid-twentieth century, increasing numbers of Chinese emigrants went to Nanyang. Whether as merchants, artisans, or manual laborers, they would occupy a place sandwiched between the colonial masters and the indigenous populations, virtually indispensable to the other two categories of people but also resented by them. Thus third-party nations, the colonial powers, came to influence Chinese emigration and Chinese settlement abroad.

The Century of Mass Emigration (1842–1949)

The large-scale international migration of Chinese laborers began with the defeat of China by Britain in the First Opium War (1839–42). This new phase of emigration had two notable characteristics. First, Nanyang, where Chinese merchants had settled for centuries, became the destination of a large number of unskilled workers whose numbers would eclipse the category of merchants. Second, the Chinese went to other parts of the world that were relatively or entirely new destinations. Within one century, from the end of the First Opium War to the founding of the People's Republic of China in 1949, Chinese migrants left in record numbers, bound for countries of all inhabited continents. The narrators whose life stories, thoughts, and sentiments you will read in this book are descendants of those who left China during this period.

This century of massive emigration was characterized by the demand for laborers in different parts of the world, the impoverishment of the Chinese people in a context of foreign encroachment on China, and the weakness of the Chinese government to defend the country. But it all began under very different circumstances.

Opium Trade and Opium Wars

The closing of the eighteenth century saw China as self-sufficient and prosperous. This was best indicated in the national revenues and expenditures, measured in silver, that showed that the reign period of the Qianlong emperor of the Qing dynasty (1736–95) "enjoyed a surplus of eight or nine million taels[3] (*liang,* an ounce of silver) annually" (Hsu 2000:63; see also Spence 1990:129). One contributing factor to the overflowing national coffers was the trade surplus. Since the sixteenth century, commerce through the Manila galleon and directly with the Dutch East Indies Company, the British East India Company, and American and other European merchants had increased steadily. European and American demands for Chinese teas, porcelain, silks, and other decorative goods seemed limitless. On the other hand, China imported few of the wares that the Western merchants had to offer: woolens and clocks from England, and ginseng and otter skins from North America. A trade surplus resulted in China's favor, which not only filled the national treasury but enriched the ordinary people, particularly the coastal merchants, artisans, and farmers who produced the tea, silk, porcelain, and other goods.

In order to redress the alarming trade deficits, British and American merchants developed an innovative trade strategy in the 1760s: to import opium into China. Over the next few decades, more and more opium was shipped to China. By 1835 there were an estimated two million opium addicts in China, from the Manchu ruling class, through the officialdom and the merchants, down to the laborers (Fan 1962:12). The trade imbalance was reversed and silver began to drain from China.

After 1800 the Chinese government, concerned with the growing addiction problem, banned opium imports, production of opium, and opium smoking in China. However, the British East India Company and American merchants in collusion with unscrupulous Chinese adventurers and corrupt officials resorted to smuggling. When the Chinese government destroyed the contraband near Guangzhou in 1839, Britain declared war on China. China was no match for the superior military technology, especially the steam gunboats, used by the British. China's defeat in the First Opium War led to devastating demands from Britain: indemnities of 21 million silver dollars for the cost of war and the destroyed opium; opening of five ports to foreign merchants; ceding Hong Kong to Britain; allowing Christian missionaries freedom to make converts; and granting Britain the most-favored nation status so that any import tariff imposed by China on British goods could not exceed 5 percent. Moreover, any privileges accorded by the Chinese government to any other nations would automatically be enjoyed by Britain. Separate treaties with the United States and France in 1844 extended most of the privileges to these two nations. In addition, the principle of extraterritoriality was greatly strengthened such that Europeans and Americans involved in legal disputes in China, civil or criminal, would be handed over to their respective consulates. This meant that Westerners would not be subject to Chinese laws.

The pattern of aggression by one or more imperialist powers, China's defeat, and compensations and concessions made by China were to repeat many times during the next century, until China was nominally independent but in effect very much colonized, not by one power, but by a group of Western powers and later also Japan. This phenomenon is referred to as "semi-colonialism" in Chinese history.

One immediate result of the First Opium War was the dramatic increase in opium imports — though still illegal — from 20,619 chests in 1830 to 52,925 chests in 1850 (Fan 1962:81). By 1855 over 69,000 chests were imported every year (Zhu 1994:139). Another devastating consequence was that China, the loser, had to pay indemnities again and again for wars waged by the imperialist powers. The lasting impact was the impoverishment of the tillers of the land and of the lower social classes because on them would ultimately fall the burden of taxation. Because payments were to be made in silver, the unstoppable drain of silver from China pushed up its value in relation to the copper coins that were the currency in general circulation. A high official, Zeng Guofan, who was to prove invaluable to the Manchu rulers in suppressing the Taiping Rebellion, described in a report to the throne in 1852 the dire poverty of the common people because the price of silver had doubled in terms of copper coins in the ten years after the war. Harvests of rice could fetch less than half the former price. Consequently farmers' tax payments more than doubled because the tax collectors demanded the regular amount (Chen and Zhang 1994:523).

The people of the Guangdong Province were particularly hard hit. Guangdong was the province where in 1839 the smuggled opium was destroyed, thus precipitating the war. At the end of the war, Britain demanded damage compensation directly from Guangdong. Moreover, the province had to shoulder 70 percent of the 21 million-dollar indemnity China had to pay for the First Opium War. During the war, the provincial and local governments had had to pay subsidy to the Qing army, which had proved virtually useless. All in all, Guangdong was levied a price of 19.5 million taels of silver for the war! This was the equivalent of the total revenue of Guangdong for eighteen years (Zhu 1994:139).

Several peasant rebellions broke out in different parts of China in the second half of the nineteenth century, both reflecting and compounding the misery in the countryside. The largest was the Taiping Rebellion, which lasted from 1850 to 1865. Under the conditions of unrest, the Chinese people, especially the residents of the coastal provinces, sought opportunities overseas to escape the heavy taxes and worsening poverty. In a 1935 study of the relationship between Chinese overseas in Nanyang and the coastal provinces of Guangdong and Fujian, 70 percent of the respondents claimed economic pressures as the reason for going overseas (Zhu 1994:251–52).

Other factors strengthened the economic motivation of the emigrants. According to demographic studies, the population of the entire country had been rising rapidly during the Qing dynasty. Between 1685 and 1759, it doubled to 200 million in less than a century. By 1840, the time of the First Opium War, the national population exceeded 400 million. But the growth in Fujian and Guangdong was particularly staggering. According to estimates, the population of Fujian rose sharply from 7 million in 1661 to 19 million in 1840, while the increase in Guangdong was fivefold, from 4.2 million to 25 million during the same period (Zhu 1994:137). In the midst of rapid population increases, rampant graft and corruption among the Qing officials made it easier for big landlords to amass more and more land from the poor farmers, a trend that intensified after 1840. By then, the Qing government was weak and ineffectual, unable to resist foreign aggression and incapable of administering a vast country. These desperate economic and social conditions were the reasons why laborers wanted to leave China.

International Demand for Labor

Meanwhile England during the eighteenth century had been transforming its economy with commercialization of agriculture and development of manufacturing industries, shifting its emphasis from mercantile activities to production of commodities. By the early nineteenth century England was the world's first industrial capitalist society. Other western European countries and the northeastern part of the United States soon followed in developing industrial capitalism. All these countries increasingly turned to Asia in their competition for colonies. The colonies were to supply raw materials and prospective markets for manufactured goods. Large-scale extraction and processing of resources in the Asian colonies complemented those in other colonies around the globe or in immigrant societies where Europeans had settled in previous centuries. Thus the globalization of economy proceeded, involving a mixing of people and materials from all over the world to produce commodities that would also be moved all over the world. One example illustrates this globalization. Brazil had the monopoly over wild rubber, a native plant of the Amazon, during most of the nineteenth century. Sir Robert Wickham smuggled rubber seeds to England in 1876. Rubber plantations were established in the British colony of Malaya by 1900, with workers imported mostly from India. Rubber was also produced in Dutch Sumatra, with workers imported from Java and China (Liu et al. 1979). Local villages became company towns (Wolf 1982:329–30). Rubber was of course an essential raw material in the burgeoning automobile industry, for making tires, as well as in other industries.

The Western powers had always regarded Chinese workers as diligent and reliable. Since the sixteenth century, there were occasional episodes of Portuguese, Spanish, and Dutch sailors and colonial authorities seizing Chinese men, women, and children from Chinese ships on the open seas or through raids of coastal villages to meet their labor demands in Goa, the Philippines, and the Dutch East Indies. But with the advent of the nineteenth century, demand for labor became more urgent. Between 1786 and 1820, when Britain through the British East India Company acquired Malaya and Singapore, Chinese laborers were recruited to develop the region (Chen 1991:155–56). In 1810 the Portuguese shipped several hundred tea workers to Brazil. Demands were heavy and the problem of labor shortage was acute because earlier in the nineteenth century Britain and other countries had outlawed the lucrative African slave trade. Then slavery itself was banned by the British government in 1834, a move that affected all British colonies, including the West Indies, and by France in 1848 (Zhu 1994:147). Alternative sources for cheap and disposable labor were sought in populous countries like India and China to meet demands in Asia, the Americas, Australia, and Africa.

Chinese Labor Exodus

While the 1672 ban on private trade did not stop private merchants and sailors from going abroad, it did prevent large-scale emigration up till the mid-nineteenth century. By then the Qing government, following China's defeat in the Second Opium War (1856–60), had to give in to the demands of Britain, France, and Russia that it *must* allow the Western powers to transport Chinese laborers to work abroad. An agreement between the United States and China, broached by the American former diplomat Anson Burlingame in 1868, also made it possible for more Chinese to work in the United States.

There were four ways whereby Chinese laborers went overseas to fill that need: the coolie trade, the contract-labor system, the credit-ticket system, and paying one's own way.

COOLIE TRADE. The word "coolie" is often used to refer to all Chinese emigrant labor (see Pan 1998), but some writers reserve the term "coolie trade" specifically for "the seizure and sale of cheap human labor" (Chan 1982:39; also Takaki 1989). The word "coolie" might have been derived from one of the Indian languages. The Chinese term for it is *kuli,* meaning "bitter strength." And bitter was the lot of the Chinese who were unfortunate enough to be sent abroad to work. The slang for the coolie in the Guangdong and Fujian dialects was *zhuzai,* meaning pigs, because the workers were bought and sold just like pigs, and they were treated so inhumanely throughout their overseas experience that their lot was like that of the beasts.

The coolie trade began in 1845 with a shipload of able-bodied Chinese from Xiamen to the French Isle of Bourbon in the West Indies. Foreign-owned companies, some operated by the British government, would contract with a Chinese agency who sent out recruiters, known as "crimps," to round up the would-be laborers for export. Men became coolies mostly because they or their families were landless and in debt; some had gambling debts. Some were kidnapped. Others were deceived or tricked with the promise of good wages and opportunities abroad. Quite a few were even drugged (Pan 1998:61; Chan 1982:39).

Once the workers were in the hands of the crimps, they were virtual prisoners. From recruitment centers such as Xiamen, Shantou, and Macao, the coolies were sent to Hong Kong, then a British colony, where they were transferred to ocean-going ships. As one coolie trader, by the name of Tait, was a consul in Xiamen for the Netherlands, Spain, and Portugal, these three countries were among the most involved in the trade. The coolies landed in their colonial territories, such as Peru, Panama, the Dutch East Indies, Cuba, and other Caribbean Islands. The ships were described as floating hells. Each ship would carry more human cargo than it was permitted to have. The coolies were given one meal a day, often consisting of rotten meat and moldy rice. There was a limited supply of drinking water, but the navigational route the ships followed was mostly around the equator, and the heat was oppressive all year round. Complainers were badly beaten. Coolies died in great numbers en route of illness, starvation, thirst, beatings, and even suicide. In 1857, during one passage to Peru, 285 coolies died after eating tainted meat. The death rate on board the ships was on the average 40 percent in the 1850s and early 1860s. Conditions improved somewhat later, and the death rate declined to about 20 percent in the second half of the 1860s (Zhu 1994:157–60).

Once the ships reached their destinations, the coolies would be auctioned to plantation or mine owners. The price for each coolie at the point of recruitment was three to ten U.S. dollars. All the expenses involved in recruitment and shipment would total $120 per coolie, but the average price per head at the auction market was between $200–500. The ships used were mostly British-, American-, or French-owned. The profit from one shipment of coolies would be enough to cover the cost of building one fast ship in the United States (Zhu 1994:159–61).

A coolie was obligated to work for a number of years, ranging from three to even ten, during which period the master or the company owned the coolie absolutely. Food and shelter were provided, but the coolies received little or no wages. Treatment of the coolies on the plantation or in the mine was hardly better than in the "floating hell." Workload was heavy while food was scanty. Punishment for any infractions was brutal, often resulting in severe injuries to limbs, eyes, teeth, and internal organs. Many committed suicide. The overall death rate among the coolie workers in Cuba, during the period while they were still indentured, was estimated to be 75 percent (Zhu 1994:161–62).

CONTRACT LABOR. The seizure-sale method declined after 1874 (Pan 1998:61) as a result of protests from the Qing government against the treatment of Chinese laborers overseas, rebellion of the workers themselves, and criticism from international antislavery groups. It was modified and then replaced by the contract-labor system. At the point of recruitment or at the point of embarkation, there was a contract between the coolie and the representatives of the establishments overseas. However, in many cases, the contract was a sham, as illiterate workers were tricked or coerced by the agent.

Contract laborers were recruited for continental railway construction and mining companies in the United States and Canada. Recruitment agencies in Hong Kong and China advanced passage money to migrant workers and received repayments from them for many years after their arrival in North America. The Chinese workers were assigned to the most dangerous operations, such as installing and igniting explosives, but received wages lower than the white workers (Hu 1991, 1:234; Su 1986:36; Chan 1982). Many contract workers were indentured for a specific number of years to the sugar planters in the Sandwich Islands, as Hawaii was then called. They received free passage and also wages, food, and lodging (Chan 1991:27). During World War I, the governments of Britain, France, and Russia entered into agreements with the Chinese authorities to use contract workers in Europe. About two hundred thousand workers went, mostly from North China, a departure of the usual trend of the southerners leaving for work overseas. They dug trenches, buried the dead, and built airfields but were paid about half the wages of a British private (Bailey 1998:64–65). Other contract workers were indentured in mines and plantations in Malaya, the Dutch East Indies, other Nanyang locations, and Australia. Working conditions for the contract laborers were sometimes just as harsh, dangerous, and inhumane as in the seizure-sale practice (Liu et al. 1979). But insofar as the contract system demanded more accountability from the recruiters and employers, the conditions of some contract workers were better than those of the coolies (Chan 1983:45).

The last documented case of contract workers was in 1940, when over a hundred men were shipped to the tin mines of Indonesia. Thus the contract-labor system lasted until the eve of Japanese occupation of Southeast Asia (Liu et al. 1979).

CREDIT-TICKET SYSTEM. The third way whereby Chinese workers went abroad was the credit-ticket system. The workers would venture abroad independently, borrowing money for the fare of passage overseas and any embarkation fees. Upon reaching the destination, they would pay down their debt plus interest with wages earned. Most of the workers were men, but a small number of women also sought opportunities abroad.

While agents might provide credit for the passage and employment prospects abroad, the emigrants relied heavily on members of their families, clans, or villages or towns of origin to find out about the opportunities overseas, and for assistance in the entire process of emigration. It was through these kinds of connections that settlement patterns of Chinese overseas yielded specific groups in particular destinations. For example, the emigrants to the Philippines were mostly from Fujian Province, whereas the vast majority of those to Canada and the United States were from the four counties of Taishan, Xinhui, Kaiping, and Heshan in Guangdong Province under the credit-ticket arrangements (Chan 1982; Su 1986).

SELF-FINANCED EMIGRATION. The last method of emigration was paying their way entirely on their own. Those who financed their own passage were mostly merchants and students, and some workers. While most of the emigrants between 1840 and 1949 were workers, merchants and entrepreneurs continued to be part of the diaspora. For example, in the early days of British colonization of Malaya, Chinese were allowed to own and operate tin mines. In the United States and Canada, the governments banned the immigration or entry of Chinese in 1882 and 1923 respectively (see Hong 2001 and Chan 1982). However, three categories of Chinese were exempted: merchants, students, and diplomats. Merchants, but not workers, could bring their families to those two countries during the bans.

Paper Son and Paper Daughter

Some emigrants utilized another innovative strategy. It depended on any of the methods of emigration described above and the fact that children born to Chinese immigrants in the countries or territories of residence usually had the status of legal residents. When the parents and the children visited China, they would sell the legal papers to other families who might have children of similar age. The original paper-holders might remain in China or might have died. In this way, thousands of "paper sons," and to a lesser extent "paper daughters," made their way overseas in place of the original legal residents. In the narratives in part 2, one paper daughter made her way to the American protectorate of Hawaii, and one "paper son" went to Cuba with the paper of someone much younger.

This innovative strategy was most in use in the first half of the twentieth century to gain entry to all parts of the world, but it was particularly prevalent for those wishing to enter the United States because of a certain loophole in the U.S. citizenship laws. Although Chinese immigrants could not become naturalized American citizens until 1952, their American-born children were by law American citizens from birth. Moreover, the children of American citizens, born anywhere in the world, are also automatically American citizens from birth. The citizenship paper of an American child, fathered by an American and born in China, could be sold to another family eager to send a child to the United States.

The greatest opportunity for many Chinese immigrants to the United States came after the 1906 San Francisco earthquake. The ensuing fire destroyed most birth and immigration records in that city. Many Chinese immigrants claimed to have been born in the United States, and it was virtually impossible to disprove. This gave rise to a whole generation of "paper children" in China fathered by the alleged American-born Chinese Americans. Given the fact that the total number of Chinese female persons in the entire United States was 4,522 in 1900, if all the claims to birth in America were genuine, one estimate suggests that every Chinese woman living in San Francisco before 1906 would have to have given birth to 800 children (Takaki 1989:235–36)!

Citizenship laws were different in other countries. In another narrative in part 2, the father was born in Australia and held an Australian passport, but his children born in Hong Kong were not recognized as Australian citizens.

Political Reasons for Emigration

While most emigration after the mid-nineteenth century was for economic reasons, there were also political exiles. In the second half of the nineteenth century, peasants and laborers in China, oppressed with heavy taxes and inhumane treatment at the hands of unscrupulous landlords and officials, waged many rebellions. When the uprisings were put down, the participants had no choice but to flee. When uprisings of the Small Knife Society in Fujian and of the Heaven and Earth Society in Guangdong failed, some of their members escaped to Nanyang. Dr. Sun Wen (Sun Yat-sen) is revered by the Chinese today as the father of the nation for his role in overthrowing the Qing dynasty in 1911 and establishing the Republic of China. He was an exile and used connections among the Chinese communities in Nanyang, Hawaii, North America, and Europe to evade the Qing authorities and to raise funds for his political cause.

After 1937, when most of the eastern half of China came under Japanese occupation, many Chinese in the southern provinces again sought refuge in Southeast Asian countries only to find later the Japanese occupation of some of those places as well.

Scope of Emigration

It is difficult to come up with firm figures of emigration between 1842 and 1949. A conservative estimate for the period between 1840 and 1911 is that at least three million left China. This did not include thousands in the underground trade, because the number of coolies on board ships was always under-reported. There were also men and women who used or purchased immigration papers belonging to others. Thus the real figure was probably a few million higher, possibly up to ten million. Between 1911 and 1949, an estimated six million emigrated (Zhu 1994:225–26; 301).

An estimated 300,000 Chinese arrived in the West Indies, British Guyana, Cuba, Peru, and Panama between 1851 and 1875. British Malaya and the Dutch East Indies probably had the highest numbers of Chinese immigrants, estimated at a million for each territory between 1851 and 1925. Between 1851 and 1875, over 160,000 Chinese went to the United States, and 55,000 to Australia. But between 1876 and 1900, the numbers of immigrants to the United States and Australia fell to 12,000 and 8,000 respectively (Pan 1998:62). The decrease was due to anti-Chinese immigration legislation passed in both countries in the last decades of the nineteenth century. Between

1901 and 1925, about 55,000 Chinese went to Transvaal, South Africa (Pan 1998:62).

As has been mentioned above, at the end of the Second Opium War, the governments of Britain, France, and Russia demanded that the Chinese government allow Chinese laborers to work abroad. The Burlingame agreement allowing the entry of Chinese into the United States was based on the principle of the "free migration of aliens" (Chan 1982:42). The 1672 Qing Edict prohibiting the Chinese from going overseas was officially repealed in 1893. The irony is that around the same time in almost all the countries and colonies to which the Chinese emigrated, there began to appear a ban on Chinese immigration, restricting the number or the type of Chinese, or both, that would be allowed to enter.

Sojourners and Settlers

In discussing the phenomenon of the Chinese diaspora, a question often raised is whether or not the Chinese who went abroad had intentions of permanent settlement in their countries of residence. Those who argue that the Chinese emigrants were only sojourners point to the Chinese word *qiao,* which means "a temporary stay." According to this argument, insofar as the Chinese emigrants, and their descendants who never set foot in China all their life, are sometimes all referred to as *Huaqiao* (meaning Chinese in temporary stay abroad), the Chinese never intended to be permanent settlers in their countries of residence.

The sojourner view of the Chinese diaspora has come under critical scrutiny in recent years. The fact of the matter is that in the long tradition of agriculture in China, people and families are necessarily tied to the land. Since the land could not be moved, people moving away from their family land base would be considered to be on a temporary sojourn elsewhere. The ideal culture was the family staying together and tilling the land together. Throughout Chinese history, whenever people and families left their native village for any length of time, whether to sit for the civil service examination or to conduct trade, the travelers would be called qiao, that is, sojourners in another region of China. Even when people migrated southward and westward within China, for economic and political reasons, they could still be regarded as qiao residents, at least initially, in their new locale, although they were there to stay.

The people of the coastal provinces, who moved to Nanyang and elsewhere, were simply following the age-old custom of finding better opportunities in a new frontier. Nanyang was certainly more accessible than the mountainous western parts of China. Moreover, trade ties with Nanyang went back hundreds of years, and there were Chinese communities founded by earlier generations. These factors lessened the hardships of dislocation.

Merchants in the past centuries would often bring their families from China or form new families in their countries of residence. Family formation was the basis of a community and a proof of permanent settlement. There is ample evidence of such old communities throughout Nanyang. Malacca in Malaysia, Cebu and Manila in the Philippines, and Jakarta in Java are prime examples.

However, the emigration waves of the period 1842–1949 had a few unique characteristics. First, most of the emigrants were laborers; only their physical strength was needed in their land of residence. Second, most of the laborers who went abroad were too poor to have families in their countries of residence. Marriage or family was out of question for most coolies. Even for most of those using the credit-ticket or the contract system, their wages were too meager to support families in their countries of residence. Their wages would be of greater value to their families if their parents, wife, and children would stay in China, because the cost of living in China was lower. Last, but not the least, in most countries of residence, once the urgent demands for labor were met, the government or local residents restricted or banned the immigration of family members, or prohibited the immigration of Chinese altogether. There were even attempts to drive the men from their countries of residence. In many places, Chinese immigrants were subject to special taxes; they were not allowed to become naturalized citizens and, therefore, could not enjoy political rights given to other immigrant groups; they were prohibited from buying land, living in certain neighborhoods, or entering into certain occupations; and they were not given police protection in times of violence against their person or destruction of their property. Thus Chinese immigrants were legally constrained from participating in the political and social life of the societies to which they immigrated, and could not take political action to effect any change (Stanley 1996; Chan 1982; Chan 1991; Anderson 1995; Pan 1998).

Despite these obstacles, of the millions who left China by whatever method, most did not return to China. If the workers survived the indenture, some would renew the contract. Others would stay on to become small traders if they had saved enough money. Of those who did return to China, many would leave for opportunities overseas again. Other emigrants remigrated from one society of residence to another. There were also students whose stay abroad was intended to be temporary but who settled permanently there instead.

In many overseas destinations there developed among Chinese immigrants a phenomenon of bachelor society, composed of men who were never married or whose families back in China could not join them. Under the circumstances the nostalgia for one's homeland was acute, and the longing to be buried in one's native village with one's ancestors according to the customary ideal would be even more intense. Some workers returned to China, but others died and were buried abroad. The fact remains, however, that yearnings for the native land, by itself, cannot be taken as not wanting to settle abroad. Laws prohibiting inter-racial marriages in various jurisdictions, such as in thirty-eight American states, including California (Chan 1991:59–60), or the poverty of the men made it impossible for many of them to marry local women. Thus external factors, far more than Chinese cultural values, prevented thousands of workers from establishing families as settlers in their countries of immigration.

That most of the Chinese emigrants intended to settle in the foreign countries of employment and residence was well recognized by the Qing government, as revealed in the comments by Huang Cunxian, the Qing consul-general based in San Francisco, to the Canadian Royal Commission on Chinese Immigration in 1885. He pointed out that the charge against Chinese emigrants of only wanting to earn money and then return to China was untrue. Since the great migration had begun thirty years earlier, large numbers of Chinese had settled permanently in Nanyang and the Caribbean Islands with their families. Many in Cuba and the Hawaiian Islands had married local women and looked upon the islands as home. He further pointed out that the Chinese immigrants coming to Canada were denied all the rights and privileges extended to other citizens and, therefore, were compelled by law to remain aliens. Huang remonstrated that if the Chinese were allowed to be naturalized and could enjoy privileges and rights, they would remain in Canada permanently with their families (Canada 1885).

Since only merchants were allowed or could afford to bring wives from China in many countries of immigration, the Chinese communities in those places, such as North America, would remain small until the middle of the twentieth century. But when the Chinese diaspora is taken as a whole, through time and space, especially in Nanyang where Chinese emigrants had gone for centuries, marriages and families were formed, and permanent communities established. Here again the Chinese overseas showed some ingenuity in ensuring family formation. As will be seen in one narrative in this book, an unmarried male emigrant had a marriage arranged by his family back in China. The bride was married by proxy, according to local customs, to a rooster in a genuine wedding ceremony. Because she was considered a real wife in the eyes of the family and kin, her husband could then apply for legal immigration on her behalf. She would eventually join her husband in the country of immigration.

1949

The Qing government was overthrown in the 1911 revolution, and China became a republic the next year. However, the humiliation and exploitation of China by foreign powers that began with the opium trade did not stop. During the first half of the twentieth century, China was fragmented and dominated by regional warlords, foreign powers who held territories in many cities, and eventually Japan, whose military occupied most of eastern China. The Nationalist party, backed by the landlords and industrialists, nominally ruled over all China but lost its moral authority in the eyes of most Chinese because of its lack of will to resist Japan and corruption among the high officials. After the end of World War II, the Communist People's Liberation Army defeated the Nationalist army in province after province until the People's Republic of China (PRC) was formally declared on October 1, 1949. The Communist rule put an end to foreign aggression against China and landlord exploitation of poor peasants.

Emigration from China came to a virtual stop after 1949. In fact, there were several waves of migration to China by Chinese overseas from Southeast Asia in the 1960s and 1970s. One notable case was from Indonesia following the coup by General Soharto and the massacres of about half a million Chinese in Indonesia in 1965. Another was from Vietnam in 1978–79. There were also similar incidents of remigration from Burma and India. Words such as "return" or "repatriation" would be misnomers because most refugees of Chinese ancestry were never in China before. They were quite simply people not wanted by their countries of birth, or they were too fearful to live in these places.

International political conditions for migration changed after 1949, resulting in the liberalization of immigration laws in many countries in the second half of the twentieth century. The familial and cultural connections of post-1949 emigrants with China, Hong Kong, and Taiwan are vastly different from those whose families emigrated in the 1842–1949 era. The experiences of the post-1949 emigrants lie outside the scope of this book.

In this book, all the narrators have ancestors who left China during the century of 1842–1949, even though a few of the narrators were born in China or Hong Kong. This book explores the experiences of living overseas by individuals whose families have a history in the diaspora, often enduring incredible hardships in that century of mass migration. The Chinese overseas will share with the reader their life experiences and their reflections on being Chinese. This book reveals the remarkable phenomenon of people perceiving themselves as being Chinese when they are a few generations removed from China, and when their links with China for the most part have become quite tenuous.

II Voices from the Diaspora

Eating Cats

T.Y. (United States)

Grandparents

My family name is really Leung. Young was the last character in the name of my paternal grandfather. It became the "last name" and, therefore, the family name.[1]

My paternal grandfather and great-grandfather, from Zhongshan of Guangdong Province, were merchants and, therefore, able to get a visa to come to the U.S. They first set up shop in Massachusetts. Then they went down to New York City. However, they returned to China often because my great-grandmother was still there. Also, they tried to arrange a marriage for my grandfather, but that did not work out. My grandfather ended up marrying one of the first Chinese born in New York City Chinatown in the late 1800s. Her parents were also born in Zhongshan.

After they got married, my grandfather went back to China with his bride. They returned to the U.S. in the 1910s or early 1920s. My dad and his younger brother were born in New York, but his two elder brothers and an adopted brother were born in China.

When I was a kid, I used to sit with my dad and watch John Wayne movies. I would ask him, "What do you think of the Second World War?" He told me that his mother corresponded with and sent money to the extended family members in China up until the war. Then all communication stopped because of the war in the Pacific. They found out after the war that the village had been completely wiped out by the Japanese army. There was no survivor. So we no longer have any relatives, on either side of my grandparents, in China. One uncle, who had been in the village as a boy and could remember landmarks, did go back there before his death, but it was totally different, occupied by another clan.

My maternal grandparents were from Taishan. My gonggong's (maternal grandfather) elder brother was one of the scholars that took the last imperial examination, but he was attracted to Dr. Sun Yat-sen's[2] independence movement against the Qing dynasty and went to Europe and North America to raise funds for the uprising. My gonggong accompanied his brother and traveled extensively throughout the U.S. When he went back to China, his marriage was arranged with my porpor (maternal grandmother). I think they came over here probably because Gonggong got a student visa, as he had been here in the past. They started off in California, where they had two kids. Then they went to Nevada, where my mother was born. They eventually made it to New York with many daughters; two twin sons died in infancy. Theirs was not a happy marriage. They really hated each other. As soon as they could, they separated. Gonggong remained in New York City Chinatown and Porpor eventually lived with us for a number of years.

War and After Years

Being Chinese has been a prominent feature in my mother's character. She grew up in the isolated enclave of NYC Chinatown. My mother said that they never moved outside the confines of Chinatown until they went to high school. One just never crossed Canal Street. My mother and father grew up in the same Chinatown tenement. The families knew each other but they were not dating. In their minds, my mom and dad would have never thought of marrying anyone who was not Chinese.

My father served in the U.S. Army in World War II. He was in a division that was comprised of some Asian but mostly Native Americans. He saw frontline action in Italy and North Africa. He rose in the ranks quickly and ended being a lieutenant mainly because he survived, one of five out of a large division with over a thousand men. As my mother puts it, he was the only one who came out with his eyesight, hearing, and all four limbs intact, as the other four survivors either lost a limb or an eye.

My mom was in Germany for over a year after the war with one of the U.S. agencies servicing the post-war effort. By the time she came back, my dad was already decommissioned. He was just having a hard time being back and having no support system. He tried committing suicide two or three times. The last time my mom saved him and took him to the emergency room. After he recuperated they started going out seriously. That's why they got married.

So when I asked my dad about John Wayne movies, his response was, "This is Hollywood, this is not real, or that happened a long time ago." This, in retrospect, was his coping mechanism. My mom, to this day, will say, "Your dad until he died still had nightmares. For the first ten or fifteen years after the war he would wake up screaming from nightmares, drenched in sweat. He did try to kill himself because it was so overwhelming."

My dad would say, every once in a while, "Well, you know, I had to marry your mother because no one else would marry her." Actually, I think, for him here was someone whom he could talk to possibly for the first time in his life. My mom gets along with many people but never had any super-close friends. My dad was her best friend ultimately.

Parents

Both my parents saw themselves as loners and outsiders within the small Chinatown community. They moved out of Chinatown, first to Astoria Park, and finally right outside of NYC to Long Island. Yet there was a conscious effort on their part to maintain ties with the community because that's where the comfort zone was. When we were kids it was important for us, every weekend, either to be with my paternal grandmother, or with my porpor when she was not living with us. There were clear and explicit rules of conduct: "This is how you greet your grandmother every single time, and this is how you behave." The implicit message was that this is how Chinese are, or this is how we are. There were also Chinese in the areas where we lived. My mom was involved in the Queens Chinese circle and later the Long Island Chinese circle.

My dad went into service with the Narcotics Bureau. Because he did undercover work, for a while he was somewhat of a pariah in the NYC Chinatown. There was the time when my dad was involved in a kind of precedent-setting discrimination lawsuit against the Immigration and Naturalization Service of the U.S. Department of Justice. I think there were seven complainants from different ethnic backgrounds saying that they were all denied promotions. It took them three or four years. When it was settled finally, the case set the standards for promotions in the federal government.

Up until then, about 1973, my parents were certainly struggling financially. They helped to support my father's mother and my mother's mother. We had relatives and friends' kids living with us. It was all very Chinese because my parents were the first ones to get a house. Above all, they both emphasized education very strongly, to the point that my dad uncharacteristically told my mom to go back to work because they didn't have enough money to send all the kids to college. He said, "Look, here is this new program in special education at Brooklyn College and you'll work with crazy kids. This is perfect for you." That's how my mom got a master's degree in special education. Then after the lawsuit was settled, my dad was promoted and received back pay. My three younger siblings benefited from that economic windfall, whereas for my older brother, older sister, and myself, it was clear that we had to get our own scholarships to college.

My mom does not go back to NYC Chinatown now. There are all the new Fujian immigrants. She doesn't know anyone. Everyone that she grew up with has either moved out or passed away. She lives with one of my sisters. Another sister works near Chinatown, and she would get Chinese groceries for my mom. I think if my dad were still alive, my mom's orientation mentally would be very different. He would have just dragged her along to visit so-and-so in Chinatown. My dad died of lung cancer in 1992.

Marrying Chinese

I did not set out consciously to marry an ethnic Chinese. I never went out with any Chinese when I was in high school. Coming from New York, I had some Jewish boyfriends and I also went out with a couple of Puerto Rican–Afro guys. I do remember watching Kurosawa's movie *Seven Samurai*, and just falling in love with the samurai who dies living for his art. I was about thirteen then. So I did have standards and they leaned towards the Asians.

I went through my teenage years and young adulthood exploring my identity. I knew that I wasn't a blue-eyed blond that you see in the magazine or TV. It was important at that time to understand who I was through my visual artwork, as I was training to be an artist. In college I also became interested in women's studies and Asian American studies. I was involved with the Chinese Students Association. I went out with one fellow from Hong Kong and a Singaporean Chinese. I met a lot of international students and minority students in the Third World Student Association. I went out with some of those guys, but not a lot. I mean, I wasn't that way. I think I was consciously making friends with people of diverse backgrounds.

I do remember going out with this white Italian guy from New York who at one point asked me, "I heard that Chinese eat cats, is this true?" I was just disgusted and nauseated. I think that that might have been one of my turning points. I said to myself, "Oh, wait a minute, wait a minute! There are some real, fundamental differences here with someone from the dominant culture that I don't know if I'll be able to bridge." I was in my early twenties at that point, and I was starting to say consciously that this is not for me.

After college I was recruited to teach English at a private university in Taiwan. It was a great experience, and I had the opportunity to learn Chinese. That's where I met W., my husband, and it worked out. He was also an American-born Chinese, teaching at this private university. He is four years younger than I am. My in-laws almost had a fit! They should be so happy that he married someone who is Chinese and has a college degree! We have three sons and one daughter.

I think that I was different from my sisters in this respect. Something of that Chinese orientation my parents tried to instill in us stuck inside of me. I still talk to my mother about that, because none of my siblings married Asians. All their spouses are Caucasians. Though my mother loves all her grandchildren, and she does really love her children-in-law, she feels closest to my husband because she can sit down and talk about things. There are certain assumptions that they don't have to go over. There are things she can say much more freely because he is Chinese. When she talks about her growing up, or her parents, or how she orients towards life, she is much more comfortable with him.

And W. and I talk about it. We understand that other people make other choices. But knowing ourselves the way we do and seeing our relationship, we know that for ourselves it was a pretty conscious choice to marry Chinese. It would be very hard for us not to.

At our house now we speak a smattering of everything: Taishan dialect, Guangzhou dialect, Mandarin, and English. I think there is a part of identity that is connected with language, but language is not the only defining aspect of identity. Whatever exposure W. and I can give them via language will hopefully provide them with a broader base for their own individual sense of who they are. On the other hand, I don't know how realistic it is for us to say that our kids are Chinese and, therefore, they have to learn Chinese. Given the neighborhood we live in, my kids can easily attend Friday evening or Saturday morning Chinese school. They don't because I don't want to overschedule them. Frankly I don't want to be driving the kids all over the place every single day. I don't want to impose Chinese language on them, but as a parent I say, "This is important to me and it will be nice if it were important to you. If it's not, that's okay." I think that all three boys, anyway—the baby is too young yet—have responded well, perhaps because it has not been forced down their throats. So with every little opportunity we have, we stick in some more language. The example is the two-week Chinese language camp in the last two summers. They actually come back learning a little bit more. They also play *Weiqi*.[3]

Chinese Spirituality and Religion

There was a Christian missionary in my porpor's village, so the entire village was exposed to Christianity. Being very close to her, my siblings and I were exposed to a unique, idiosyncratic Christian and Confucian blending when we were growing up. There were, of course, missionaries too in NYC Chinatown. My father actually went to a Lutheran Church and my mother to a Methodist Church. My siblings and I all went to Sunday school and the Methodist church up to the age of twelve or thirteen. Then we were given the choice to continue or not.

I am not a practicing Christian; neither am I an atheist. W. was raised with absolutely no religious indoctrination at all. When I think of my kids, I ask myself, Should I expose them to religion? Or is it too late? Or does it matter? And I have a spouse who essentially thinks that it doesn't matter. My basic fear is that one of my kids will become a born-again Christian like the Tammy Faye types, or go into the army, because we have not provided our kids with some early exposure to religion. But I do talk to my kids about world religions and explain the various festivals like Easter and Passover.

As parents we are quite careful about how the kids pay respects to their grandparents. W. and I are pretty conscientious about explaining to them about *Qingming,* the ancestors' day.[4] We visit his grandfather's grave and do a little ceremony. We do the bowing. We talk to the kids about who are their ancestors on their father's side and who are on their mother's side. We do things like that and think that some of it penetrates into their little brains. We talk with our kids about inner feelings and thoughts. Going to the great-grandfather's grave on Qingming provides a spiritual side of life.

For me at this point being Chinese is my reality, and a good percentage of how I perceive myself. Perhaps I can only talk about being Chinese very indirectly. I think it has been an incredible source of strength for me as an individual. I hope that it becomes that too for my kids. I feel so privileged that there is so much that I have inherited through my parents, and through their parents, and through their parents. I can access that through studying, through my work as an art gallery manager, and in my social networks. Having gone through the struggles of being an American teenager, when you ask who am I and what am I, I know that being Chinese is normally a source of anguish or anxiety. But it has become an incredibly positive aspect to who I am. Being Chinese plays a very prominent role in the way I view the multiple facets of myself. Talking about being Chinese further strengthens that elusive notion of being Chinese; so it becomes a cathartic process. I think that I am becoming more Chinese as a Chinese American.

3

Paper Son Meets Father
Joaquin Li (Cuba, United States)

I WAS BORN IN Taishan, Guangdong, in 1920. My family was poor. There were three brothers and three sisters in my family. Shortly after I finished elementary school, the Japanese invaded China. There was no work. We fled the village and went to Guangxi Province. I did construction work building barracks for the U.S. Air Force.

My wife is from Kaiping. We were married about half a year after the Resist Japan War, as World War II is known in China. We were matched; our families did not know each other before the marriage. The matchmaker wrote down the names of three generations of ancestors on both sides on a piece of red paper. They were taken to the fortune-teller, who said that the union would be an auspicious one. There was very little *lijin,* the customary gift money for the bride's family to buy things for the trousseau. There was nothing to buy after the war. The bride, wearing the traditional red ceremonial dress, was taken to my family in a sedan chair.

I emigrated to Cuba in 1949 as the Chinese Communist Army was pushing south. My father was already in Havana. I don't know much about how the older generations went to Cuba, except that in the old days many were sold there as zhuzai (coolie, see chapter 1). My father went there before I was born. He had come back to the village for a visit, and then I was born, his youngest child. I was born in September, but he had gone back to Cuba in June. I did not see him until I was almost thirty years old! By that time I was already married and had a son myself.

When I went to Cuba, I had to buy someone else's paper because of restrictions on Chinese immigration. I bought the paper of a young man also named Li, but he was eight years younger than I, while my second brother got the paper of someone who was ten years older.

My father had a general store in the Havana Chinatown, but it was for a Cuban clientele, as it did not carry specifically Chinese merchandise. Most of the businesses at that time were in the hands of the Spanish or the Chinese people. I worked for him for two years with no pay, learning the retail trade. Eventually my father had three general stores, each managed by one of his sons. I earned $75 (U.S.) a month. It was hard work. I learned to speak Spanish on my own.

At the time I was in Cuba, there were about thirty or forty thousand Chinese. Most of them worked in the laundry business. Some had restaurants. They did quite well. They would work eight hours, four in the morning, a siesta break for two hours, and another four hours in the afternoon.

The Chinese in Cuba had all kinds of organizations: the Benevolent Association, the Freemasons, various clan associations, and the Nationalist party. It was predominantly a male community. Some were bachelors. Others left their wives and families behind in China. It was not that women and children were prohibited from going to Cuba. It was the financial problem. With US$75 a month it was hard to bring over and maintain a family in Cuba. Most of those who had families in China would send remittances home. Some would save money and go back to China in old age, to build a house in the village or buy some land. There were Chinese schools for those born in Cuba. We associated with Cubans, too, in and outside of business.

I went to Hong Kong for a visit in 1958 because by that time my wife and son had moved there from Taishan. My younger son was born after that visit. Shortly after I came back, Cuba came under the communists. The government took over the grocery stores in 1959. No more private business. Many Chinese, especially the young people, left Cuba. Some tried to flee illegally by swimming to the United States. A few drowned. Those who stayed behind became government employees. There are very few Chinese in Cuba today. The old died and the young went away, to the U.S. Some went to Hong Kong, and others to PRC.

I was in Cuba for nineteen years. After the revolution in Cuba, I could not send any money to my family in Hong Kong. I left for the United States in 1968. I was not allowed to bring anything with me, except what I was wearing. When I arrived in Miami, I was given $60

Joaquin Li and his wife, Chun Woon Ng, in Miami

as refugee relief by the U.S. government, and I could go wherever I pleased. At that time there were very few Chinese in Miami. I went to San Francisco for a week and then on to Los Angeles. I did not know anyone. I had no friends. People from Hong Kong were opening up new restaurants. Just heard people say that such-and-such restaurants were hiring. I would go and apply. I was told that I should not mention that I was from Cuba. If I did, no one would hire me. I don't know why, even though I was from Taishan and many of the Chinese in L.A. were from there. If one didn't speak Taishan dialect, one would not be able to find work at all. I found work in restaurants as a dishwasher, not through any recommendation from anyone. I was paid $250 a month. My hands got swollen from washing dishes. My wife and the younger son came to the United States in 1972. The older son was studying at the National University of Taiwan and did not join us until 1975.

The person-to-person relationships in Cuba were better than those in the United States. If any Chinese had no work or nothing to eat, he could go to this place or that and would always be given a meal. No one would refuse to feed or look after him. There was a depth of human feelings *(renqingwei)*. After work, in the evening, we would visit each other and chew the fat. We would get together on Chinese New Year, other festivals, and various occasions. It was great fun. When I first worked in the kitchen in L.A., the experienced chefs did not want to teach me anything, such as how to roast the duck or how to fry shrimps. They were afraid that I would learn the trade secrets.

Eventually we settled in Miami, as did my brothers' families. There might have been eight or ten Chinese families when we first came. We couldn't buy any Chinese grocery. There was no teahouse either. Although there are a lot more Chinese from Taiwan, Hong Kong, and Vietnam living in Miami now, they are scattered all over. There is still no Chinatown as a centralized area of Chinese shops. We still have to walk for half an hour to get Chinese groceries. Two Chinese churches.

My wife and I live in a house by ourselves. Our younger son is not married. He lives on his own and works in the shipping industry. There are many Cubans in our neighborhood, so I speak Spanish with them.

Although life was freer in Cuba then, on the whole, I like the U.S. better. Better housing, cars, air conditioning, more material comforts. Pay is higher. If one works for a few years here, one can have enough money to go back to Hong Kong for a visit. In Cuba, even when one worked for many years, one could not afford a trip home. There is social security for old folks at age sixty-five here. Nothing like that in Cuba. However, because my age on the Cuban immigration paper is eight years younger than my real age, I came to receive my social security benefits eight years late. I tried to rectify the discrepancy when I came to the U.S. But to no avail.

The Chinese value I emphasized to my children is diligence in studies. My eldest son was very studious: he would study even when he was eating. He won many scholarships and has a Ph.D. in mathematics. I am proud of the fact that the Chinese are very hardworking, saving money. Of course, there were lazy workers among the Chinese in Cuba.

Our grandchildren were born in the U.S., but my wife and I cannot talk to them. They speak Mandarin and we speak Taishan dialect; we need interpreters.

I have been to the People's Republic of China twice, visiting a sister in her eighties. I don't think I would like to live there: cannot get used to the plumbing—no shower, no flush toilet—and too many mosquitoes. Even in the new apartments, on the sixth floor, there were mosquitoes. No elevator. Social problems are on the increase too: heroin addiction, gambling, robberies, and organized crimes. The years following liberation were good, no such crimes. Freedom came too suddenly after so many years of totalitarian rule. Now that we are accustomed to the way of life here, it's difficult to live in China.

4 My Country and My Origin
Tan Chong Koon (Malaysia)

Chinese Settlement in Malaysia

My family contains quite a bit of the history of Chinese settlement in the Malay peninsula. One of my great-great-grandmothers on my father's side was a *Nyonya*. This term is for the daughter of a Chinese father and a Malay mother, while the son of such a marriage is called *Baba*. Her father came from Fujian Province around 1830 when the British gained control of the Straits Settlements of Penang, Malacca, and Singapore. He was a small trader. This Nyonya ancestress of mine was born in Malacca around 1850.

My father still remembers what his grandfather (that is, this Nyonya's son and my great-grandfather) said about her. At that time the Baba and Nyonya children were brought up to regard themselves as Chinese, apart and different from the Malays. But in their daily life they actually incorporated quite a bit of Malay culture. Apparently my great-great-grandmother always wore the Malay dress called sarong, combed her hair in a bun the Malay style, cooked a lot of Malay food, and spoke Chinese mixed with many Malay words and phrases. However, she was not a Muslim but followed the Chinese customs, which combined rites of veneration of ancestors with Buddhist and Daoist practices. She apparently also told the story about the cow herd and the weaver maid, tales from the *Romance of the Three Kingdoms*,[1] and other folklores to her son, my great-grandfather.

So my great-grandfather grew up as a Chinese, but with quite a bit of Malay culture. His father, this Nyonya ancestress's husband, nevertheless, made sure that he had a Chinese education even in Malaya. Besides, my great-grandfather was sent back to China, to our hometown Yongchun, to marry a Chinese woman. My grandfather and his siblings were born in Penang, but they studied for a while in Xiamen, Fujian Province. My grandfather came back to Malaya and married my grandmother, who was born in Kuala Lumpur. By that time, the family had become more culturally Chinese again. This was undoubtedly due to the influence of my China-born great-grandmother. But I think it was also due to the impact of the mass migration of the Chinese that was taking place then. Since the late 1870s, the British colonial authorities encouraged the influx of Chinese to work in the tin mines, rubber plantations, and sugar farms. Initially mostly men came without their families. But there were always merchants who often had their families here. Later there were restrictions on the immigration of Chinese men, but Chinese women were allowed to enter. As a result of more families, Chinese communities flourished and most of the Baba and Nyonya became more culturally Chinese.

Today my family is quite distinctly Chinese, almost as if there were no Baba or Nyonya in our family at all. We eat Chinese food, we speak the Fujian dialect or Mandarin at home, we keep all the Chinese festivals, and we are still members of clan and ancestral village associations. We have Malay business associates with whom we get along well, but our close friends are Chinese.

There are, of course, still Baba and Nyonya today. They are more Malay in their culture and, I would say, in their view of themselves. Most of them speak Malay at home. Some of my Baba classmates in the Chinese school spoke Chinese at home, but that would be the minority.

My father's family was originally involved in the rubber industry and banking. It was my father who got into the construction business after his marriage to my mother. I think my mother's grandparents were sugar merchants with some land holdings in the state of Selangor, where Kuala Lumpur is situated. Her father began the construction business. He, my maternal grandfather, was an only child. Although he had four children, only my mother and her sister survived the Japanese occupation during World War II. His son and another daughter died in childhood, as no medicine was available during the war. My father went to an English school when Malaya was a British colony. His command of English is very good. He helped my maternal grandfather run and expand the construction company in and around Kuala Lumpur. My brother, three sisters, and I were all born here. I am the oldest among the five.

Post-1969

Malaysia gained full independence in 1963, but Singapore seceded in 1965. At present the Chinese are less than 30 percent of the total population. In the years leading to independence, the Chinese leaders failed to gain equal rights for the Chinese. The terms of independence ensured not only Malay sovereignty but that the Malays would have special rights over people of Chinese or Indian ancestry. The years immediately following independence saw the Chinese gaining and expanding their economic dominance in Malaysia while the Malays wielded political power. Then ethnic tensions intensified and came to a boil in 1969. Beginning on May 13 that year, rioting, looting, and burning of Chinese properties, and killing of Chinese, went on for several days. Things changed after 1969.

The new economic policy that was adopted after the riots had a lot of discrimination against the Chinese built into the system. For example, if you want to open a company, the law requires that 30 percent of the shares must be owned by the Malays. Some businesses can only be owned by Malays. When new houses are built, a certain portion must be occupied by the Malays, and the selling prices of those houses are also lower than those for the Chinese. These government regulations apply even to the houses built by private developers. So there are many laws and regulations that give the Malays preferential treatment. We still abide by them. The Malays are still dominant politically today and they have gained economically.

Perhaps it is because of these conditions that the Chinese in Malaysia are always striving to get ahead. Because we are discriminated against, we will sink even lower if we do not strive to achieve or are not hardworking. We must fend for ourselves. We must seek opportunities, be resourceful, and become more productive in general. The Chinese who slacken off will be losers.

Education

I went to a Chinese school, from kindergarten all the way to the end of secondary school. The Chinese schools are private. The Chinese donate money to build and maintain these schools. We do learn three languages: Chinese, English, and Malay. All the instruction is in Chinese. There are over sixty Chinese secondary schools in Malaysia. There is now a Chinese college with emphasis on commerce, computer technology, and Chinese. The college is intended for students graduating from the Chinese secondary schools. Another government regulation after 1969 has been that the enrollment of Chinese students in government universities and colleges cannot exceed 30 percent, even if the grades of the Chinese are higher.

The government runs the Malay schools, where the Malay is the medium of instruction. It is hard to compare the Malay and Chinese schools because the curriculum is so different. The standard in mathematics is usually higher in the Chinese schools.

I was already in school when the riots broke out in 1969. Of course we were kept at home and, therefore, did not see the violence first hand. But I remember the grown-ups being very worried and talking about the events. When my younger brother began his schooling a couple of years later, given all the government regulations and sanctions against the Chinese, my father decided that it would be better to send him to a Malay school so that at least one member of the family would be more familiar with the Malay ways. He did very well. In fact he was one of the 30 percent to be admitted to a national university. He even gained a scholarship, something not common for a Chinese to win. But he did not go to university in Malaysia.

My younger sisters did not go to the Malay school; they attended Chinese schools too. I guess my parents wanted them to associate with the Chinese. Even in my generation — and we were all born in the 1960s and early 1970s — marrying a Malay was and still is unthinkable. However, memories of ethnic conflicts and violence are fading and there are more interracial marriages now.

My brother, my sisters, and I all went abroad for college education. They went to California eventually; one sister studied for a year in England. I went to Australia and studied mechanical engineering. I met my wife in Sydney. She was born in Ipoh, Malaysia. We were married in Kuala Lumpur, but we left for California soon after, as by that time my brother and sisters were all studying there. I received a master's degree in business administration at the University of California, Berkeley. Our two daughters were both born there.

At present, my wife, my brother, and one sister all work in the family construction company. My wife is the bookkeeper. I help to take care of the computer systems of the company, but I have a small computer consultancy business of my own. We all live very close to each other; in fact, on the same street except for two sisters. One sister is married and working in Singapore, while another is pursuing an advanced degree in genetics in the U.S.

Being Chinese and Malaysian

Like most Chinese families in Malaysia, we have a shrine of the ancestors in our parents' house. There is also a Buddhist shrine upstairs. My grandmother used to say that we should not make offerings of meat to the Buddha Sakyamuni, but we must offer the best food—fowls, fish, pork, fruits, and vegetables—to our ancestors. The shrines are still separate. In my house, we have a shrine of the Bodhisattva Kuanyin.

I feel that my family has been very blessed in the sense that our parents provided us all with excellent education. But they also emphasized the virtue of diligence and modesty. While studying abroad, we all had part-time jobs, working in the college library stacking books or washing dishes in Chinese restaurants. And we always helped each other out. While we were still very small, my father demonstrated that he could easily break one bamboo chopstick. But he could not break any when five chopsticks were bundled together. That was a powerful lesson. However, the best example is still provided by my mother. She is very hardworking and yet so modest. I really respect her.

In many ways, my brother who went to the Malay school is even more Chinese than the rest of us. Maybe it is to make up for what he missed then. In the Chinese school, for example, we celebrated

Chinese New Year of course, but also the Dragon Boat and the Mid-Autumn Moon festivals. For the Moon festival, there would be lanterns all over the campus and the students would compete in solving challenging riddles. We had a lot of Chinese drama, song and dance performances. Well, he missed this kind of school activity, although all the festivals were observed at home. Now I find that he is very conscientious about cultivating and maintaining relationships. He has *xiao* (filial piety).[2] He drives my mother wherever she wants to go. Lately my brother has taken up playing the Chinese drums. The largest one is about one meter in diameter.

One interesting aspect of living in Kuala Lumpur is that the Guangzhou dialect seems to be the speech of commerce among the Chinese, even though its native speakers are not necessarily the majority, and only Mandarin is used in the schools. So I grew up speaking the Guangzhou dialect. The ability to do so came in handy when I was studying abroad. Not only was I able to buy groceries and order food in the restaurants in the various Chinatowns in Australia or the U.S., but I was also able to find part-time jobs there. Last year, when I was visiting the New York Chinatown, I heard quite a bit of Fuzhou dialect. Although that dialect is different from my native tongue, the Xiamen dialect, I could follow most of it. Being able to converse in different Chinese dialects so far away from home gave me a feeling of belonging to a much larger group.

I see Malaysia as my country even though the Chinese in Malaysia are treated unfairly. The Chinese do try to fight for their rights. My father, my brother, and I belong to a national political party. We campaign for our candidates during elections. At the moment things are calm, and the relationships between the Malays and the Chinese are not hostile. But if the government puts more restrictions on the Chinese, if something like the riots of May 1969 should happen again, we will seriously think about leaving this country. I think it is comforting to my parents that my children can claim U.S. citizenship by virtue of being born there. If conditions become tense again, there is at least an escape route. The Malays obviously are more patriotic than the Chinese and the Indians. The fault lies with the government. If it treats us fairly, we would certainly be very loyal. As things stand now, we are citizens of Malaysia, but we feel very Chinese. During the Olympic games, I always watch and root for the Chinese athletes.

I am proud of being a Chinese. The Chinese in Malaysia are essentially like the Chinese in China, the same ideas about history and tradition, and the same feelings towards parents and family. In fact, I think, we the Chinese in Malaysia may have kept more of the old customs than the people in China. For example, when my children were born, my parents made sure that not only did the characters in each of their names have propitious meaning, but the number of strokes and the radicals in each character must harmonize with our surname. I don't know how many parents in China pay such attention to their children's names, although I hear that these customs are coming back to some areas in China. Naming is very important to us.

Three years ago my wife went with her parents and grandmother to their ancestral village. My brother and I would like to take our parents to our ancestral village in the next year or so. Since we still have so many kinsfolk there, we have to be very careful about what presents we should give to whom and whom we should invite to dinners so that we won't hurt anyone's feelings. We have not come around to such detailed planning yet.

Family relationships are the living ties to China. They express some of the good qualities of the Chinese, like perseverance, modesty, always working hard, and taking care of one's family. These ideas can be traced all the way to Kong Fuzi. I feel that my roots are in these traditions and customs that our ancestors brought from China. China is not my country, but it is my origin.

From Liverpool Chinatown

Sylvia Marie Chinque (United Kingdom)
& Natascha Chinque (Germany, Canada)

Sylvia Marie Chinque (Grandmother, United Kingdom)

My father, Chow Sing, was a seaman from Guangzhou. My mother, Bridget, was half-English and half-Irish. She met my father through a friend who was married to a Chinese already. She was eighteen and he twenty-three. They were married in three weeks, I believe, in 1906. He didn't speak English and she did not know any Chinese. They were together for over forty years. I was born in Liverpool in 1914, the fourth among four brothers and eight sisters. My father didn't speak Chinese to us. The only Chinese we knew was things such as Good morning! Have you had your rice? Would you like a cup of tea? I think my mother eventually understood what he was saying in Chinese, but my father's English was atrocious. We used to tease him that we didn't understand what he was saying. It was a lovely childhood.

My father never went back to China after he got married. He sent money back to his mother for several years until her death. As Liverpool was a port, it was mostly seamen in Chinatown. My father had two horses and a cart. He would take the luggage for the seamen from the ship to their lodging. The stables were at the back of our house. He later became the manager of the Chinese Seamen's Boarding House. We were not rich; we were not poor. We always had pretty dresses to wear and beautiful jewelry. My father was always able to get beautiful gold chains and jade. I remember seeing other children walking around without shoes in those days.

I grew up in Liverpool Chinatown. You could walk the street any hour of the day or night and nobody would attack you. We had a house that was on the corner, next to the police station. We later moved to a house which was sandwiched between a brothel and an opium den. At that time my Irish grandmother was living with us. She always told us not to talk to the ladies of the brothel. They were pretty but did not wear much makeup. They were English girls, and the clients were Chinese men without families.

There were laundrymen and eventually some restaurants, but not very many businesses. I used to like going to the Chinese restaurants, especially every Sunday morning when we had *dim sum*.[1] We would watch *hakou, siumai,* and all the other delicious treats coming out of the great big bamboo steamers. Barbecue pork bun was two pennies each. There were two Chinese grocers who were related to each other. They brought their wives from China. Those ladies did not speak English. My mother's friends were English ladies married to the Chinese.

There were Chinese organizations, too: the Benevolent Association, *Chee Gong Tong* (the Freemasons), the clan associations, and *Guomindang* (the Nationalist party). My father was one of the grand masters of the Chee Gong Tong. He had to give that up when he became a Catholic on his deathbed. By then it didn't really matter; he was sixty-three. The old Chinese were very, very kind. At Chinese New Year, they used to give us red packets with gold sovereigns in them! Yes, gold sovereigns. We would give them to our mother, and she would replace them with copper pennies, and we were satisfied. The old Chinatown was bombed during World War II. Many people died. A new Chinatown was built in a different part of the city after the war.

My parents believed in education and made us go to school when not all children did. My younger brothers and sisters went to the Chinese school on Saturdays, but I never did, as there was none when I was growing up. I went to a Catholic school. My eldest brother was the first Chinese to graduate from the University of Liverpool. Another brother was a schoolmaster. One of my sisters had voice training for singing. One sister played the violin, and another the piano.

My sister the violinist met this Guomindang lieutenant who was a student in Scotland. After he returned to China, he wrote and asked her to marry him. So she went to China and they were married in the Qingdao cathedral. She took Chinese lessons and could speak Mandarin fluently. They moved to Taiwan in 1948, by which time he was

Sylvia Chinque (center) with sister Beryl and niece Nuan

an admiral. They came to visit Liverpool for their ruby wedding anniversary. She died in her sleep the night she returned to Taibei.

Only one sister and I are living. I lost four siblings in two years. I am still grieving for them. Michael, the youngest, stayed close to Liverpool Chinatown all his life. We were very close. I miss him desperately.

I had spinal trouble when I was seven and was hospitalized for over fifteen months. I had to lie in a frame. My mother couldn't come to see me because she was pregnant with another baby. My sister was allowed to visit once a month. I was so homesick! After I came home I wore a frame on my back for three and half years. They told my mother that I would never walk and could never bear children. They were wrong. I have eight beautiful children.

I met my husband, Samuel Chinque, when I was fifteen and married him at the age of seventeen. He was also a seaman. He will be ninety-three next week. My parents approved the marriage; I would not have gotten married without their blessing. My eldest sister married an Englishman against my father's wishes. In fact they eloped. She died when she was only twenty-three, leaving behind two children.

My husband was born in China and then taken to Jamaica, where my father-in-law had stores. He was six when his mother died, and was taken back to China to be educated. While he was about eighteen, he got married. The wife died in giving birth to a child. Then his father died, too, so he had to go to sea. He still has family in Kingston, Jamaica, but he didn't keep in touch with them, neither with the son he had in China who is living in the U.S.

When we got married, my husband knew that I was a Catholic and that our children would be brought up as Catholics. After World War II, he bought a house in London, and we moved there in 1952. He was the editor-in-chief of New China News Agency in Europe and of a communist Chinese newspaper. As a communist he was an atheist and did not want the children to be brought up as Catholics. We eventually parted. He is remarried now.

After my divorce, I went to Taibei for five months, after which officials began asking my brother-in-law questions about me and why I was there for so long. I emigrated to Canada to live with a daughter. Sadly I could not settle there. I was fortunate to get a beautiful cottage after I came back to England. There are about fifty cottages run by a charitable organization with money bequeathed by a nineteenth-century philanthropist. The cottages are meant for elderly women who could not afford to buy a place of their own. I have a large living room, a bedroom, a kitchen, and a bathroom. There is a lovely garden in the front, which the organization maintains in excellent condition. I have been living in the cottage for almost twenty-five years.

My children are scattered all over the world: one daughter in Switzerland, two sons in Germany, two daughters in the U.S., a son and a daughter in Canada. Only one child is in England — he lives in Yorkshire. I have grandchildren and great-grandchildren. All my daughters have children, but only one son has children. He has five.

For my eighty-fourth birthday, one daughter arranged a beautiful party for me. She invited her brothers and sisters to join her if they wanted, but she planned and arranged it all. It was a party for all my good friends, held in a hotel. My daughter reserved rooms for my friends to stay there overnight. We had a wonderful time. Six of my children were able to come. I hope that all my eight children will be able to come for my ninetieth birthday. One last reunion before I die.

I am full of aches and pains, but I count my blessings. I read a lot, and I knit. I can't go to church every day, but the priest will come to see me. I love to talk to people. I do some *taiji* and *qigong*[2] every day. My son in Toronto taught me; he first learned it from my husband. I'll watch some television, and go to bed at the drop of nine o'clock.

I don't cook at all; I gave all my pots and pans away. I have hot meals delivered to me. I just make some sandwiches for myself, but I don't have any appetite. I never liked cooking. My mother cooked English meals. My father didn't cook at all. My husband did. He is an excellent cook, and the children are all good cooks. Sometimes I would love to have a Chinese meal. I used to cook a simple favorite meal sometimes: a bowl of rice, with shredded cabbage and lean pork, cooked with garlic and onion. I found it delicious and yet so simple. When I cooked too much, I would give some to my neighbor. She loved it.

I am a mixture of Chinese, English, and Irish. The Irish bit is where I got my Catholic faith, which is a great support to me, the most important thing to me. Most of my family look more European; I look more Chinese. I remember when I was in school people used to call me Chink. I used to wonder, I am not yellow, how can they tell? But children can be very cruel. I was a very quiet child. There was no physical bullying. They just said very hurtful things. Somebody once asked me if I wished that I weren't a Chinese. I said, I am proud of being a Chinese. My children prefer to be Chinese rather than English, very proud of their Chinese blood. And me too.

Natascha Chinque (Granddaughter, Germany and Canada)

My father was born to a Chinese father and half Chinese mother in Liverpool in 1941. Thirty years later I was born in Frankfurt, Germany, to my German mother and my three-quarter Chinese father. My four brothers and I are all three-eighths Chinese, half German, and a bit of English and Irish for extra flavor. We were raised to be proud of our heritage and diversity.

According to my father, our name Chinque is Chin and Que. Chin was my grandfather's family name, and Que was his mother's family name. At one time, Grandfather had a choice in a name. So he took the names of his father and his mother and joined them together. It even used to be written differently: Chin-Que. Over the years, we ended up with Chinque.

Throughout my childhood, either we would drive up to England, or my father's many brothers, sisters, cousins, aunts, and uncles would visit us in Germany or Spain. Many of those visits revolved around delicious food, often Chinese. My grandfather makes the best Chinese stew I have ever tasted.

My grandfather introduced me to Chinese medicine, Chinese cooking, and taiji. We spent a lot of time together when I was a child. I fondly remember a three-week period in 1982 when our grandfather came to the south of Spain to take care of my brother Mark and myself while our parents were in the U.S. He started every day with at least an hour of taiji on the terrace. He tried to teach us, but it was too slow for us. We always had a great time with him; he treated us with kindness and patience. I also remember visiting him at his London home on many occasions. He has a picture of Mao Zedong in every room. The smell of mothballs still reminds me of the scent in his home today.

My brother Mark and I used to beg our father to tell us stories about his youth. He has always been a great storyteller, and he walked us through his childhood. He built soapbox cars with his friends, explored old abandoned buildings, and was always finding ways to make some pocket money. He described how all the children bathed in the same bathwater: an inch or two of water for the youngest child, Jui Ling, and then a little water was added as each child took their turn. I have always been impressed with his memory, such as the gifts the children gave each other and their mother. It appears that they grew up during difficult times in Liverpool and London, but something about their upbringing sounds so basic and romantic.

Natascha Chinque

As a child in Germany, I was completely oblivious to any prejudice directed toward me. My parents split up when I was five, and at age eight, my father, stepmother, and younger brother moved to the south of Spain. My father went into early retirement to raise my brother and me. We lived a life of leisure. If we weren't at dinner parties with friends, we were playing tennis, swimming, horseback riding, or fishing. Many of my current hobbies and activities developed during that time. Whilst in Spain, I experienced some prejudice, mainly against my German background. I was fortunate in having attended a German, Spanish, and English school during those years.

At age thirteen, we moved to a suburb of Toronto where I went through a major culture shock adjusting to the large metropolis. During the next few years, we moved to the Muskoka region in northern

Ontario, and St. Catharines in southern Ontario. By the time I graduated from high school, I had attended about nine different schools. It
was not easy to adjust to so many different schools, but in retrospect,
I appreciated the exposure to different cultures and people.

At age eighteen, I moved to Vancouver to attend the University of
British Columbia. I have been in Vancouver ever since and love the life
I have made for myself here. Vancouver is a city full of transplants; it is
a bit of a challenge to find someone who has been born and bred in the
city. I am very fortunate to have such a multicultural background, as it
taught me to accept people for who they are rather than where they
come from. I believe being three-eighths Chinese has helped me get
closer to other Chinese. Oftentimes I am invited to come along for
what everyone knows to be my favorite meal — dim sum.

There are a few Chinese influences in my life. I like to arrange my
apartment to encourage the free flow of energy according to *fengshui*.[3] I sometimes consult the *Yi Jing,* the *Book of Changes,* for
guidance. And I like playing mahjong on the odd occasion when there
are three others who enjoy playing. My gambling habits usually lean
towards poker, which my father taught me as a young girl. I usually
play with friends at someone's home but have been known to go to
the casino on the odd occasion. I am always surprised to see how
many Asians visit casinos.

The rest of my life revolves around friends and family, cooking
and eating well, bike riding, yoga, reading, being in the great out-
doors, traveling, working with wonderful people, and searching for
enlightenment. Eventually I hope to find the man of my dreams and
raise a family.

6

Leong Wong-Kit the Paper Daughter

Rochelle Wong de la Cruz (United States)

MY GRANDMOTHER'S NAME was Leong Wong-Kit, and she was born in Guangdong Province in 1895. She came to Hawaii in 1900 with a Honolulu family who took their two daughters back to China to be raised by grandparents. When they returned to Honolulu, they brought back two other girls with the Leong family paper, and one of them was my apo (grandmother). I always read about paper sons, but Apo was a paper daughter.

I gave my daughter the middle name of Leong, for Apo. Later my aunt told me that it was her Honolulu family's name, not her real name. But she was known only by that name, or her married name. We called her Apo (Grandmother) but others would call her Ah Mu (Mother) or Mrs. Wong-Kit. But this name Leong Wong-Kit is on her gravestone. I'm not sure whether anyone knew her birth family name in China or even her personal name.

She and another girl were brought to Honolulu to be helpers in the Leong household, like maids. She told me that the family tried to send her to school, but she always ran away. It was probably a Chinese school, as they lived in Honolulu Chinatown. She spoke Chinese and the pidgin English (Hawaii Creole), but she was literate in neither English nor Chinese.

Hawaiian Islands

In the nineteenth century, the most important crop was sugar, and there were plantations on all of the islands. When the white plantation owners couldn't get the Hawaiians to work for them, they imported labor, first from Europe and then from Asia, and that's when the Chinese started coming, in the 1860s. At first, the men came as indentured workers with the idea of doing their servitude for four years and then going back to China. But many of them stayed and intermarried with the Hawaiians. Not many Chinese women came until the 1900s. After the Chinese came the Japanese, and later the Koreans and the Filipinos. My mother's father came from Korea, and her Portuguese mother was born in Hawaii. In 1893, the American cabal overthrew the queen of Hawaii, Lili'uokalani, in order to control the resources.

Apo married my gonggong Wong-Kit when she was fifteen. He was maybe ten years older, also born in Guangdong Province, and came to the island of Maui to work on the plantation. After he did his four years of labor, he left Maui, married Apo, and opened a store in Honomu, on the big island of Hawaii. I'm sure it was an arranged marriage since Apo and Gonggong were on different islands.

My father and his sister, Aunty Gnit, were born in Honomu. Apo had my father when she was sixteen. This part of the island had many sugar towns, and every town had a plantation store, owned and run by the plantation. Workers had to buy most of their necessities at the plantation store, so the money just circulated within the plantation system. Gonggong and Apo sold Chinese dry goods and items that the Chinese workers couldn't get at the plantation store, so they were not really competing with the plantation store. They lived above the store in Honomu, in a old-style plantation building on stilts; it is still standing.

My father remembered a strike at the Honomu plantation, in the 1920s or early 1930s. The plantation had separate living quarters for the workers, so there were a Chinese camp, a Japanese camp, and so forth. This kept the workers apart, but eventually they got organized. During the strike, many workers stayed under Gonggong's Chinese store, which had a running stream beside it. Apo cooked for them and Dad remembered eating with these striking workers.

When the Great Depression of the 1930s got to the Hawaiian Islands, Apo and Gonggong had to close the store and move to Hilo, about eighteen miles away. They tried to set up the same kind of store selling Chinese goods, but Hilo was a bigger city with well-established Chinese markets and stores. They ended up with a small

Mrs. Leong Wong-
Kit at the Lono
Street house

snack shop, selling preserved plums and melon seeds imported from
China. But the mango seed and the very black salt lemon came from
the island, made by a Hawaiian-Chinese family. Apo displayed these
seeds on large blue and white platters that many years later, when I
got married, my mother gave to me. Apo recognized the platters
when she came to dinner and the very first time I served something on
them. That made both of us happy.

We know very little about Gonggong because he died in 1935.
One thing we do know is his connection to the Lin Hing Society,
which he and about thirty other immigrants, mostly bachelors from
Guangdong, formed on the Big Island. With the pooled financial resources from the members, this mutual aid society not only helped the
immigrants but became the extended family and the hub of social life
for many contract workers.

When my father was old enough, Gonggong made him a member of the Lin Hing Society. Even though Gonggong could read and write Chinese, he needed Dad's help with the English, so my father was put in charge of the books. The Society even had its own building in Hilo, which housed Chinese bachelors until the 1960 tidal wave (tsunami) severely damaged it and it had to be demolished.

Toward the end of his life, my father became concerned about being the last remaining member of the Lin Hing Society. Some members had family who inherited their share of the proceeds; others did not. Dad had faithfully kept the books and was adamant that the money could never be for personal use. In his last years, my brothers and I discussed with him the possibility of setting up a scholarship at the University of Hawaii, in the name of the Lin Hing Society. He thought that was a fitting use of this money. Before he died in 2001, he turned over the entire funds of the Society to the UH Foundation, which now provides two scholarships a year for students of Chinese descent from the big island of Hawaii or from Guangdong Province, China.

The Bar

It must have been at the end of Prohibition when Apo and Gonggong added a bar in the shop. So the Hilo store sold snacks in the front, and there was a small bar in the back. Gonggong even built the bar counter himself. A few years after his death, Pearl Harbor was bombed. Soldiers arrived in Hilo, and Apo's bar did very well. She bought a house on Lono Street at the beginning of the war years and moved everybody in: my parents and my oldest brother born in 1939; Aunty Gnit, her husband and son; and Apo herself. In 1941 my second brother was born. I was born in 1945 and Apo played an active part in my adoption; she was by then so well known for her generosity that people would approach her with many requests. I was brought into the family right after my birth and grew up in the Lono Street house that Apo bought.

The bar was very busy during the war years, and everyone had to put in time and work there. Apo made a lot of money and invested it in Hilo Ice House and Hawaiian Electric stocks and lived on those dividends for the rest of her life. When you think about the fact that

Apo couldn't read or write, her success might appear remarkable, but not to us because she was, as we say in Hawaii, very *akamai* (smart).

The Lono Street house was typical of older houses in Hawaii, with a basement on the ground level and the main floor upstairs. In the basement were two extra bedrooms that were always available for whoever needed them. Abaji, my mother's father, lived there for a while, and one of my father's friends, whose entire family and house had been washed away in the 1946 tidal wave, also lived there.

There were also many gatherings and parties at the Lono Street house. Apo gave all her grandchildren a *lu'au,* which is the custom in Hawaii, but I think it's also a Chinese custom. You have a big party to celebrate the baby's first birthday. In our family scrapbook is a faded clipping with a picture of Ronald Kai Sheong Wong, taken at his baby lu'au at the house of his grandmother, Mrs. Wong-Kit.

Good Luck Jade

Apo used to buy jade stones from a troupe of Chinese actors and actresses that traveled regularly through the Hawaiian Islands, and later had these stones made up into rings. These are imperial green jades that we hardly see anymore, except in antique jewelry. Everyone in my father's generation wore jade rings, and all of us grandkids received one when we graduated from high school. But by now, the 1960s, the young men were not wearing such jewelry. My older brother used to put his on only when he knew he was going to see Apo, but inevitably, he would forget. She'd ask him, "Where your ring?" And he'd say, "On my bureau — I forgot it." He never told her of course, but didn't think the jade gold ring was too cool. But she said to him, "You wear your jade. Jade is good luck."

In pidgin she would tell the story about a man who was jumping from roof to roof with everyone chasing him. He finally had to jump to the ground, thinking that he would probably die in the fall. "If he jump down, he *make* ("die" or "dead" in Pidgin) but no can help. He jump and . . . Ayah! He no make! But he look and he see his jade crack! His jade good luck. You wear your jade, for good luck."

But did my brother wear his jade after this story? Of course not.

Bai Sam

When my Aunty Gnit moved to Honolulu, Apo went with her but returned to the Big Island a couple times a year for *bai sam*,[1] because Gonggong is buried in Hilo. It was usually in April or May I think, and sometimes she came in October. She brought from Honolulu the stacks of square papers she needed for bai sam, which we had to fold. Only the women could fold, and only if we weren't having our menstrual period. We all sat on the floor — me, Apo, my mother, sometimes my aunt from Honolulu — and we'd be folding papers for days. Apo would string them and explain: this is the clothes, the money, et cetera. She also brought a sheet of paper with Chinese writing on it that she got from the Daoist priest in Honolulu.

She spent time cooking certain kinds of food: the boiled chicken, the shrimp and fish. Maybe it was only in our childish mind, but the food had a certain heavy smell that my brothers and I hated, and we called it "graveyard food." It was different from the food she usually cooked. When all the food was prepared and papers folded, the car would be loaded up. I remember Apo running back and forth, making sure that she had things like matches, the bottle of gin, all the cups, the candles, and the joss sticks.

We all went with Apo to Gonggong's grave and participated in the ceremony. She put the special paper with the writing on the gravestone, securing it with a small rock so it wouldn't blow away. She arranged the food dishes on a tray, and poured the gin into jiggers, sprinkling it around the grave. She burned the folded papers, and then my father lit the firecrackers. Following her, we'd all take our turn showing respect, bowing in front of Gonggong's grave with the joss sticks in our hands. We did this every year the entire time we were growing up.

My father belonged to the Chinese Cemetery Society in Hilo. It still holds regular gatherings for bai sam twice a year, in the spring and autumn.

Paper Daughter Home Again

Apo lived to be eighty-five and was still quite alert at the end. I was living in Honolulu then and feel thankful that in the last few years of her life, I was living in the same place as she was and could visit her regularly. My children loved to visit Apo because she was always giving them candy.

Apo died in her sleep. She went to bed the night before and simply did not wake up the next morning. We should all be so lucky!

She had a Chinese funeral, with a Daoist priest officiating. He explained that he would be ringing the bell and chanting our Chinese names as he implored, on our behalf, for the gates to be opened for the new arrival, Apo. I listened hard for Kai Sim, my Chinese name. When he said it, I felt satisfied. I wanted those gates to Chinese heaven to open after all, for Apo. My father and his sister had converted to Catholicism by that time, but they agreed that Apo should be buried with Daoist rites, in her tradition. But they were nervous about how and what to do because except for bai sam, they didn't know much more. Apo had beautiful jewelry, so my aunt wanted to bury her with one of her pins. One of Apo's adoptive sisters—a few of them were still alive and came to the funeral—told my aunt, "The pin—no good! She can get hurt on her trip." So my aunt took off the pin, but she and Dad felt bad because they didn't even know little things like not putting a pin on her!

So she was buried in Honolulu with Daoist ceremony but not in the Chinese cemetery in Hilo. My father and aunt made all the funeral arrangements. They told me that she wanted to be buried in Honolulu and had, in fact, bought her own plot there. Maybe she always considered Honolulu her home. We don't even have a Chinatown in Hilo. I just feel sorry that she is not in a Chinese cemetery where we could do bai sam for her. Nobody I know does bai sam now except for the Hilo Chinese Cemetery Society priest. But I would like to do it for her. Maybe I still can. What would be stopping me?

Apo never talked about her birth family back in China and always referred to the Leong siblings as her brothers and sisters. Before my brother went to China recently, he wanted to know about the town and the village where Apo was born. Even Aunty Gnit couldn't get any information. By then, Apo was gone and so were most of her Hawaii Leong family.

Apo never even talked about the fact that she was born in China. I always thought that she was born in Honolulu but knew that Gong-gong was born in China. I was told that she never talked about it because of her fear of deportation. It was only after the amnesty, in 1962 I think, when Apo got her paperwork in order that the fact of her being a paper daughter could be known. But once I found out, I was reluctant to bring it up because she never talked about it. Maybe because she was so young when she came and had been quiet for so long, her birth family was not anything that she thought about or even remembered. Maybe she didn't even know her real name. What a huge relief it must have been to have the fear of deportation finally lifted. Can you imagine living with that fear for all those years?

Thanks for the opportunity to talk about Apo. She is an important person in my life. I feel lucky that she was also my apo.

Fighting for Education
Fay Chung (Zimbabwe)

[The first part of the narrative is excerpted from Fay Chung's unpublished memoir.]

IT WAS IMPOSSIBLE to grow up in colonial Rhodesia without becoming aware from the earliest age of the deep hostility between the races. The land issue was the main bone of contention. At the age of four I would listen to my (maternal) grandfather talking about the land issue with his old friend, a Somali who owned a butchery near my grandparents' café. My grandfather, Yee Wo Lee, had come to Rhodesia in 1904 as a youth of seventeen, the fifth son in a large Chinese peasant family. As the fifth son, he did not inherit any land in China. Instead he was given an education. He had gained initiation into politics as a schoolboy follower of Sun Yat-Sen, and as a result was very sensitive to the colonial situation. He was one of the first people to provide financial support for black nationalists, and his bakery, Five Roses Bakery, situated very centrally in the middle of Charter Road, and near the Railway Station (in the capital city Salisbury, now renamed Harare), soon became the meeting place for many nationalist leaders. He was later to pay the rent for ZANU.[1]

With the peasant attachment to land, he came to Africa in search of land, but his ambition was thwarted by the racial laws instituted by the colonialists. These laws forbade the sale of the best land to all but whites. Grandfather was unable to buy the farm he yearned for. From a very early age we learnt that the whites were greedy, and would not allow other races to own land.

Instead of farming Grandfather began his career as a chef at the then Grand Hotel. All his life he loved cooking, and in the Chinese tradition, made it into an art. In my grandparents' household it was

Grandfather who did all the cooking whilst Grandmother ran the business. . . .

My mother died when I was three years old, leaving my father with three young children. My father was busy running his business, and we were left in the charge of our nanny the whole day long. It was in that situation that we soon picked up a working knowledge of Shona, one of the main African languages in the country. We also came to understand our nanny, her views, her character, and background quite well as we followed her around. We knew her friends and what they talked about. It was in those early and impressionable days that I came to understand the situation in the country. I did not understand the problem of land from my nanny and from the other servants in the house, but I quickly heard about education. The black people around me felt that they were being deprived of education because whites did not want blacks to be too educated. One of the old workers in my father's business, who was called Zakia, told me that whites would only allow black people to know the Bible, but kept all other knowledge to themselves. Certainly black people knew a lot about the Bible, and we were taught Bible stories and sang hymns such as "Jesus loves me, this I know." My nanny and subsequent nannies were also excellent at craftwork. I learnt to knit at an early age, and was able to knit myself a jersey before I was ten years old.

Education, or rather the lack of it, was an area that caused bitter resentment. Children were separated by race. White children attended "European" schools. Black children attended "African" schools. There was a third category of schools known as "Coloured and Asian" schools that we attended.

I attended a primary school for Asians. It was called Louis Mountbatten School, named after the British Viceroy for India, as most of the pupils were Indians. Our headmaster, Mr. V.S. Naidoo, a South African Indian from Durban, drummed into our heads from the earliest grades that since we were not whites, we would only make our way in the world through education. This message obviously fell on fertile ground, as both the teachers and pupils were exceptionally dedicated to learning. It was many years later that I learnt that it was not very usual for primary school children to be conversant with Shakespeare

Fay Chung

and Jane Austen. By the time I went to secondary school I had already covered quite a lot of the secondary mathematic syllabus. . . .

Up until the 1950s there was no secondary school for Coloureds and Asians. I first became aware of this problem when I was about seven years old. My mother's youngest sister had completed primary school at the age of eleven. A brilliant scholar, she was unable to enroll in a secondary school because she was Chinese. My grandfather went to every secondary school in the city to try and get her enrolled, but these schools were for whites only. She was forced to repeat the last grade of primary school for five years until she left school at the age of sixteen. This was the fate of all Asian and Coloured students except for the few whose parents could afford to send them overseas or to South Africa for secondary and further education. Education, like land, was for whites only.

The situation for blacks was slightly better than for Coloureds and Asians: in the 1950s there was already one secondary school for blacks, Goromonzi High School, which served the whole country. In contrast, there were over twenty secondary schools for whites, although whites then constituted only 4% of the population at the time. Whites had compulsory and free primary and secondary education, whereas blacks had limited access and also had to pay for what little education they could obtain. A handful of blacks were allowed to obtain secondary education so that they could serve their own communities as teachers and nurses, and also assist the colonial government as lower echelon civil servants and clerks. Blacks who wanted more education would have to go to South Africa. . . .

I was fortunate that by the time I completed primary school, the first secondary school for Coloureds and Asians, Founders' High School, was opened in Bulawayo. Our primary school head, Mr. Naidoo, a dedicated educationalist, spent a whole day persuading my father to allow me to attend this school as a boarder as the school was in a different city, Bulawayo, four hundred miles away. My father, a conservative and traditionalist, did not really believe in educating girls, particularly in a boarding school far away from home. But Mr. Naidoo was persistent and persuasive, and my father finally relented.

I spent two happy years as a boarder at Founders. Our headmaster, Mr. Baldock was an Englishman. For most of us this was our first experience of having a head and some teachers who were whites, as our teachers had so far been either Indians or Coloureds. Mr. Baldock had a strong sense of justice, and did not utilize corporal punishment, a system which we had become accustomed to in our primary school. Mrs. Baldock found out that Chinese were allowed to enter the whites only cinemas, and once asked me to accompany their two small sons to watch a Walt Disney film. Blacks, Indians and Coloureds were not allowed in most of the cinemas. Apartheid allowed the Chinese some privileges, and this was one of them. . . .

At the end of my second year at Founders', St. John's School, a well-known Roman Catholic school for Coloureds, established a secondary section. My parents decided to transfer me to St. John's immediately so that I would be nearer home. Moreover my father had great faith in the nuns, and believed they had special powers to improve people's character and morality, and as he placed great value on character and morality, I had to leave the Government school for a Roman Catholic school. He was not very confident that a Government school like Founders' would provide the right moral background.

It was at St. John's that I came to understand the colonial set-up more intimately. St. John's was also an "orphanage," but the "orphans" were not really orphans. Many of them were the offspring of white men with their black mistresses. The children of such unions were usually rejected by their fathers, and sometimes also by their mothers. The totally abandoned children were raised by the Dominican sisters. They were easily identifiable as they were invariably given the names of Catholic saints such as Francis Xavier or Martin de Porres. They had developed a hard exterior, often persecuting children like myself from more privileged backgrounds. They did this by stealing our panties and our soap. Actually they were deeply sad children who knew no home other than the school, and no other family than the nuns and priests. I spent two years at that school, and it made me appreciate the privilege I enjoyed of being a spoilt child from a middle class family.

Such was the racialist consciousness that some of these children of mixed races would themselves despise and reject their black mothers. One of my most vivid childhood memories was of a black mother coming to visit her ten-year old daughter at St. John's. As the school had very few visitors, crowds of children would usually gather round to stare at every visitor. So it was that when Hilda's mother arrived to see her, I was one of the crowd of children who had turned out to stare at her. Ten-year old Hilda was mortified that her black mother had come to the school. This incident made me think. Hilda constantly talked of her father, a white farmer in Sinoia. She was very proud of her father who had rejected her, but she did not want to know her own mother who had come to see her. I was amazed. As a child who had grown up without a mother I found it appalling that someone would reject her own mother because of race.

I learnt at St. John's that Coloured children placed a premium on white skin and straight hair. Many Coloured children were indistinguishable from whites, and they were envied. Many others were indistinguishable from blacks, and they were either despised or pitied. Teenage girls spent an inordinate amount of time trying to make their skins whiter and their hair straighter. Chinese girls like myself, in contrast, spent our time trying to make our hair curlier. We all had the image of the perfect beauty, who was Caucasian. . . .

On completion of my [secondary education], I was accepted at the local University. This was the first opportunity for us to meet with students of all races on an equal footing. . . . It was during this period that I met some of the black students who would later become part of the ruling elite in Zimbabwe. We had to learn to juggle personal, social and political relationships within a racially segregated society. My friend Irene Steblecki, who had been at St. John's with me, and myself were the only two women students who were neither black nor white. We were given the privilege of having a whole corridor, complete with a large sitting room to entertain our guests, to ourselves, in Swinton Hall, the women's residence, as the University authorities respected local racial prejudices by separating us by race. There were only four black women students, two of them from Zambia, one from Malawi, and only one from Zimbabwe. They too had a whole corridor and sitting room to themselves! . . .

The leading intellectual light at the University was the History Professor, Terence Ranger. He, together with other anti-racist lecturers and students, organized peaceful protests against the color bar. This was my first experience of protest. We would go in a racially mixed group and have tea in an all-white restaurant. Innocuous as that sounds today, at the time it was a courageous challenge against the color bar. We found that we were never chased out when the group consisted of women only. However, things became pretty rough when men were involved. One violent incident that occurred was at the Salisbury Swimming Pool. For some reason swimming pools and bathrooms were particularly sacred to whites, and a violent incident took place involving Terence Ranger being pushed into the swimming pool by some irate white racists. . . .

It was as a university student that I first became interested in education. I began teaching at the University Night School which was run by lecturers and students for the house servants and other workers in the nearby upper class suburb of Mount Pleasant. I soon became the head of the primary section of the School, a position I held until I graduated three years later. I encountered the thirst for knowledge of my black compatriots. They indefatigably arrived for their evening classes day after day, year after year, despite the fact that most of them worked a twelve-hour day. On the other hand it was a battle to ensure that the university students who had volunteered so enthusiastically to teach at the beginning of the academic year continued to do so consistently. . . .

Having taught for three years at the Night School it was natural for me to think of education as a career, and I decided to enter African Education on graduation. . . .

When I applied for a post in African Education, I found I was received with less than enthusiasm. I was told that I should apply to teach pupils of my own race. As there were only a few hundred Chinese in Rhodesia this was a laughable suggestion. Although all the Chinese children attended the same school, there were so few of us that it was virtually impossible to find two of us in one class. Then I was told that there were too many teachers in African Education, and that there was no need for more teachers. However, I had done my research into the area, and I knew that there were in fact very few university graduates within African Education. Even if it were true that there were too many teachers in African Education, it could not be said that there were enough graduate teachers. At any rate I refused to be turned down, and after some time my application was accepted. . . .

[The white Rhodesians, under Ian Smith, rejecting black majority rule, declared independence from Britain unilaterally in 1965. Years of liberation struggle by the blacks followed. After teaching in secondary schools in Gwelo (now Gweru) and Salisbury (now Harare) for five years, Fay Chung spent three years at the University of Leeds, England. She went to teach at the School of Education in the University of Zambia, Lusaka, Zambia, in 1971. It was there that the struggles for the independence of Zimbabwe forced her "from being an intellectual observer, political analyst and commentator to an actual participant" (Chung 1996:61). She remained in Zambia until August 1975, when she had to flee to Mozambique, as her safety and life were threatened by the Rhodesian Secret Service agents operating in Zambia. Thus she became a full-time freedom fighter. She was part of the ZANU delegation to the Geneva Constitution Conference in 1976. She established educational programs for the children of thousands of Zimbabweans living in refugee camps in Mozambique. At times she was caught in the internal conflicts within the liberation movement. She did not return home until Zimbabwe won independence in 1980. Since then she has shown time and again to be an indefatigable educator both in Zimbabwe and around the world. The following is an account, in her own words, of some of her work since Independence and her thoughts on being a Zimbabwean of Chinese ancestry.]

Even though there were conflicts within the liberation movement, I stayed on, not knowing how soon success would come, because I looked at it this way: Internal conflict was unavoidable and to be expected. Nearly all the people who joined the liberation movement were against Ian Smith but were all different. There were people who were idealistic, people who were mercenary, people who were conservative, even fascist, one could say. But they were still opposed to Smith because black fascism was against white fascism. Then on the other side, you had socialists and Marxists. They all had different ideas, but everybody was against colonialism. They were united by their opposition to Smith and also by the issue of race because the colonial regime was very racist. So it would not have been realistic to expect the struggle to be rosy. Then also I looked at it this way. We could have run away but the ordinary people could not. It was better for us to participate than for only the people who had nothing to lose.

Education in Zimbabwe

After Independence we only had about 35 percent of the children in primary school and about 2 percent in secondary school. Our task was to ensure that we had everybody in primary and secondary school. My first job after Independence as the head of education planning in the Ministry of Education was to plan a system which could provide education to everybody. We relied heavily on the parents and communities. We initiated the policy which said that if the parents built the school, we would pay the teachers and pay for the educational materials. In other words, we would share in partnership with the parents the responsibility for the education of their children. There were some simple rules. They had to write down the number, names, and ages of the children who wanted to come to school. We had some regulations about the size of the classrooms, safety features, the kind of toilets, and other technical kind of criteria. Then the parents built the school, with some subsidies from the government. Community ownership of the school was such that once the communities got organized, they went from strength to strength. So the major success was due to the fact that the parents were interested in educating their children. They more or less paid half the cost by building schools.

We invented a system of training good teachers cost-effectively that has become quite well known. It's a four-year course. The idea was that only one-third of it was in college, and two-thirds of it in the schools. The student teachers were placed in teams of threes to a school. They held weekly seminars, attended weekend and holiday courses, and so forth. It was one of the most successful in-service teacher training courses, I think, worldwide.

Of course we did not have the teachers, buildings, laboratories, workshops, or equipment as we expanded secondary education from an enrollment of 2 percent to everyone. To provide secondary schools effectively with all those handicaps, we utilized a system of distance education. Take science for example: how to teach the first four years of high school science without science teachers. We chose six of the best science teachers in the country. They prepared the lessons for four years. Then we prepared a science kit where all the chemicals and equipment were packaged so that each week the students did an experiment. They would open the kit for the week, follow the instructions, and use the chemicals to do the experiment, and so on. Many teachers were unqualified. They might have had eleven or thirteen years of schooling but were never trained as a teacher. Or they might have been trained as a religion or African language teacher. Now they would be teaching science, using the lessons prepared by the six best teachers. Then we integrated that with radio and holiday courses for teachers. We did that for lots of subjects: math, geography, history, woodwork, metal, technical drawing, food and nutrition, fashion and fabric, and construction. Through the use of distance education, the six best teachers instead of teaching six classes were reaching out to 800,000 students. It was a very successful program. Some of these ideas evolved from the educational programs instituted in the refugee camps in Mozambique.

After educational planning, I was the head of curriculum development from 1983 to 1987. We needed a modern post-Independence curriculum rather than following the colonial curriculum. We updated the curriculum from grade one to form four (grade eleven), quite strong in science and technology. I became the minister of education from 1988 to 1993.

Did the fact of my being Chinese make any difference to my work in the Ministry of Education? Yes and no. I think actually in Zimbabwe in the years immediately following Independence it was easier for a non-black woman to rise to the top. In the civil service when you looked at the women at the top, it was more likely that you would find nonindigenous women: white women, or American blacks married to Zimbabweans, or Asians like myself. There was much more prejudice against indigenous women than there was against people like ourselves. Of course, as I said, the people who were against colonialism could be anything politically. For example, in 1990, we had a teachers' strike when I was the minister. A group of teachers demonstrated against me. They held placards saying, "Go back to India!" I think everybody was very embarrassed but I was the least embarrassed. I think that the whole country felt very upset by these teachers and their placards. They did not even know my country of ancestry.

Education Around the World

I resigned from being the minister in 1993 and joined United Nations Children's Fund (UNICEF) as the head for education. I thought it would be a way to extend my experience and knowledge by going from a national position to an international one. UNICEF supports educational programs in over a hundred countries.

One area we worked on was supporting girls' education. Probably in ninety-nine out of one hundred countries, when you find children who are not in school, the likelihood is that they are girls. I looked at the institutional strengths, one of which for UNICEF was that it was very decentralized and decision-making was done in the country. This allowed us to emphasize again the community part of the education equation, for very few educational systems would succeed without strong community support, particularly parental support.

If we wanted all girls to go to school, we asked how could we do it in country X or country Y. There were slightly different answers but more or less the answer was that schools must be controlled by the parents. It must be cost-effective. It must be relevant to the lives of the people. They must feel that they were going to gain a whole lot of things from being in school, and that education would make their lives better. That meant that the curriculum and the processes must be relevant to the aims of the community. I think we made some positive changes in that area.

Of course, UNICEF has traditionally worked in emergency and reconstruction areas. We streamlined and improved our work in education under those conditions in Rwanda and Somalia. We developed something similar to what we did in Zimbabwe. We had all these kits in UNICEF. We called them "Edukit." Sometimes they were called "school in a box." It was linked to in-service teacher training. So our experience in Zimbabwe influenced UNICEF.

UNICEF also worked on the issue of human rights, particularly the child's right to education and how that would affect what is done in school. If you look at a country with only 35 percent of its children in school, it means that the other 65 percent are being deprived a basic human right. I think that changes your whole picture of how you regard education. If you look at children not in school as being deprived of their human right to education, then you need to look at legislation and political debates. This would also change the debate on human rights. Very often the debate has been narrowed to looking at China and saying the dissidents are not allowed to express their views. But you have to look at other areas of human rights and see if they are not being contravened. One can analyze governments or political parties fighting in an election whether they are putting education as one of their top priorities. One can use that as an indicator of how far a government is a good government. If it neglects education, then it cannot be a good government, even if it builds good roads.

Gender, Ethnicity, and Culture

Overall gender and ethnicity have made some differences in my career. Coming from a traditional Chinese family, which placed value on sons and not on daughters, it was necessary for me to assert my own direction in life rather than following in the traditional paths of obedience, marrying into a wealthy Chinese family, being a housewife, et cetera. I decided when I was a teenager that I wanted to go to the university and to have an independent career.

Ethnicity has been important insofar as I have fought against identity based solely on ethnic grouping all my life. It is my belief that human beings have other values that are more important than their racial, ethnic heritage. This is one of the reasons that I have identified with Africa and with Zimbabwe rather than with my own ethnic grouping, i.e., with the Chinese. I feel that although I am racially Chinese, I am much more Zimbabwean and African in my interests and background. I have also had the benefit of an international education, which is above ethnic identification.

I feel that there is the issue of race and there is the issue of culture. I think race is not the most important characteristic of people. You could have a number of attributes which are across races, say, intelligence, kindness, charity, or moral strength. I think these attributes are more important than race. Then, in terms of culture, obviously there are different cultures that are linked to different nations or religions. Obviously there is a Chinese culture. I think one of the strengths of Chinese culture is that, on the one hand, it has certain moral values which are not based on religion. I think this is a feature of Chinese culture that it is not essentially a religious culture. On the other hand, I think the Chinese are very adaptable, and are able to absorb the competence and values of others. My own family, for example, has adapted very well, compared to other groups. That is valuable. I think one should value one's culture, but there is no need to reject other cultures. It is important to find common values. If there are different values, and if you don't accept the values of other cultures, you have to understand why other groups have different values and respect their need to be different.

For myself it is very valuable to have had inherited Chinese cultural and moral values. I do feel that they have been helpful to me. In particular, I have been fortunate in always being supported by my family in all my enterprises.

Lotus in the Swamp
Laileen Springgay (India)

Jamshedpur

My name is Laileen. It means "beautiful lotus." I was born in Jamshedpur, a steel city with a population of two million, in the state of Bihar, not too far from Calcutta. Both my grandfathers came to India around 1911 from Guangdong Province.

My paternal grandfather was from Shunde. He first worked on the railroads all over Northern India. While there, he was introduced to a Chinese family in the Nainital area, and a marriage was arranged with my grandmother around 1925. She was born in India. Her father, my great-grandfather, was one of about ten Chinese tea experts that the British brought to India around 1890 to grow tea. We still have a picture of him in his pigtail.[1] He went to different parts of India before he found the perfect soil for the Dumlot tea in the Kumaon region in the foothills of the Himalayas. He settled near Nainital, and owned some tea estates, walnut groves, and farms. His wife, my great-grandmother, was from the nomadic tribal people along the India-China border. We were told that she wore a long dress in the Tibetan style. Although not a Han, she was Chinese because her daughter, my grandmother, used kinship terms according to the Chinese custom.

My maternal grandfather, Hsieh, was from Sihui and came to Calcutta via Hong Kong. At that time he had a wife and two kids back in China. He was supposed to send for them once he was settled, but they died. After leading a bachelor's life for a few years, a marriage was arranged by a go-between. My grandfather sent all the immigration papers for the bride. She was married to a rooster standing in for the groom, and came to India as Mrs. Hsieh.

Both my grandfathers eventually worked in the steel factory. There were nine or ten Chinese families in Jamshedpur, three of which were mine. The other large families were those of shoemakers, dentists, and restaurateurs. There were also some "bachelors" whose families were still in China.

I was born in 1951, and we lived with my paternal grandparents until 1961. My mother used to work full-time, so I had a very interesting upbringing at the hands of my paternal grandmother. This grandma, who was raised in Northern India, did not like to cook and was also a bit uppity. She expected the servants to do the housework and did not like us to mix with them. I was not allowed to eat their spicy food. But the housekeeper would let me taste some on the sly. I would also pinch some dough with which I made little gecko lizards and stuck them in my grandmother's prayer book to scare her.

Direct Link to the Village

After we moved out of my paternal grandmother's house, we lived across the street from my maternal grandparents. It was wonderful at their house. My mother had eight sisters and three brothers, and they did not have servants. There was always something happening in that household. Dinner was a big production every evening. We would sit around this huge round table, picking tiny stones from the rice, peeling vegetables, shelling peas, or cleaning fish. If it were someone's birthday, there would be a gathering of about thirty of us at dinner. As my grandma came from the village, she made everything herself and taught us to make these things. We used to make noodles for long life on birthdays, sweet fermented steamed rice cake for the Hungry Ghosts festival, and all kinds of delicacies for the Chinese New Year and other festivals. I learned to make salted preserved spinach, Chinese sausage, and a variety of dim sum, all in a little city in India where you hardly saw any Chinese or came across a Chinese book.

To make dim sum items, we had to buy sticky rice in Calcutta, as it was not available in the local market. Before we could knead the dough, the rice was pounded in a device designed and made by my maternal grandfather, who was a carpenter in Hong Kong. It con-

sisted of a vast wooden vat for the rice and a pestle, which we operated with our feet. The mechanism was like a seesaw, with two of us
pressing down one end by turns to raise the pestle on the other. As it
came down it would pound the rice in the vat. As kids we loved
making the rice flour, chatting and sometimes even reading a book as
we worked away with our feet.

Previously in my paternal grandmother's house, we did not follow many Chinese traditions partly because she was a Catholic, and
partly because she was born in India and was isolated from many
customs. Here in my maternal grandparents' house, we celebrated all
the Chinese festivals and observed the customs. For example, you
were supposed to wash your hair on New Year's Eve so you could
wash away all the old misfortune down the drain. Often we would
visit them on Sunday after church, where in those days we wore white
veils for the mass. If we wore a white veil in their house, Granddad
would mumble under his breath, "Who has died that you are walking
around in white?" He was happier when we were dressed in red.[2]

They had the *bagua* with the mirror in front of the house.[3] In the
entrance hall of their house was the ancestral shrine with the family
name. They lit the incense the first thing in the morning. We never ate
any delicious birthday food like the *baizhanji* (plain steamed chicken)
until the food and rice were offered to the ancestors first. There was
the kitchen god altar. We had the same incense burners, pots, and
pans as those in my grandmother's village. They kept the first and the
fifteenth days of the month in the Chinese calendar (the new and the
full moon respectively), with prayers and an extra chicken. They
visited the graves of relatives on the appropriate day. They would say
not to put this piece of furniture here or that ornament there because
it is black, or it's square, or whatever. There were many do's and
don'ts related to fengshui, and they were all part of normal life for us.
I remember the time my aunt lost her baby. They said that it was a
consequence of her moving her bed or leaving scissors on it.

Years later, after I was married and living in Hong Kong, my
Chinese friends would be amazed that for someone who grew up
in India, I not only could make all the Chinese food from scratch
but would know when to make it and for what festival. There in

Jamshedpur, a part of our life was led according to the old culture from Grandma's village. I am so proud of having this direct link to Chinese culture.

1962

I went to a Catholic convent school. It was an English school but we also had to learn Hindi, the Indian national language, and Sanskrit, the classical language. I learnt to speak Guangzhou dialect in my maternal grandparents' household. But we did not speak Chinese in our own house because my parents knew that we would otherwise have a hard time in school learning English or Hindi. They didn't want us to speak market English or Hindi. Moreover, after 1962, they knew that we would not live in India forever. They thought that a good English foundation would help us move on, and any other language we picked along the way would be just fine. They were right because eventually we left India.

I did go to the Chinese school, for a total of six or seven Sundays, and I loved it. My mother's brother married a Chinese schoolteacher. She came from Calcutta and ran a one-room Chinese school. Ten or twelve children did not go to an Indian or English school but attended this Chinese school full-time. Then some of us went to English schools during the week and to the Chinese school for a few hours on Sunday. I loved practicing page after page of Chinese characters. I learned to write my name and a few other things.

India and China had been bickering over the border for some time and they actually went to war in 1962. It was extremely difficult to be a Chinese in India during this time. The little Chinese school closed. Many Chinese lost their Indian citizenship. Overnight my family became stateless. The other choice was to become citizens of the PRC, which could lead to deportation. Because we lived in an important steel city, security was heightened and there was fear of being sent to concentration camps in Rajasthan.

We had blackouts every night. We had newspapers plastered on our windows. We tried to do our homework by the light of a little flashlight or a very tiny candle, as we couldn't have our lights on.

Because of the war, the Chinese came under the Defense of India Rules, which meant that we could not leave our local jurisdiction for more than twenty-four hours. If we wanted to go even to the neighboring city, we needed the permission of our city police. When we arrived in our destination city, we had to report to the police there. When we were ready to return home, we had to report to the city we visited, and then to our local police. It was almost impossible to attend any wedding or funeral in another city. Chinese had to obtain permits to stay and work in India. It was harder for young people to get jobs, and many young Chinese men were working as waiters in restaurants and hotels.

The war and the restrictions really affected me. I was a lost soul at that time. I think as a young person I hated that I was Chinese. I was the minority; I stood out. I could not speak, read, or write Hindi as well as I thought I should. The Indian girls could talk about Hinduism and living in India generations upon generations, but for me only my parents were born in India. Even though it was a private school, kids still picked on you if they did not like you. It was bad enough being teased about your flat nose or slant eyes, but being considered the enemy was very scary. When the war came along, I wished I could just blend in with the majority. I wanted to disown my background.

We could not tell our Indian friends what was happening. India was also at war with Pakistan. If you had Muslim friends, you really did not want to be close to them; otherwise you could be in double trouble. Not only were you perceived as an enemy because you were ethnically Chinese, but you were now befriending Muslims who might have connections to Pakistan! So we kept distance from our friends, as we did not want to get them into trouble. That was very hard for a child. Why can't I talk to so-and-so? Why can't she come in? Why can't I visit her? We couldn't.

I remember going to college a few years later. The kids in the street threw rocks at me. Back in the 1950s, when Jawaharlal Nehru was the prime minister of India, and Zhou Enlai, the prime minister of China, came to visit, there was a slogan: "Hindi Cheeni bhai bhai!" meaning "Indian Chinese brother brother." I would never forget how these kids would taunt me with that slogan while throwing stones at me. You just walked with tears streaming down your face. You didn't really feel that you were Chinese, because you never lived in China. I felt that I was as Indian as they were; this was where I grew up, as did my parents. Although we weren't religiously or culturally Indian in our ways, we spoke the language and ate the foods. I just felt like I was nobody. This was home and yet I was being ostracized. I wished that someone had explained to me that this was a difficult time but you were always going to be Chinese at heart. I guess everybody was in turmoil; everybody was trying to survive. It was a matter of am I going to be here next year? Will I have a job next year? Will they put me on a boat and ship me off somewhere? As children the fear of being shipped off to China was even worse because neither of our grandfathers had any immediate family there, we had no ties to China at that point, and I couldn't speak the language properly. It was really, really a hard time. The war first broke out in 1962, and my family lived there for almost another twenty years, through the two Indo-Sino wars and the Indo-Pakistan wars.

There was something, thank goodness, that kept us reasonably sane. I remember one incident when I was in grade seven or eight. I could write an essay in Hindi but did not have the floral characteristics of someone who was conversant with Indian literature. I wrote an essay on Prem Chand. He was an Indian who wrote about Hindu and Muslim conflicts. I guess he hit a nerve, and I took to his books. I sort of purged myself of all the hurt by focusing on the issue and relating to it on a personal level. When I wrote, something simply flowed through me. My essay was so good that the teacher read it to the class. My classmates were incredulous that I, a "foreigner," a "pug-nose," and a "nobody," could write so well in Hindi. The teacher, Miss Lily — I'll never forget her — told the whole class: "I know you are all amazed that a student can write Hindi this well even though it may not be her first language. You may think that this person's background is not like yours. But sometimes the most beautiful thing is found in the most unexpected place. If this surprises you, just remember that you can find a lotus flower even in a swamp."

I thought, I am going to remember that. I shall always be a beautiful lotus, but I am getting out of this swamp! It was perhaps a little thing that you heard as a youngster. However, when your life was in turmoil, because of external factors, a little thing took on a new meaning. That statement did stick, till today.

Bloom Where You Are Planted

I heard another saying years later: Bloom where you are planted. It conveyed a similar idea. You may be planted in a swamp, but bloom. Be a lotus.

I met my husband, a European Canadian, in India. But I was coming to Canada even before I got married. I became a Canadian citizen a year after our marriage in 1975. I was really happy that for once I could be a citizen of someplace that was willing to accept me. There are many Chinese in Canada, and you can be Canadian and still ethnically Chinese. As I traveled more and more — my husband is in the Canadian foreign service — I felt blessed that I grew up with both Chinese and Indian cultures in my life: the history, the religions, the architecture and art.

Growing up in India, at first I thought that I was part of the Indian scene. Then I did not know what I was. We had to suppress our Chinese heritage. Once I got past the teen years, I realized that being Chinese had always been an intrinsic part of me. When I was young, seemingly all alone and everything was happening around me, I was just absorbing Chinese culture consciously or unconsciously. It had sunk in over time. I feel closer to the Chinese culture in spirit as opposed to just knowing how to read, how to write, or how to sing. I don't do those things because I wasn't given the opportunity. But through the value system, I can connect with someone in the village in China. I don't think I am a practicing Chinese in some ways. But I definitely feel more Chinese, closer to that culture than anything else. I am very proud of my background. If you had asked me this question thirty years ago, you would get a different answer.

It's hard to impart all this to my kids. Even when they were very young, I used to tell them to greet their grandmother in Chinese and bow their head a little. They should ask her if she had her tea and offer things to the grandparents with both hands. They should not reach for the food first. I just feel that my children should keep these little things that my grandparents passed on to us. Yes, this part of us is Chinese. I think the time will come when they too will appreciate their Chinese heritage. Our daughter wants to take a year off to study Mandarin when she graduates from high school next year.

Back in 1981, when China was just opening up to the West, we were based in Hong Kong. I went with my husband on a trip to China and met some wonderful Chinese officials in Shanghai. I was speaking Guangzhou dialect the way my grandparents did, the way people spoke in the early part of the twentieth century. Those officials were astonished that I could say those things in that formal, polite way. The director said, "We are surprised that you have such good manners. It's not usual to see this traditional way of greeting. Obviously you were raised in India, but you understand." This older gentleman came to the airport to see us off, with an interpreter because he only spoke Mandarin. He called me a daughter and said to me, "Welcome home. You know, I never do this but I have to come to do this at the airport. I want you to remember a very beautiful Chinese saying: 'When a sapling grows to be a big tree, the branches and leaves spread all over. Yet as the leaves fall, they always come to the roots.' You always remember your roots and be proud of them." I have never forgotten that!

9

Pomelo

Walter Keoki Quan (Canada, United States)

I AM A fifth-generation Chinese American, and third-generation Chinese Canadian. My great-grandfather, my paternal grandpa's father, came to Canada from Kaiping some time after the 1858 gold rush in the Fraser River Valley. He scoped things out and then went back to China. Grandpa was born in 1892, and came in 1904. He was a houseboy in Shaughnessy in Vancouver for a while, sold vegetables, and then ran a green grocer's store on the side of the current courthouse. My father and his siblings worked at the store too. It closed down in 1965.

My mother is from Hawaii. She is fourth-generation there. My maternal great-great-grandfather was a rice planter on Kauai Island. My great-grandmother and grandmother were born there. They all spoke Hakka.[1]

My mother studied biology in Hawaii. She got her Ph.D. in parasitology from the University of Nebraska in 1958. She has been teaching at Simon Fraser University. She was the Woodward Chair in women's studies at SFU in 1990. Lately she has gotten very involved in women scientists' issues. Her focus is women and science, encouraging girls to go into science and finding scientists as role models for them.

I was born and raised on the west side of Vancouver. It is upper middle class and affluent. My high school graduating class, at Prince of Wales Secondary School, had 250-odd students, and there were maybe ten from the visible minorities, most of whom were Chinese. That was in 1980. Now it is totally changed so that the Asian kids are the majority. It's changed the dynamics of that school quite significantly. I used to hang out with the Asian kids. We certainly all knew who each other were. I was not sure whether it was because we were segregated so we would hang out with each other, or we were drawn to each more naturally.

I am trained in Canadian labor relations. I work as a grants program administrator in the British Columbia provincial government mostly for writers, visual artists, and filmmakers.

Gay and Asian

Being gay and an Asian, I am very blessed. There is certainly a discussion among the gay Asians about not fitting into the Asian communities, nor into the gay communities. The gay male culture is built around the "buffed" Caucasian male: pumped biceps, beautiful body and appearance. If you don't look like the ads in the magazines, you are marginalized. You are not seen as desirable as others. This is something that some support and discussion groups want to deal with.

When we came out, Mama was teaching in Women's Studies at SFU. This is not a place for the timid of heart because there are women who either have been involved in feminism, are lesbians and out of hiding, or militant! Father is a notary public and has an office in downtown Vancouver. He had been notarizing domestic partnership agreements for a long time. I was twenty-six, and Andy, my little brother, was nineteen. He was attending Trent University in Peterborough, Ontario. He had heard that people in Vancouver were spreading word about him being gay. He decided that Mom and Dad would hear about his being gay from him first instead of someone else. He wrote to them saying that he had something important to share with them the next week. And they said, "O god, he is going to quit school and become a poet!" In a separate note to me, Andy gave me warning that he couldn't keep it a secret any longer and he would have to tell them.

We don't necessarily consider siblings as sexual beings. He guessed it about me, but I hadn't a clue about him! We weren't as close as we are now. I called him saying, "I know I cannot tell you not to write the letter. But you realize that it is going to be a package deal." He replied that he knew but he had to tell them. He wrote his letter and it arrived. I knew it was coming, and I just stayed out late that evening with some friends. Went home and it was there. I penned my own letter and left it. The next day, my parents went out, so we didn't talk about it until much later in the day. They said, "Well, we sort of guessed about you, but we never guessed about him. Perhaps a little bit about him."

It was tough for my parents, harder than they let on. But they have been supportive always. There are stages of coming out, to ourselves, to our family, to our friends, to our co-workers, and to the greater community. There is a similar process for your parents or those close to you because they also have to come out as parents of gay children. I think Mom and Dad are pretty out about things; they have certainly shared with most of their friends by now. But that is a tough thing to face and deal with.

I think I was able to apply some of my experiences in working on Chinatown issues to gay issues. In the early 1970s, activists in Vancouver Chinatown put up an effective opposition to building the freeway through Chinatown. I was only in school then, and I thought that I was ten years too late. My very first summer was working for the Vancouver Chinese Cultural Centre, on a series of tourist brochures. The coordinators put together this project for us to discover and write some texts about Chinatown, that it wasn't just bad parking and restaurants, but that it was a living culture with a living history.

Also, I would show up at the city archives looking for my family history. They were articles about my father's siblings who grew up to be brilliant scholars. So discovering the cultural identity as an Asian Canadian was already in me.

I used to go to the store in San Mateo, California, that has all the interesting Asian American materials. When I came out, I was fascinated to be able to go into the gay bookstore, the Little Sisters, in Vancouver for the very first time. Wow, it's just like that store in San Mateo except it's gay! This is what I mean by transferring the search for family and ethnic identity to establishing the gay identity.

I am active in the community largely through music. There is no gay band here in Victoria, but I sing in the Victoria forty-five–member choir. The gay and lesbian choral movement is huge. There are over 150 choirs, mostly in North America, but also in other parts of the world. Every four years they do a big international meet. There is a Canadian choirs meet too.

Since coming to Victoria, I became one of the co-conveners of the lesbian and gay provincial government employees' association. There was an article in the newspaper and one of the columnists predicted that the association was going to ask for quotas, and it was going to be like affirmative action. My boss asked me, "What do you think of this?" I replied, "We won't want quotas; we would have to downsize if we did." He laughed and laughed and laughed and laughed!

Pomelo and Icono'me

Mama kept her American citizenship, so I have Canadian and American passports. Culturally I am Canadian.

I think there is an essence of being Chinese. I used to take great umbrage at being called a banana,[2] because in my metaphor it is not a person of the Chinese diaspora. For many of us, there is an inner core that is yellow (i.e., Chinese). There may be another layer which is very white, and the outside is yellow. The pomelo is much more my metaphor: big white pith inside, with a yellow exterior and a core that is still yellow.[3] This metaphor is interesting because I don't know how to imagine not being Chinese.

I would gravitate towards cultural signifiers. I use the term "icono'me." Icons are those signifiers. Icono'me is my homonym of those cultural signifiers, those icons, of me. I merge them together into icono'me. I am not sure whether it means anything outside. Various things are signifiers of me: the Buddha mask, the wall hangings, the way we eat, the way we have food, the way we manifest kinship. These objects we keep tie back into our heritage.

My brother from Hawaii was visiting the other week. I managed to spend a day with him, his girlfriend, and Mom and Dad. I think we ate most of the time, or we were shopping for food. I don't know whether it is specifically Chinese, but I know it resonates with my Chinese friends when I said, "You know, we got up, we ate dim sum, we shopped, we ate dinner, we shopped, we went to the night market and then we ate *siuye*."[4] That's definitely one of the ways we manifest kinship.

I went to a session many years ago at the Chinese Cultural Centre

in Vancouver, and I was absolutely outraged because there was someone talking about the notion that you couldn't be Chinese unless you
spoke a Chinese dialect. His approach was that the language carried
the culture. I took Chinese Mandarin 101 in University of British
Columbia and nearly flunked out in my first year. I would love to
learn Guangzhou dialect, but no one teaches it now, only Mandarin. I
was very angry at this man because over time, I have thought about
how it is to be Chinese without the language. I concluded that the
operative language for our period of Chinese Canadian communities
is English; at least that is all I had. By nature I like to be the go-
between, brokering cultures. Even though I do not have the Chinese
language, I think my ability to manifest many things in Chinese culture to others in English is still very important.

For example, there are two Chinese medicine schools here in
Victoria. Many practitioners graduated from these two schools. I still
find people asking me whether I know any of the herbal medicine. I
say, I don't know Chinese but I certainly know some of the herbs and
some of the bark, and so forth, that Mother used to cook up for us.
Even though I have no expertise in Chinese medicine, I am quite
happy to explain the things I know. I go to this Chinese herbal doctor
if I need someone to read the pulses. The herbs will smell up the
house, but he is really quite good. I won't like buying the herbs from
him too much because his prices are high by comparison to Vancouver. When I go to Vancouver and buy the patent medicine, it is dirt
cheap.

On the metaphysical side, I am involved with an energy healing
group. It's called *linqi* in Chinese. In Japanese it is *reiki*. The *ling (rei)*
is the universal spirit, the essence that comes down first, and the *qi
(ki)* is all the very different ways in which energy is manifested on
earth. That makes sense. Our essence, whatever it is, is Chinese. How
it is manifested in form differs from person to person. For some people who try not to manifest it in form at all, does that change their
essence, the spirit? I don't think they can change essence.

I do remember the Mandarin I learned. One of the first questions for conversation was: "You are of what country? *(ni si nai guo
ren?)*" I happened to be in a section that was all ethnic Chinese. The

instructor, a Chinese, looked at us and said, "You are all Chinese."
She was quite convinced, and she had no problems in saying that we
were all Chinese. Of course in UBC, the answer was: "I am a Canadian." We got different teaching assistants who would say, "You are
not Chinese; you are Canadian." So we fought back and forth. What
the answer was depended on who was in the room and what their
state of mind was.

After that I did go on the Taiwan trip, colloquially known as the
"love boat tour." There were sixty of us from Canada, three hundred
from the U.S., and a few from other places. Their whole approach was
that, in Taiwan, they were the provisional government overseas. The
communists were running the country over there in a bad way. Were it
not for the fact that the Chinese were a strong people, they would all
fall into the ocean or some such thing. It was very strange. Their
headspace was: You are all Chinese and this is your motherland.

My grandfather was active in the Guomindang overseas. The trip
organizers would check your pedigree before you go. It was very
interesting being with all those Chinese from all over the world.
There were amazing moments, even with all the propaganda. We
toured the military college. We sat down with the soldiers, male and
female, at supper, although we couldn't talk to them because of the
language barrier. Then they put on this incredible variety show for us
in the evening. We were made to feel like the younger brothers and
sisters from overseas. The crowning part of it was the send-off. There
were many buses to take 460 of us all at the same time. As we left the
auditorium, they had set up a torch parade, winding down this path-
way to the buses. They had paper garlands, and little keepsakes that
were handed to each and every one of the 460 of us as we went down.
Propaganda tool or not, it worked because they as our Chinese brothers and sisters were greeting us, hugging us, and giving us all these
keepsakes. By the time we got to the buses we were all completely
emotionally overwhelmed. It was a fascinating trip in many ways.
There were mixed-race kids on our trip who were being fully recognized as Chinese also for the first time. A friend from Arizona with
whom I keep in touch a little bit, still, is half-and-half. But she was
there and being Chinese. There was no question in anybody's mind
that she was. Funny tour.

10 The Musician
Fook Poy Woo (United States)

American Citizen

I was born in the Taishan countryside but grew up in Hong Kong and Guangzhou. I came to Seattle in 1968 on a U.S. passport. My father did not explain why I was an American. It was only later, from reading the newspaper, did I piece together an explanation. It was sometime around 1932 when the U.S. Congress passed this law that should anyone, from anywhere in the world, after residing in the U.S. for at least ten years, return to his native land and father children, his children would be considered U.S. citizens.[1] My grandfather first came to the U.S. over one hundred years ago. My father, born in China, was an American citizen because he had lived here for over ten years. He went back to China, got married, and had children. His children were automatically Americans.

My father returned to the U.S. shortly after I was born, and I did not see him again until more than thirty-eight years later. I did not know what kind of person he was. When we met at the airport, needless to say, we were both very glad. But it was like acting in a play. For people of my father's generation, it was important to see one's flesh and blood. He had deep emotions. When he saw me, his son, virtually for the first time at the airport, he was very moved. He tapped me on my shoulder and asked, "Fook Poy, you are my son, aren't you?" I replied, "Yes, I am your son." Hot tears swelled in our eyes and we wept. Thirty-eight years.

My mother was also separated from my father. She came a bit earlier, in 1960. With my grandfather, my parents, my children, my grandchildren, and myself, there have been five generations of us in the U.S.

People from Taishan

Of the Chinese old-timers in the U.S., the majority was from Taishan. They came to the Gold Mountain to make a living. Every U.S. dollar was worth a lot of money in China. But in the early part of the twentieth century, coming to the U.S. was a risky venture. A man from the neighboring village wanted to come but he was not legally qualified. He tried to smuggle into this country by bribing the captain and taking passage on board an American steel ship. The U.S. government at that time knew about this kind of smuggling; not only the Chinese but people from other parts of the world were coming illegally. When the ship was off the west coast of the U.S., the Coast Guard came aboard to search. It was a tense situation. The captain panicked. There was nowhere to hide. Even if the smuggled migrant were dropped into the ocean, he could still be seen. So the captain ordered that the man be thrown into the furnace. The poor chap was incinerated. There was no evidence. I know that man's sons; we keep up contact.

Another device was to buy paper. Many immigrants, after spending enough years here, would return to China and father a child, preferably a son. Even a daughter was valuable. Any offspring of an American, regardless of birthplace, is a U.S. citizen. So the paper of a child, especially that of a son, carried a very high price, in thousands of dollars. However, if the child is too old, then it would not be so valuable. I had an elder brother who died in infancy. He had a paper too. I think my father sold the paper. I never asked him, as it would be improper.

The older generation of Taishan people was full of *yiqi,* a strong sense of loyalty, righteousness, and camaraderie. My father talked a great deal about it in those days. If they could come to this country and make a living, however marginally, they would save money and help the relatives at home. Very generous and loyal, not like the people nowadays.

Look at that restaurant over there. It used to be Yee Yuan. Our village as a whole used that name to rent that building, for about a hundred years. But a few years ago, a couple of village brothers did something illegal — well, I dare not say that they operated a gambling

Fook Poy Woo
playing pipa

den. The government closed it down. Otherwise we would still have
the hall. It was for our clan, the Woo. When it was Yee Yuan, our village hall, I was the manager for a short time. My father stayed there
too when he first arrived. He worked as a cook in the hall, earning less
than a hundred dollars a month. Those who worked on fishing boats
in Alaska all used the hall as a base. Also the newcomers from China.
There were thirty or forty iron beds for the men to stop over. When any
clan brothers arrived, with no parents or friends, they would stay and
eat in the hall, and my father would look after them. He was very kind-
hearted. I still hear some of the old-timers say that my father treated
them better than he did me because he spent more time with them.

Music

When I was seven years old, we had to flee from the village to Hong Kong because of the Japanese invasion and occupation of China. We stayed with this clan uncle who had just gone to Hong Kong to get married after a long stay in the U.S. He loved to play music. I was deeply impressed by my uncle, who would invite friends, men and women, to play music and sing together. Everyone had a great time. We lived in that kind of old house with a large balcony, so there was plenty of space for gathering and singing. I thought then that I wanted to become a musician when I grew up.

After the Japanese occupied Hong Kong, we went back to the village. I begged my mother for an *erhu*.[2] She bought the instrument, but it was too long for me. We cut off part of it. I started to learn how to play erhu and other instruments. Aside from eating, I seemed to be playing every minute of the day. There were many teachers, and the tuition fees were costly. As I also developed an interest in acting, I joined a Guangdong opera class and played in the orchestra for several years in Taishan.

After the Communist Revolution, the provincial South China Music Conservatory came to recruit students. I took the examination and went for an audition. Out of about one hundred applicants, I was one of the three chosen. After I joined the conservatory, I found out that the way I had been playing was not quite proper. The way I sat or held the instruments, the interpretation, theory, and so forth were all incorrect. I had to learn all over again. I was already in my twenties. It was not easy. I had to put in quite a bit of time and effort. After six months of probation I was accepted into conservatory as a regular member. It was during this time that I learned the *pipa*,[3] my favorite instrument. But that was not part of my regular curriculum, as my specialization was playing the *sanxian*.[4] This is a very ancient instrument. But during the time of the Nationalist government (1912–1949), it was not popular and few knew how to play it. After the Communists came to power, the government wanted to revive it.

The conservatory had high standards and enjoyed a certain reputation. It ranked fourth nationally, after Beijing, Shanghai, and

Wuhan. Whenever there was a political campaign, it would take the message to the people and perform all over the country. It also performed overseas, but I never went abroad.

Gold Mountain

I got married in 1959. I knew my wife Yuen Fong from the village. Then she applied to go to Hong Kong to study. My mother left for the U.S. in 1960 and I was in Guangzhou by myself. I could go to the U.S. because I was an American citizen, but I wanted to leave China legally. I applied for an exit permit and was eventually allowed to leave.

Before I came to the U.S., I thought everything would be smooth-sailing and I would have a good time and enjoy life, like in the big cities of Shanghai and Hong Kong. When I suddenly found myself in Seattle, everything was strange and unfamiliar. First of all, there was the language problem. Secondly, not everyone would play with you. Everyone had to work. I almost thought about returning to Hong Kong, as I was not accustomed to the way of life here.

When I first came, I was lazy. I don't quite have an explanation for this. When I was a kid studying in Hong Kong, English was not my strong suit. I could speak some English. But in the last thirty years or so, I have forgotten totally the little English I knew. I really have to blame myself. As a new immigrant I could have studied English, without having to pay tuition, at a school about two blocks away. In fact, I could have received $80 a week for attending the English as second language classes. I did not attend the ESL classes. You see, how foolish I was. I was afraid. Then later, there was an opportunity, but I did not know enough English. It was at the university. There was a European American lady who had returned from Taiwan. My niece, who accompanied me to a function where I played the Chinese instruments, knew her. This woman tried to persuade me to teach music at the university. But I had not the courage. My English was so poor, how could I take on the job? She said that it was not a hindrance as she could arrange to provide interpreters. She promised me such and such a sum as monthly salary. She came to my house to ask me to teach. I dared not take up her offer.

When we first came to the U.S., we had two little children. They were born in Hong Kong. A third son was born here. My wife was employed as a seamstress soon after we arrived. Someone had to stay home and look after the children. We reasoned that we should arrange our schedules so that we would be home at different hours. It would be the best for the children. I knew quite a few couples that both worked outside the home and the children did not turn out so well. Some children would not obey their parents and, worse still, there was no emotional bond between the parents and the children. So I stayed at home. The children would have their father with them even if their mother had to work outside the home. I would play with them and talk to them after they came home from school.

My wife, Yuen Fong, is a fine woman. Since our arrival in the U.S., I never really had any employment. She has not been feeling well in the last few years. She is diabetic, and it has affected her eyesight. She had to undergo eye surgery twice. All these years, she never nagged me about going out to find work, or about not having enough income. Not one word of complaint. My father and mother were good to me, too. Although my father was not a rich man and his earnings were those of a workingman, he would say to me, "How are things? If you don't have enough, just let me know." He would give me some pocket money every month. That's how we got along. The two oldest sons have been on their own for over ten years. The youngest one finished university and has a steady job. I don't need to provide for him. He is still living with us. Our burden is lighter. We lead a quiet and unexciting life.

11

The Sinologist
Adrian Chan (Australia, New Zealand)

Out of Australia

I was born in Hong Kong of Australian parents. My Chan great-grandfather and grandfather went to Australia in the 1880s. In the early decades of the twentieth century, Australia had a very bad anti-Chinese policy. By the 1920s, my great-grandfather had died already. My grandfather, who had a business in Fremantle, wanted to take his family away from Australia. His children, my father and his siblings, were all born in Australia. They all spoke English at home. They went to Hong Kong, which was of course a foreign country to them. Hong Kong was Chinese with a little bit of the cool British dialect thing. My father went to the University of Hong Kong, where he read English. He taught in Hong Kong as a secondary school teacher till he retired.

My mother was born in China but grew up in Hong Kong. She became an Australian citizen after marrying my father. My father kept his Australian citizenship. At home we spoke Chinese to our mother and English to our father.

I had my early education in Hong Kong and went to an English school. Because my father did not have much formal Chinese education, he tried to make sure that his children would get some. He hired a private tutor, an old guy, to coach us several times a week in classical Chinese, which at that time I did not like very much. We wrote essays in classical Chinese, couplets, and things like that. In other words, we studied another culture after school.

There are five of us in the family: I have three brothers and one sister. We were sent over to Australia to finish high school and university. We traveled to Australia carrying the Hong Kong British passport. That didn't matter much, as I was a student. After I finished my first degree, I taught English in a state high school. Then I applied for

Adrian Chan

the position of an education officer in the Australian Air Force. I was given a commission. I had to be an Australian citizen if I was to wear a uniform. It was the end of 1965. I wrote to the Immigration Department, applying for citizenship, as my parents were Australian citizens. They replied that since I obviously was not a European I had to wait for fifteen years. Well, I said, stuff it. Then I got this offer of a teaching assistant position in a New Zealand university. So I went over there, first to the University of Otago in Dunedin in the South Island, and then to the University of Canterbury.

My wife is a New Zealander of French and Scottish background. We got married and I became a New Zealand citizen. Five years later, I returned to Australia to pick up a scholarship to do my Ph.D. at the Australian National University. After my Ph.D., I taught political science, political theory, development studies in Asia, and integration. I was tenured at the University of New South Wales. I worked for a year (1979–1980) in China too, teaching in University of Science and Technology in Anhui Province. I took early retirement in June 1996.

There is no ethnic Chinese elected to any lower house in any part of Australia, state or federal. Neither political party would put an ethnic Chinese up in a winnable seat. There is one or two Chinese in some state upper house. The guesstimate is that there are about 100,000 Chinese in Australia. It is no longer necessary to mark one's ethnicity in the national census. In those days when we had to check one of the disparate categories for race in the census, my whole family put down "human." Race is not a scientific term; it is our humanity that matters.

Sinology

I became interested in China in graduate school. Part of my misspent youth was in a theological college until I worked myself to a position where I didn't think that the concept of God was necessary. I am sure that I am one of a few sinologists who have read the Christian Bible from cover to cover. One of my majors in undergraduate studies was English literature. My graduation thesis was on Thomas Jefferson. I came back to China intellectually, as it were, via my interest in Karl Marx. And given my earlier education in classical Chinese, I was very much an oddball. I was brought up in such a way that I thought my experience was quite normal. Of course it wasn't! My Ph.D. was in the development of ideas. The dissertation was on the development of the concept of communism in China. I was looking at ideas rather than at party political machination. Basically, I am not a traditional historian but a historian of ideas.

In a course on classical Chinese political thought, students of course read the translations. Where there were dubious translations, I would say, "Well, in Chinese it means this." Like the word *tian*: it is often translated as "Heaven" with an uppercase "H," which is obviously unChinese. It's an example of Orientalism. So I explained that "Heaven" with an uppercase "H" has a special connotation in English. But in the Chinese context, the word "heaven" does not have such connotations.

The term "Confucianism" is not a Chinese term either. You

cannot translate the concept back into Chinese; it would have been *Kong Zi Zhuyi*. This is foreign; there is no such a thing in Chinese. The Chinese term would be *sixiang* for "thought." *Zhuyi* is a certain doctrine or worldview of foreign origin, like *Ma Keshi Zhuyi* for Marxism. There is no such a thing as *Mengzi Zhuyi* for the philosophy of Meng Zi (Mencius). In a sense, my early education in classical Chinese has helped me, for which I am grateful.

What started me off was that I came across a lot of missionaries proclaiming that the Chinese were anti-Christian. Basically, Christianity was very unsuccessful in China, even under the Nationalists (1912–1949). To the missionaries, the leading anti-Christians were the Chinese moralists, the Confucians. So I started from there, but I sort of dropped it for a while. Then I came across Edward Said's book *Orientalism* (1979).[1] I put the two together and it clicked. If you are a Confucian, you have to reject Christianity, and vice versa. The Confucians openly came across: There is no creator. In the Chinese language there is no sin because there is no one to sin against. But the missionaries needed rampant sin. It was the rationale for their vocation. So the early missionaries used the word *zui,* which is crime or transgression against temporal authorities.

Of course, for anyone to be a Christian, one must accept one's inability to be saved or to be morally perfect, and will accept the free gift of the savior. However, to the Confucians, the Chinese moralists, moral perfection is through one's own efforts. As Confucius said, "I start at 15 . . . and hope by 70 what I want to do coincides with what I ought to do" (*Confucian Analects* 11:4). So to the Confucians, the Christian way is moral cowardice. To the Christians, the Confucian way is spiritual pride. They have to reject each other. The missionaries complained while they did not quite understand.

Right from the beginning, the European missionaries made translations of Chinese philosophical texts but rejected the Chinese concept of the cosmos. They could not have a people not created by god. They had to reject it. So they gave Chinese culture a god. They gave Chinese culture sin, and they gave Chinese culture Heaven with a capital "H." Right from the earliest missionaries, Matteo Ricci[2] and the Jesuits to James Legge, they translated Chinese cultural texts with a Christian slant. I came across references to Ricci knowingly distorting his translations to suit the Europeans. He made the Chinese texts appear to carry European ideas. There were willful distortions of Chinese culture from the start. For example, the Chinese are supposed to have the Central Kingdom mentality. But those who discovered this syndrome also located China in the Far East! Now where is the center? In British London? Those who did that exhibited in a sense the mote and beam syndrome identified by Dr. Luke.[3]

And the distortion continues. The language of discourse is very important. As I was brought up bilingual — Chinese and English — when I started applying Said's critique of orientalist thought expressions to sinology, I found so many sinologists theoretically inadequate. You may be aware, especially in America, that in the late 1980s and early 1990s, many sinologists were searching for the civil society in China. Basically, they were barking up the wrong tree because they misapplied Jurgen Habermas's idea of civil society. They misread him. Habermas's ideas were based on seventeenth-century England and eighteenth-century France before their respective revolutions. He said that his conclusion was based on historically specific conditions and could not be transposed. Yet the sinologists did just that. The problem is that too many sinologists were monocultural. They study China, but they don't know their own culture. The translator of Habermas said that seventeenth-century England and eighteenth-century France were high European Middle Age! What nonsense. I find too many Western sinologists having little exposure to the history of their own civilization.[4]

The Cold War, in fact, has a most enduring impact on the understanding of the communist movement in China. One Canadian, Paul Evans, wrote an interesting book called *John Fairbank and American Understanding of China*. It shows that Fairbank saw the Harvard Asian Studies Center as training intelligence officers and teachers taking part in the containment of China program. Then, of course, he was the doyen of China studies in the U.S. The sinologists in that tradition would not accept for publication views that are against theirs. If you don't play their game, they make sure that you are ostracized, and you won't get a good job in a university. It is unfortunate.

I found out when I was a research student. I wrote a paper and sent it to the prestigious *Journal of Asian Studies* in the U.S. Two months later, the editor informed me that both reviewers recommended publication. However, I strongly criticized Professor Martin Wilbur in the article. The editor asked me to remove Wilbur's name as he was then the president of the Association of Asian Studies, and they would publish the article. When you were a Ph.D. student and given a chance to publish in a well-known journal, you would jump at it. But I thought that it was too much of a compromise. I said that my idea of academic freedom and freedom of speech would not allow me to do that. They did not publish it.

Just recently, the Cambridge University Press was going to publish a series of books on political thought, one century per volume. The English editor of the twentieth-century volume asked me to contribute a chapter on Asian Marxism. So I submitted a six-page detailed synopsis in which I said that there are basically two types of Asian Marxists: one group learned and adopted Marxist praxis independently of the Russian Bolsheviks, and the other was connected to the Comintern (the Communist International), which was led by the Russian communists after the October Revolution of 1917. The first kind was the Chinese and Japanese communists, and the rest of Asia was of the second type. The editor thought that that was very controversial. Scholarship in the English language largely takes the view that Asian Marxism was of the Comintern type. I was uninvited. It's kind of an embargo on truth. If the Cambridge History of the Twentieth-Century Thought were to publish an article by Adrian Chan, it would effectively challenge the whole Harvard scholarship on the communist movement in China and Japan. The "received scholarship" in that tradition is that the Chinese Communist Party (CCP) was really not Marxist but a Russian Bolshevik creation. But Chen Duxiu,[5] who was one of the founders of the CCP, published an article in 1915 in which he discussed at length European socialism, from Babeuf at the time of the French Revolution through Saint-Simon and Fourier to Lassalle and Marx. He regarded European socialism as one of the major gifts to civilization. The first Japanese Marxist started writing on Marxism in 1916. In both cases, they became Marxist socialists and published their ideas before the October revolution of 1917. This is totally against the established tenet. The first generation of Chinese communists read Marx carefully, understood his theory of exploitation and revolution, and was emphatic about not adopting the Bolshevik methods blindly. That kind of argument and evidence put forward in an important book like Cambridge history would be pulling the established sinologists out of their seat. They can't have that.[6]

In a way I took the propaganda of the free world for granted. In that sense I was a bit naïve to think that in a free world there was free exchange of ideas among scholars. Alas, not so!

I spent a semester at the Hoover Institute in Stanford University doing research for my Ph.D. dissertation. While I would love to work with the Hoover Institute collections, I found that I could not work in America. While it's a big country with a lot of opportunities, I had to change my thinking if I were to work there. I was not prepared to do so. I have always been pretty outspoken. I just felt that I wouldn't take that kind of nonsense. Some people may say that I never grow up.

In my retirement, basically, I am doing full-time research. I go to academic conferences delivering papers every year, in this country, Europe, and Asia. I just finished a book on Marxism in China. I am in the process of writing a book on Orientalism in sinology. I am borrowing Said's ideas. He does not deal with China, and his book is essentially concerned with the Arab world. After working on it for six months, I realized that most of the sinologists were Orientalists.

In addition, I write a column for a newspaper in Australia. I also have a weekly column for an English paper in Bangkok. The topic is pretty much up to me. In several hundred words a week I talk about Australia and Asia connections, and Australian attitudes towards various things Asian. I am perhaps in the right place at the right time. I have time on hand to do it.

New Zealanders

My years in New Zealand were happy. What interested me about New Zealand was the democratic socialism. There I embraced the idea of equality. I came to respect a person for that person's achievement, not because of the accident of birth, or who the parents are, or how deep is that person's pocket. New Zealand was a very good social democracy. In those days, there was a sense of community, caring for each other, which I found very attractive and welcoming. Also, I find that New Zealand treats their indigenous people far better than Australians do theirs. New Zealand had its own nineteenth-century anti-Chinese period too. But the indigenous people fared much better there. Already at the beginning of the twentieth century, the indigenous Maoris were made diplomats and cabinet members, whereas only two indigenous persons are part of the corresponding Australian institutions today. It was not until 1967 that the indigenous people of Australia were counted in the national census. So they weren't even regarded as part of the human race before that.

After I got an academic position in Australia, I stayed on. My wife sacrificed her career for mine. She couldn't go to France for her studies. She did the cooking and housework while I worked hard to get tenured. She went to China with me and taught there too. After she came back, she got qualifications teaching English as a second language. Eventually she got her Ph.D. in French literature after our two children started school. She is now the manager of student welfare in a college of health science studies. She teaches research and study skills, and academic English to students who come back to graduate work. Now I stay home and work.

We have two sons. Unfortunately or fortunately, depending on your view, they are not familiar with Chinese things. The elder son is not intrigued by anything Asian. He studied French in school and university. The younger son took Latin in school and became a computer nerd. He works in the field of telecommunication. They don't speak Chinese; of course one speaks French. They have an active social life. The elder son is in the local choir. Both play in the chamber music groups. They are certainly well integrated.

The elder son was born in New Zealand and the younger one in Australia. They grew up in Australia, but they don't see themselves as Australians so much as New Zealanders. The whole family carries New Zealand passports. Being a Chinese I still feel more at home there than in Australia, although there are many more Chinese in Australia.

12 I Brought Myself Up

Lillian Yuen Louie (Canada)

I WAS BORN IN Vancouver in 1911. I don't look my age, but I feel like I am over a hundred right now. I had my ninetieth birthday earlier this year.

My mother and father were from the village in Shatin, New Territories, Hong Kong. We are the Hakka people, who originally came from the northern part of China centuries ago. My parents came to Canada before the head tax.[1] But my dad paid a lot of head tax for my elder brother and his wife when they came over from China. My dad had two wives. This brother was from the first mother who died. I belong to the second mother, who had six children. I was the oldest among the six.

My father was building a business for my elder brother, two cousins, and my younger brother. He traveled all over the place. I don't know why he went to such awful places like Lilliooet and Little Fort. Finally they got it set and built this store in Little Fort. That's when he fell and hurt his back. He wanted to go back to China for better medicine. My father and mother took the three youngest children with them and left my brother and me here. I was thirteen. I brought myself up. I took care of myself. I looked after my younger brother and myself. I stayed with my elder half brother in Little Fort. I went to school there. But I also helped in the store and looked after my elder brother's young children. I worked all my life. That's why my fingers are so sore with arthritis. That's why I am so independent. Even my children say so. I never depend on anybody. I go everywhere. I take the bus and go everywhere instead of asking someone to take me there.

During the depression time it was hard going. We didn't have much money, and we had to struggle. Then I was married in 1931 and moved to Ashcroft a year later. My husband, Wee Tan Louie, and all his family were born in Shuswap, outside Kamploops, in the B.C. interior. They had a little homestead there where they grew the best strawberries in the country. Wee Tan used to drive a taxi in Seattle. He came up to Vancouver for a holiday and that's where I met him.

We lived in Ashcroft for twenty-eight years. Wee Tan fought in the First World War with the Tenth Canadian Infantry. I joined the Ashcroft branch of the ladies auxiliary to the Pacific Royal Canadian Legion in 1946 and am still a member. I served as the president and the secretary of the auxiliary. I was also the secretary-treasurer of the Teacher Parent Association in Ashcroft. My husband, children and I were all very active while we were living there. Ashcroft was a good town, busy and lively because they had the tomato cannery there and all the construction work. There was also a copper mine not too far. There were quite a few Chinese there at that time. Some worked on the farms, as Ashcroft was known for its tomatoes and potatoes. However, after the cannery closed down, followed by the mine closure, people began to move away. It is quite dead now, hardly anyone there.

I worked in the cannery for a little while. My husband worked on different jobs, like freighting tomatoes and potatoes down to Vancouver. Then he was baling hay. Later he was building all the guardrail on the highway until his health broke down and we moved down to Vancouver. We bought a house, a brand new one and not quite finished when we bought it. I have been down here for over forty years now. After coming down here, I worked at the University of British Columbia for about fifteen years. I worked in the cafeteria, serving the students.

I had four children, three girls and a boy. All were born in Ashcroft except the oldest one, who was born in Vancouver. I only have a daughter and a son left now because my husband died and then my two daughters.

My oldest daughter, Joyce, did not go to university. She took a course in business. The second daughter, Lorna, took a sewing class at the academy, the Gold Thimble. She was the first one ever to win a gold thimble. She went to the University of British Columbia and got

Lillie Louie on her 90th birthday

her degree in education. The third one, Shirley, attained the bachelor of home economics and master of business administration degrees. She was a dietitian at UBC and, towards the end, the head of food services there. She managed about eight or nine cafeterias at UBC. She worked from early morning to late at night. She wrote two cookbooks. She died quite suddenly. She had cancer.

My son went to the university once and did not like it. He attended the technical college in Alberta. He works as a telephone lineman and lives in Kamloops now. Only the second daughter has children: a boy and two girls. I have three grandchildren and three great-grandsons.

Back in the village, my mother took the children up to the hills during the anti-Japanese war. My younger sister would come down every night when it's dark to get food for them. I went to Hong Kong to visit my mother after the war, in the 1950s, for the first time in over forty years. I stayed for six or seven weeks. I stuck it out even though there was no plumbing or running water. After that first visit, I went back every five years. Towards the end I went back every two years to see my mother until she died in 1989.

I still have two sisters and a brother living in Hong Kong. One sister works for my cousin in Kowloon. The other sister and her husband lived in England for about fifteen years. He was cooking there until he retired and they decided to return to the village. My brother still lives in the village. They all had little plots of land in front of their houses for growing rice and vegetables. Several years ago the government took all their land to build highways, but they got paid by the government. (This was before the return of Hong Kong to China in 1997.) There is hardly any ground left.

I spoke Hakka dialect at home. I had to because my parents couldn't speak English. Even my two sisters who went to Hong Kong when they were very young, about three or four years old, cannot speak English. A couple of times when I was in Hong Kong, I said that whenever they decided they could just go and get their Canadian passports. They were born here and are Canadian citizens. But they never came back to Canada, all these years. When my mother was alive, the sisters looked after my mother. After my mother died, I said, "There is nothing to keep you here. You might as well come over to Canada." But they just said, "We'll see, we'll see." That was fine with me. It saved me money. I don't bother anymore. The sister in Kowloon has her family and grandchildren. They are grown up and married. My other sister who lives further north toward the Chinese border has a daughter and sons in London. My brother's sons are in London and Manchester, working in the restaurants. So my sisters and brother are all going to stay in Hong Kong.

About ten years ago, my daughter and I traveled, looking for all my cousins, nieces, and nephews that I have not seen since they were quite little. We went all over London, Liverpool, Manchester, and Scotland. We covered a lot of ground. In two weeks we found them all. They all have these take-out restaurants, like fish and chips. Now they add Chinese food to what they offer. Quite expensive.

I have had an interesting life, too, because I did a lot of traveling at one time. I have been to Tangiers and Casablanca in Africa, Jamaica, all over China and other countries. Some of the memorable events in my life were probably getting lost a few times in my travels. I would go by myself to Hong Kong, but I joined tours in going to those other places.

I see myself half-and-half, Canadian and Chinese. I follow the Chinese ways like keeping birthdays and New Year, and giving out red packets of lucky money. My parents are buried in the old Hakka way in Hong Kong. I follow the Canadian customs too, like Thanksgiving. Certain things you don't agree with but you go along with them. Like the head tax.

13

All Bases Covered

Deanna Li (Philippines)

I WAS BORN IN Manila. My mother was also born in the Philippines. She is pure Chinese. Her family had to change their Chinese surname to a Filipino one when they became naturalized Filipinos. My father traveled from his native province, Fujian, to the Philippines once or twice when he was in high school, as he had relatives there. He saw that there was a lot of opportunity for business. But he went back to China to finish his studies. That was the time of Japanese occupation in China. He decided to go to Shanghai because to him that city was very cosmopolitan, like New York. He graduated from St. John's University, which, even today, is known for having produced many dynamic and aggressive business people. My father still keeps up contact with his friends from college. He emigrated to the Philippines after graduation.

My dad was not rich. He started down at the lowest level, even with his university degree. He would peddle fruits from wholesalers to the market in search of buyers. He was also a janitor, cleaning tables and running errands for this man who is now poorer than my father.

My parents' marriage was arranged by a matchmaker; both my father's and my mother's parents were from the same village in Fujian. When they first met, my father was an employee in a textile firm. After marriage he formed his own textile firm, from spinning yarn all the way to the embroidered cloth, which was his specialty. My father was very enterprising. He spent six months in Japan learning the whole trade. He is still in the textile business and my sisters are now handling it. The firm exports embroidered cloth to Canada, Europe, and Australia, with a little to the United States. There are some loyal customers for over twenty years. It is quite amazing since many textile firms in the Philippines, even the big ones, have gone under or have been bought out by others. You see, he had branched out, into sugar and cement. These two industries are more basic and stable. His businesses are prosperous.

My father is very fair in business. Some people say it's luck. He has been very lucky in hiring very good workers, supervisors, and foremen. While workers of other companies went on strike, he was able to avoid strike, even without being able to speak Tagalog. He commands respect with his fairness. He can speak a little Tagalog now, but we would laugh at him.

Chinese School

We speak Chinese at home. Fujian dialect was my mother tongue and Tagalog my second language. I learned English in school.

My mother can read and write Chinese very well. She grew up in Cebu, in central Philippines. At that time, given the large Chinese population there, there were some excellent Chinese schools that taught everything in Chinese. Thus she learned a great deal of Chinese history and literature. About five years before I started school, the amount of Chinese taught in Chinese schools was decreased from everything being taught in Chinese to half a day of Chinese. I went to a private Catholic Chinese school for girls, run first by American nuns, and now Filipino nuns. Chinese language was taught by Chinese teachers. I understand that nowadays there are only two periods of Chinese of forty minutes each. At the other end of the school playground was a similar Chinese school for boys. Their school had a higher standard of Chinese.

At the time I was going to school, almost 99 percent of the students were Chinese. Now, 60 percent are Chinese, and 40 percent, Filipino. For the Filipino students, Chinese is a third language, after Tagalog and English. They are sent to Chinese schools because the successful businesses in the Philippines are mostly owned by the Chinese. Their parents want them to make contact with Chinese children, for future business connections, and learn Chinese so that they will have the language in doing business later. Actually, the need to

Deanna Li and her husband, Hon Li, in Manila

learn Chinese is declining. My generation can speak Chinese because our parents were from China and we had to speak Chinese at home, although we may not be able to read or write very well. But the generation after us can hardly speak Chinese despite the fact that my siblings and I all married Chinese spouses.

Going to a Chinese school would make you quite aware that you are Chinese. It was when I went to the University of the Philippines, which is run by the government, that I began to assimilate into Filipino culture. There were still quite a few Chinese, and I associated mostly with the Chinese until the third and fourth years, when I mixed more with the Filipinos in my major, mathematics.

Martial Law and Emigration

Martial law was imposed in the Philippines by former President Marcos on September 21, 1972. Many Chinese were scared, not knowing what was going to happen to them or their businesses. To show that he was serious, Marcos executed the first martial law prisoner by firing squad. He happened to be a Chinese. At that time Canada was opening its door to immigrants. My father applied in 1976 and got approval to immigrate. Then the question was who in the family should go. He extended the visa for a year, but unless some of us actually took up residence in Canada, the chance would be lost. At that time, I did not want to go because I was finishing my university studies and was afraid that my credits would not be accepted by Canadian universities. My brother was studying medicine and, therefore, in the same situation. He would have to start all over again if he had gone to Canada. So two of my younger sisters, who were fourteen and eighteen, went to Vancouver, Canada, in 1978.

In 1979 I graduated from the University of the Philippines. Since I had not immigrated to Canada like my younger sisters, the only way to go abroad was to go to graduate school. I did not want to go to Canada because I suspected that they would not have taken any of the credits I earned in the Philippines. So I thought that maybe I would go to Washington state, which was close to Vancouver B.C., and I could travel back and forth. I applied to the University of Washington and was accepted. Both my sisters who immigrated to Canada finished their studies. After they graduated from college and got their citizenship, they went back to the Philippines.

My brother eventually went to Canada also and got his citizenship. My father obviously had to protect my brother and have a place for him to go just in case the political situation in the Philippines should become unstable. I am not sure how he got his immigrant status. As I got married to a Chinese American I could stay in the United States. So everyone is protected and has some place to run to if anything happens, except my youngest sister. She was so young back in 1978 that she did not immigrate to Canada.

Ancestors and Burial Ground

My maternal grandparents were buried in the Philippines. Our rites for the deceased ancestors are half Filipino and half Chinese. My mother, sisters, and I were converted to Catholicism when we were in school. Following the Catholic feast of All Souls Day, November 2, the Chinese Filipinos would go to the cemetery and stay there all day. They would bring food and games to play, as for a picnic, and even books to read. My mother would bring fruit, burn paper money and incense at the grave, and make us bow. I remember my grandmother's funeral. At a certain hour, the Catholic priest celebrated Mass. After that a Daoist priest came and said some prayers. That was followed by the Buddhist monks performing some ceremony. There was the statue of the Blessed Virgin Mary on the side. Over at the end was the statue of Kuanyin, the bodhisattva of mercy. My father said that this way everything was covered. This could just be our family.

It was hard for many Chinese who emigrated to the Philippines to get citizenship. Only the Filipino citizens can own land, even now. So many Chinese immigrants could not own land. But they could buy a plot for burial. Since they could not build houses while alive, they would see to it that they could build miniature houses on their grave plots, the one piece of property they could own. Some of those houses are very elaborate, a couple of stories, six feet high, complete with air-conditioning. The Chinese cemeteries in the Philippines are quite a tourist attraction.

Chinese Values

I am very happy that I was born Chinese. I like the values that are in place: respect for the elders, high achievement, and the sense of togetherness as in a group.

I remember one time when my father was really ill in San Francisco and I flew over there. After he got well and came back, he told my daughter, "I hope when you are grown up and your mother is old, you too will do what your mom did." I hope it went into her brain. But at that time she was only five years old. The separation was so hard on her that she just wanted her mommy back.

I like the notion that the Chinese push their children to achieve. Even though the children's goal is to stop here, we push them beyond that goal. This is quite a tradition among the Chinese. They emphasize study a lot although I am not sure whether this high achievement orientation is just in some Chinese families or most Chinese families. My husband's family never did want him to study, even though he had his Ph.D. of all things. His parents did not see why he would want to get that degree, as it was of no use. They would rather see him open up a business.

In the Chinese tradition, being alone is not good. You always have to have company. I know it was instilled by my Chinese friends if not my parents. My friends would tell me not to eat alone or study alone. What would usually happen was that they would say, "Oh, there is a bunch of us over there, why don't you join us rather than being alone?" I found it shocking when I first went to the United States to see people eating alone in the cafeteria. I was not used to that, eating alone or studying alone. I think, in the United States, independence is so much emphasized that you become a loner. I on the contrary like the whole idea of companionship, the sense of unity.

I feel that these qualities have helped me in my career. The only thing I think that was detrimental to my development was the lack of self-esteem. The Chinese upbringing did not foster self-esteem. I know when people praise me or my work, I find myself saying, "Oh, no, it is not good, it is not good." Deep down, I feel it is not all that good either while in fact it is good. I just feel that the confidence in oneself is lacking. Maybe the family has been too close-knit so that we all depend on one another. Because there are too many people around you, when suddenly you are by yourself, you feel quite lost, not knowing what to do. That was how I felt when I was first in the United States on my own. I was not even sure what I was going to wear the next day. Then the confidence that you could do this or that was gone too. Or it was not there to begin with.

They stress self-esteem a great deal in the United States. Do you know about the study of American and Korean students in which both groups were given a math test? After the test, when asked about it, the Americans said that they did very well while the Koreans said that they did not do quite well. The result came out just the opposite. I was like the Koreans, not sure of myself.

14 The Financial Wizard
Peggy Chow (The Netherlands, United States)

I WAS BORN IN Hong Kong in 1946, the second among three sisters and four brothers. At that time the family was rich. Then in the 1950s everything just went downhill. My father had a grocery store, and we always helped out there on weekends. It was a very difficult time; we had to struggle. I came to have a particular view about money. I once told my mother: "I'm not afraid to die, but I'm afraid to be poor." Death comes only once, sooner or later, but poverty is nagging and fearsome. I was not ashamed to beg for piecework from the factories. I had all kinds of jobs in the putting-out system, like beading sweaters and gowns, assembling plastic flowers, filling up matchboxes, and packaging sunglasses. The younger siblings also helped. We would hand back the finished articles and get paid right away. Filling up 1,000 matchboxes earned us HK$1.00. Then I would give the dollar to my grandmother to buy food for the day. That's how we lived. The alternative was to borrow money from my paternal aunt. It was very pitiful. I would go to my aunt's house, borrow $5 or $10. My aunt would give me a lecture. That was why I feared poverty very, very much.

Life was hard, but my mother insisted that all the children must attend school. My elder sister was an excellent student. I was not at all good in studies. I was not stupid, and I have photographic memory, but I failed in math and English. I did not understand the reasoning, and memory alone was not enough for learning math. I refused to study English because I thought that I would always be living in Hong Kong. I was so stubborn and ignorant. It took me more than twelve years to finish schooling as I had to repeat grades.

An Arranged Marriage

When I finished secondary school, my father was out of the grocery store business and was a cosmetics salesman for some import company. I went into cosmetics sales, too, because my skin was very beautiful. I was able to save some money. In 1966, the convulsions of the Cultural Revolution in China threatened the stability of Hong Kong. My mother was anxious that the family should leave Hong Kong. My elder sister already had a teaching job and was planning to get married. The younger sister was under age. My mother said to me, "Perhaps you should find a husband overseas, daughter. Then you can bring all the younger brothers and sister there eventually." As I always wanted to please my parents, and we were beset with financial difficulties, I agreed. There were a couple of matchmaking sessions, but they didn't work out. One was very old, and my mother objected. The other one thought that I was too young and would run away once I got to the U.S. So the idea of marrying overseas was put aside for a few years.

Then one day a schoolmate of my aunt's phoned my mother. She was a professional matchmaker for overseas Chinese who came to Hong Kong looking for a bride. She had a bachelor from the Netherlands eager to get married. That was Ken, now my husband.

We all met in a restaurant. He brought his maternal grandmother while my mother accompanied me. Well, it was awkward. He was quite quiet; I did not say much either. His grandmother liked me, and my mother him. My mother asked him what was his occupation. He pointed to a waiter and said, "I wait on tables." My mother asked him how much money he was making. He said about one thousand gulden a month, which was about HK$1,600. He said that he would do his best to take care of his family. He planned to work hard and open his own restaurant someday, but he could not promise my mother any particular future. My mother liked that. She thought that this young man was honest. He did not lie about what he was doing in the Netherlands. If he did, no one would have known any differently.

His grandmother then suggested that he and I should go to the cinema. So we went to a movie and strolled about afterwards. We did

Peggy and
Ken Chow
on their
wedding day

not say much. When it got dark, he took me home and met my grandmother, my father, and my siblings. I liked him since that first day because he was handsome, quiet, and straightforward, no flowery language to deceive anyone.

He phoned in the evening the next day, and we went to another movie on the third day. After the movie, he asked me whether I liked to eat potatoes. I told him that I did; I liked all kinds of food. He said, "If you like potatoes, are you willing to go to the Netherlands with me? There is no rice in the Netherlands. If you could not live on potatoes then it would not work." I said, "I like potatoes. It is not a big issue." The following day, his grandmother phoned my mother and they began to prepare for the wedding.

While Ken was still in his teens, his father was killed in a car accident. After he finished secondary school, as the eldest son, he signed a labor contract and went to work in Amsterdam in order to ease the family situation. He began as a laborer, spearing satay meat, cleaning, and cooking rice or noodle. As he was good-looking and proficient in English, he worked up to be a waiter so he was able to earn more.

Ken's maternal grandfather went to the U.S. on someone else's paper and was, therefore, a paper son. Eventually all his children were able to immigrate to the U.S. except his eldest daughter, who was Ken's mother. The birth dates of Ken's grandfather and mother simply did not match; she could not have been born in that year. So she and her family remained in Hong Kong. At the time I met Ken, his maternal grandparents had just retired from the Bumble Bee Tuna and Salmon Cannery in Portland and returned to Hong Kong for a trip. His grandfather had not been back to Hong Kong for over forty years. While they were there, they wanted to see their grandson duly married.

I first met Ken on March 16, 1971, and we were married on April 10. We had a wedding banquet because I did not want the relatives and friends to think that I ran out of town with a guy. I did not want people to know that I married a guy whom I had known for only three days. I told people that we had been pen pals for a long time and he had returned to Hong Kong to marry me.

Amsterdam

A month after our wedding Ken went back to Amsterdam to work and to find an apartment. I found out that I was pregnant the following month. I joined him in the Netherlands in September. It was a difficult time. We bought the cheapest bed, one kitchen table and four chairs. There was no furniture in the living room. There was no carpet, just the concrete floor. Shortly after the birth of our daughter, Jenny, Ken was out of a job. Sitting at home, we did not know what to do.

As I feared poverty more than death, I always had a little bit of money on the side, for a rainy day. I thought that if my marriage did not work out, I would have money for an air ticket back to Hong Kong. At that time, we had no choice but to use my savings.

Ken and I had to adjust to each other. After all we were strangers to each other and did not know one another's temperament.

Gradually we worked out the friction. Things improved when both of us found jobs. I found a job in a restaurant owned by a Chinese overseas from New Guinea and got a baby-sitter to look after the three-month-old baby.

By the time my daughter was two years old, my mother-in-law had remarried and become a legal immigrant in the U.S. She came to Amsterdam for a visit. She did not like her son working as a waiter, as there was no future in it. She wanted to sponsor us to immigrate to the U.S. We liked the idea. We were in the Netherlands, and Ken's elder sister was in Hong Kong. Both families applied for immigration. However, just after we began the application process, I was pregnant with my son. We thought that it would be better to have the baby in Amsterdam. But soon after my son's birth in 1976, Ken's sister in Hong Kong got divorced. By coincidence just at that time I was seriously ill with thyroid problems. As I was very disturbed by my sister-in-law's divorce, I asked my mother-in-law some pointed questions: "What are we going to do once we get to the U.S.? How are we going to live?" Her reply was that my husband would go back to school for sure but I was to work in the fish cannery with her in Astoria/Newport, Oregon. I could not agree to that. If my husband alone went to college in Oregon, and if he should meet some other woman and leave me, what was I going to do? I said no. I would only go to America if both of us would go to college, as both of us were secondary school graduates. I told Ken that I would not go to the States if I was to work and live with his mother and take care of two small children. I also found out around that time that my mother-in-law was quite opposed to my husband marrying me in the first place because she felt that her son had not completed higher education. My mother-in-law was not pleased with my decision. But I doggedly refused to migrate to the U.S. I thought that my mother-in-law was too strong-willed. But I was no shrinking violet either; I was not to be bullied!

Since we stayed on in the Netherlands, I began to study. I learned to speak and write Dutch. It took me four years to speak a whole sentence in Dutch.

I am very good in saving money. If my father earned one dollar, my mother would spend a dollar and half, whereas for every dollar that my husband earns, I can somehow save $1.10! I am a very smart financial manager. I have the stamina to endure. Being Chinese is being frugal. We saved money and bought a car. My husband and some friends opened a restaurant. I had a job in another restaurant, working only on the weekend. We bought an elegant house by the river in a suburb of Amsterdam. We would go rowing with friends in the summer and ice-skating in the winter. There was a big playground for toy-car racing and other fun activities. As we were the only Chinese family in that neighborhood, I made sure that my house was always spic and span. I had a group of very good friends; I associated more with the Dutch than the Chinese women. We were naturalized Dutch citizens. I thought that we were very settled in the Netherlands, with no more fancy ideas about immigrating to the U.S.

Immigrants Again

In 1979, I took the children to visit my family in Edmonton, Canada. The children were delighted playing with cousins and getting to know the extended family. Ironically, I was unable to bring my family overseas as none of them wanted to move to the Netherlands. My younger sister, on the other hand, settled in Canada after completing her education and brought all the brothers as well as our parents there.

Then I got ill. I was hospitalized three times in one year. As I lay in bed, I was worried about my children. Who would take care of them if I should die? They spoke Dutch but no English, and a little Chinese, and their relatives were all in North America. If we went to the U.S., and if things did not work out between Ken and me, I could go back to my family.

During our visit to the U.S., we noticed that there was much more freedom of choice in terms of occupations. Although we were Dutch citizens, there were still in the Netherlands quotas for various immigrant groups' entry into the professions, such as medicine or architecture.

At that time, with more immigrants coming to the Netherlands, the competition in the restaurant business was getting very stiff. Also, the government was cracking down on illegal immigrants while we made better money by hiring them. We reasoned that we would only have five more good years in Amsterdam. We were thirty-some then, still young. I said to Ken that when we first came to Amsterdam, we had nothing, then we built a house, we had two kids, we had a nice car, we had everything. If we went to the U.S., the first five years would be worse than what we had then. But we had two pairs of hands and some savings. Also, we would have our families, his and mine, to back us up. I didn't think that it would fail. That's why we came to the U.S. in 1982. People thought that we were crazy. What more did we want? For the kids, their future, my health, and our eventual financial situation, it was the right time to move.

Around that time, my mother-in-law came into some money. She told us to come over here and we could both go to school. She would take care of things. Both Ken and I attended Portland Community College in 1983. He got into the hotel and restaurant management program and eventually got his associate of applied science degree. I went back to learning reading, writing, and speaking English as a second language.

After three terms of ESL, we moved out of my mother-in-law's house. I found a job in a food services company that ran cafeterias for various corporations. My work unit was the cafeteria in the Intel Corporation in Oregon. I wish I could have bought some stock at that time, but we did not have that much money left. At first I worked on the salad bar, cleaning vegetables and setting things up. Then I was promoted to be the grill cook, earning $1.00 more per hour. Later I also worked as the cashier. Ken also got a part-time job there first as a dishwasher and later as a cashier.

In April 1984, the food services company offered me the position of a unit manager. My husband had completed his program by then. Both Ken and I have been managers in the food services ever since. My first unit was a deli in an office building downtown. But I knew nothing about management; I just wanted a good grill job. How could I be a manager? The assistant district manager who took me to the deli told me, "Make it simple, Peggy. Remember two things. First, keep your customers happy. Second, make your people work for you.

If you can nail down these two things, you will be fine." The day after I started, the cashier stole money from the till. The assistant district manager made me fire him. So I learned not only how to hire and train people, but also how to fire workers. Later at a newspaper cafeteria, I was in charge of two shifts serving more than five hundred employees. At another place as a senior manager, I had twenty people working for me.

I have been successful in managing our finances and investments. Whenever I have money or time, I always think about what am I doing now. Should I put the money in the bank, invest somewhere, or buy some property. Whenever I have a pencil, paper, and a calculator, my husband gets nervous. But I have done quite well. I made money in real estate. I helped my children invest the money they saved from their summer jobs, and put $100 every month from my own savings into each of their accounts. By the time they graduated from high school, each had more than $10,000 in their accounts to go to college. At least they had their tuition taken care of. I just gave them room, board, and clothing. That's why they went through four years of college without my putting in any money for them. When they finished college, they did not owe a dime to anybody.

Managing money is like cooking. That's my good point. I always know how to use the leftover. Put whatever leftover in my hands, and I always turn it into something fresh and good that I sell even more. Yesterday's bread becomes tomorrow's bread pudding. If there is something that you don't know what to do with, I'll just make some dough, wrap it, and bake it. It turns out to be a pie. That's why my budget is always great. Whatever goal I set, I can always beat the budget. We are affluent again.

When Ken and I worked together, we discovered that the best thing was that our marriage was arranged and we didn't know each other. We found out about each other's good points, the strengths more than the shortcomings. Over the years, I earned my husband's respect, his trust, and also his love. Sometimes we don't ask for more than just a pat on the back. With a hug or a kiss, we can die for anything. We still make compromises to each other because it is hard to be in a relationship. A good relationship is a lifetime job. Even though we have been married for over thirty years, we are still working on it. It's not a one-time deal and you say, "We are married, and we can do whatever we want." No, you get more disciplined, more caring, more mature. Nowadays people give up too fast. It's the Chinese way to put in the efforts and persevere.

15 San Ramon the Coffee Town

Juan Miranda (Peru)

MY GRANDMOTHER, my mother's mother, was born in China. Her name was Lee Chung. She came to Peru in 1905 or 1906, at the age of 18 or 19, to work on the coffee plantation in the jungle of Peru. At that time many people came from Europe and Asia as the government was giving free land to immigrants willing to go to the eastern side of the Andes Mountains. She came with about twenty families, altogether more than a hundred people, from the same province in northern China. They lived together like a family because the government provided housing for people working in agriculture. But they were really not one family, and she was by herself. She told us that she had some brothers, and their families were living in China and Hong Kong. She did not have much education.

She married my grandfather, an Italian. It was funny because my grandfather from Italy did not speak Chinese. She did not speak Italian. But they communicated somehow. They got married in 1907 or 1908. My grandmother was a very good-looking lady, short, about 152 centimeters. She had a nice face and long hair. All the people from the different colonies would go to the grocery store. That was where they met. My grandfather liked this girl and always winked at her. My grandmother would answer in Chinese, "Very, very bad." This was what she told us; I don't know whether it was true or not. They married very fast. She was very popular in her group, and she was the only one who married outside her own people. Many of those who came with her complained, "Why are you marrying someone not of your own culture?" She had some problems there. She said that some of her friends who came together would not talk to her or work with her for years. They avoided her when she walked in the street. My grandmother's attitude was kind of, well, if you don't want to talk to me, okay. It was not her fault that she fell in love with this man from Italy. It was difficult to be in love with people not of your culture or language. She would still meet other Chinese and go to their parties, because they worked together and needed each other. They were the only ones who spoke the language there.

San Ramon is a small town. At that time the population was about five thousand. Most of the people in this town were in agriculture. My grandparents had seven children. My extended family was big, seven families in this block. My grandparents lived in the big house. We lived two doors down. When I was a child, if I did not like the food in my house, I could go to my grandmother's house because they would be cooking fish or whatever. I could go over there or to my aunt's house next door. I always liked it there because I played with my cousins. We did everything together. I had to go to a bigger town about forty minutes away by car for high school. I had to live in a dormitory but always came back to my family to be with them.

I remember my grandmother very fondly because she spoilt us. She would buy things for us, cook delicious food, and provide us with everything we needed. We loved our grandmother because she was very resourceful. She knew everything. For example, she was a master in cooking. She taught us how to do things. To make noodles, you put eggs and flour together. She made her own noodles; she never bought noodles. People always came to the house to meet my grandmother. In every culture, people like to eat, I think. My grandmother was the center of everything because she was a good cook. She also knew how to sew, with all these beautiful things from China.

We lived in this small town in central Peru where there were colonies of Asians. But there was no Chinatown, not like Lima, the big city where they have a Chinatown. To go to Lima you have to go over the Andes. When we went to Lima to visit some families, my grandmother would always go to Chinatown. She would take my older sister and me to those shops where they sold fruits, like the mandarin oranges, and other kinds of food. She liked to visit with the people in Chinatown, talking to them and feeling very happy. Some of the people in Lima came from Hong Kong, and they had a hard time communicating with my grandmother because she came from northern China and only spoke Mandarin.

My grandmother never spoke Spanish. She only spoke Mandarin Chinese to us. When I was small, it was easier to communicate with her. Then when we grew up, we began to speak Spanish. She only spoke Chinese throughout her life, although she understood a lot of Spanish. When I was a kid, she would take me shopping with her. We would go to different small stores because in a small town we did not have a supermarket or a large store. When we were in the stores, she always spoke to me in Chinese, and I would speak back in Spanish with something in Chinese. The funny thing was when we had to buy something like bathroom tissue, she would be very embarrassed to ask for toiletry. She would ask me to talk to the salesperson, and I would order for her. Some people would make fun of us and say, "Why don't you speak Spanish? Why doesn't your grandmother speak Spanish?" I had to tell them the situation, but sometimes I did not say much.

My mother speaks some Chinese because she lived with my grandmother all the time. My mother speaks Italian too. My Chinese was not good because I learned it by ear, listening to my grandmother. As a kid of six or seven, I would speak with whoever that was there. In Peru, it was mostly my grandmother. She lived to sixty-four or sixty-five years of age.

In Peru, there are still some old Chinese families that have been there for generations. And the Japanese too. We have many Asians in Peru, Argentina, Brazil, and Chile. In all these countries the Asians and their cultures are very strong. The Asian cultures are very respectable in South America. If you are part of an Asian culture, people respect you more because they think that you are more trustworthy. The Chinese who were born in South America act like Latinos in their manners. They look Asian but they speak Spanish. They are very integrated.

The last time there were Chinese immigrants to Peru was in 1968, I think. They stopped coming because the economic situation in the country was not good. Most Chinese went to Argentina and Venezuela. I have met a distant aunt in Venezuela. Most of the Chinese there came from Hong Kong, from around 1984 to about 1995. Venezuela is the only country you can pay for your residency and work. The people from Hong Kong learned Spanish very fast.

My uncle has been in Australia for forty years. He lives in Sydney now. He is the nephew of my grandmother. I met him several times in the U.S. He did not speak Spanish. We communicated in English, but sometimes he spoke to me in Chinese, and I had a hard time understanding him because I was out of practice and hadn't spoken Chinese for a long time.

I see myself as part Chinese, part European, and part Latino. I feel that way always. I like Chinese culture, as I do European and Latino cultures. Chinese culture is part of my background. I went to the U.S. for my university education. I made friends with students from Hong Kong and Taiwan. We would get together and play soccer. We discussed about things, and we enjoyed ourselves. We talked about things in Peru and how the Chinese came to Peru. Some of the Latino students from South America who saw me then did not think that I was a Latino because I was always with the Asians. When I am with my friends from Hong Kong or Taiwan, I feel Chinese. I feel I am part of that group. I feel that I belong there.

I remember one time I met this Chinese Singaporean. He asked me why I didn't speak Chinese very much. I said that I only learned Chinese when I was a child. I didn't speak it anymore because as I grew up, I did not live with my family anymore. He was curious why if my last name was Miranda I should speak with my family in Chinese. I feel more Chinese than Italian because of my grandmother. Most of my sisters and brothers were closer to my grandmother.

The Latin American culture is similar to Asian cultures. There are similar characteristics the way people act and communicate in Latin American and Asian cultures. There are similar customs maybe because many years ago, before the Incas, the Asians came to South America. My grandmother always felt very comfortable with the Indians and the mestizos. In Spanish we have this respectful address of "tu" for "you" in English. When I talked to my grandmother, I always addressed her very respectfully. Sometimes I was confused about what she was saying, and she felt frustrated explaining to us. So I would say to her, "Please, I cannot understand. Please repeat again." We respected all our elders. The way we talked to them was different. I remember that I did not look at my grandmother in the eye. I looked in the face sometimes but kept my eyes down a little bit when I approached her. There was a lot of respect. However, Asian cultures in Latin America have changed now; there isn't quite the respect.

When I taught Spanish in the U.S., I would always teach about the cultural heritage. I would talk about not only Latin American cultures but also Chinese culture. I would talk about how the Chinese came to South America in the 1800s. I would teach Spanish and tell them about the culture of the Chinese people. I like everything about Chinese culture.

16

Good in Business

D.T. (Indonesia)

IN MY FAMILY, only my mother's mother was born in China. My great-great-grandparents on my father's side came from China. We have been in Indonesia for many generations.

My parents have a printing business in Jakarta. They make calendars, labels, invitation cards, brochures, et cetera. My father looks after the operations of the company while my mother is responsible for marketing. My eldest brother also works in the family business. The bulk of the business is calendars. They are busy from July till December. After that, they get nothing at all, except the small printing jobs. My mother relaxes when there is not much to do in the company; she stays at home or goes to friends' house. Not my dad. My dad always goes to his office, looking for new business and attending to old business. Even when there is nothing to do, he must work to have something to do. If he just stays at home, sits around, sleeps, and relaxes, he'll get a headache. If he works, he is happy again. He is very hardworking. He is like many other Chinese business people. They just work and work.

The thing about being Chinese is that we are good in business. Chinese control about 70 to 80 percent of the business in Indonesia. They can't sit in the government. They can't do things politically. All they can do is business, whatever kind of business. Whatever they are allowed to do, they are going to be successful — that is Chinese. The result is that they control quite a bit of the economy. They are good business people.

I was born in Jakarta in 1975, the third of four brothers. My personal name in Chinese is Jingfang, *Jing* for scenery and *fang* for square. It means looking at four sides. I was told that coins in ancient China were round with a square hole in the middle so the coins could be strung together. The coin should be a reminder to business people, especially those dealing with money. They should be round on the outside, that is, sociable, flexible, and cordial in dealing with people; but square in the center, that is, principled and honest in the inside. I am working in a mortgage company after university. But I am now thinking about going into trading. My eldest brother is in the furniture business. Perhaps I can help him sell furniture in North America. Anyway, my name seems to be appropriate for what I am doing.

Actually my two elder brothers use my father's family name. But my younger brother and I used my mother's family name. I am not too sure why this is so. It may be because there is a two-children policy in Indonesia.

Ethnic Awareness

When I was small, I didn't realize that we were different from other people; we just lived in the country where we were born. But as I grew up, I became more aware that we were different: we were Chinese and the others were natives. I think it is very distinct that we feel Chinese and different, and that there is this gap between them and us. What made me realize this was the fact that most of the natives live in smaller houses, very crowded. We Chinese live in better environment and have better education. The natives go to public schools, which are cheap and the quality is not as good as the private schools where most of the Chinese send their children. I went to a private school where my classmates were all Chinese. That's how I felt the difference. I began to wonder why. I was told that the Chinese worked harder than the others. We have this stereotype that they are pretty lazy and that explains the gap. Just because the way we were raised and because of our background, we have this stereotype. As I grow older I understand that this is not true. But the native Indonesians discriminate against us and don't like us very much. That's why the parents do not want their kids to hang out with these people.

According to my grandmother, in the anti-Chinese violence of 1965, the Chinese in Jakarta were not too badly hurt because they got some protection in the capital. But in the outlying cities, towns, and

D.T. (first left back row) with grandmother (center front),
mother (first left front), brothers, and Wei Djao

islands, it was very tragic. Thousands of Chinese were killed. Houses
were burned and shops looted. Many Chinese went back to China.
The government of China sent ships to transport them, even though
many of the refugees were born in Indonesia. But a couple of years
later, the Cultural Revolution broke out, and China was plunged into
chaos. It was not a good situation for those who went to China. Life
was hard for both those who stayed in Indonesia and those who went
to China.

The native Indonesians discriminate against us in a number of
ways. Some of the low-income natives operate the pedicabs for hire.

You say, "I want to go to this place, how much?" He would give a price. You know the Chinese like to bargain. So you give a lower price. Sometimes the operator would just tell us to keep our money and stuff like that. He doesn't want to take Chinese passengers. Some government employees are slow to serve the Chinese. It's hard to explain. It's like they seem to think that you are rich and they are poor because you are Chinese.

After 1965, we did not have serious disturbances or violence against the Chinese until the political unrest in the late 1990s. The riots of 1997 and 1998 were aimed at the Chinese stores and Chinese people. Jakarta Chinatown was burned, property was severely damaged, and people were killed. Chinese women were raped. There were looting and violence against Chinese in other cities as well.

University education is one clear example of discrimination. There is a very good university called University of Indonesia. It is a government university. Most of the students are natives. It's very hard for the Chinese to get in. I don't think there is an official quota for the Chinese to limit their enrollment. It's just that internally they do not admit students of Chinese background. They don't do it publicly. I don't know whether this is true or not but I heard that in the resident's identity card, there is a secret code that indicates whether you are Chinese or not. Somehow they know that you are Chinese. I went to the U.S. for higher education at the age of nineteen. I have a bachelor's degree in business administration.

There have been no signs or billboards in Chinese anywhere in Indonesia since 1965. The government does not allow them. It wants us to get used to Indonesian culture and just forget about our Chinese background. It wants to eliminate all those Chinese elements so that we'll forget that we are Chinese. That's why we don't see Chinese characters in Indonesia.

There used to be Chinese schools. My father was born in 1942. He went to a Chinese school, and reads and writes Chinese well. After the "ethnic cleansing" in 1965, the government banned all Chinese schools in Indonesia because it doesn't want us to keep our culture. My mother learned Chinese from a private tutor at home. In the private school my elder brothers and I attended, we learned Bahasa, which is the national language of Indonesia, and English, but no Chinese. We also had a private teacher coming to our house to teach us Chinese when we were little; my younger brother was not yet born. We studied. Then we were lazy, so we stopped. Then we learned again and stopped again. Thus we had our Chinese lessons for one or two years. The books we used were from Taiwan or China, very elementary. I also took Chinese in college in the U.S. I know very simple characters; I can write my own name. My younger brother was sent to study in Singapore at the age of nine. He learned Chinese, English, and Malay there and is fluent in all three languages. He had no problem with Malay as Bahasa is essentially Malay. He just graduated from secondary school and is attending college in the U.S.

At home my parents speak Indonesian language, Mandarin and Hakka dialect. Sometimes I can pick up what they are talking about in Chinese if it's about the simple things of everyday life. My brothers and I usually speak Bahasa.

Personal Values

I have never been to China. It's a communist country. My grandmother told me that she had to leave because the country was poor.

The part of Chinese culture I liked the most as a child was the red packet money at Chinese New Year. We would say *gongxi* to our parents, "Happy Chinese New Year" in Chinese. They were the first people we said it to; the biggest amount we got was also from them. After that, of course, we kids would go from house to house, visiting relatives, just to get money. That's quite memorable to me.

We followed the rites in memory of the ancestors. When my grandfather died, we wore the white coats and followed all the ceremony. We had to burn all these paper houses, cars, and money, so that he could use them in the next life. It's quite funny. But it's just Chinese tradition. We went to the grave after a certain number of days. In some relative's house there is a picture of our grandparents, and we have to pray at the family altar on the anniversaries. I did these things when I was a kid. Once I am a Christian, I don't do that anymore.

Our parents sent us all to a Christian school run by a Chinese church. The school was started on a different island. Ours was a branch; there are schools all over the islands. That's where we learned about Christianity. All the years we went to the Christian school, none of us got baptized. My parents did not mention anything about religion. They sent us there because it is a good school. They were Buddhists, went to the temple once in a while, and were not very active. In recent years my mother has become a much more devout Buddhist. In fact she goes to the Buddhist hall every morning at six o'clock before she goes to work. They didn't discriminate against other religions. Maybe my mother once told me not to get baptized. But of course we have been taught about Christianity since kindergarten. Later in high school I went to church regularly by myself. After I got to the U.S., I became more serious. I felt that I couldn't play around with religion anymore. I decided that this was my life and I wanted to get baptized. It was not a bad decision; it was not like I was going to meet bad people. It's just a different religion. Of course, at first I didn't tell my mother because I was afraid that she would not approve. About a year later when I was home for the summer, I told her about my baptism, even though I was nervous. I prayed and she did not mind. So I see it as a miracle. She is still a fervent Buddhist.

I don't think I'll follow all the Chinese traditions. For example, I won't keep an ancestral shrine. Also, I think some of the Chinese work too hard. They don't spend their money on leisure. They just keep the money. I don't think I'll do that. Of course I won't spend all my money. I'll like to relax with my money on the weekend. Some Chinese just spend so much time on their business. I wonder, where is your time to relax? Where is your time for your family? I notice that the Chinese want to get together with family and friends. But how can they do that when they work so much? On the other hand, I think the Chinese realize that they may need money for the future, say, a house for their children when they get married. The Chinese like to plan for the future. That's why they are good in business.

17

Filial Piety: Virtue and Demands

Joseph Huang (United Kingdom)

MY FATHER'S FAMILY was from Shanghai, and my mother's, the U.S. My parents worked in Hong Kong for many years, and I was born there. We moved to Singapore when I was four. I was thirteen when I came over to England to attend a boarding school. I have stayed here ever since.

I came in form three (grade nine). Luckily I got a nice group of friends around me, which made the whole experience very pleasant. I was not bullied or picked on. There was no pressure to smoke or do anything like that in my group. As I am an only child, I never had brothers or sisters to play with. At the school, if I wanted to play football or tennis, there was always someone who wanted to do that too.

The way I was trained to study in Singapore was to learn everything and memorize everything. Mom would watch over me doing my homework every day. In England, I didn't feel that I had to work as hard as I did in Singapore. It was less easy for the boys here to keep up. The schools here are very much into the "you must think for yourself" attitude. Don't just memorize something, but you must understand it as well. This is a good way of teaching, but not for the very young. I think I came at just the right age so that I got the best of both worlds in that I had the foundation in basic knowledge, because I memorized it all, and I wasn't allowed to choose what I wanted to learn too early. When I got here was when I started to think for myself, and it came at the right time.

The Surgeon

After five years of secondary school, I went back to Singapore for a year of army service as I was — and still am — a permanent resident of Singapore. Then I returned to England for five years of medical school in Bristol, and a year of internship. After another year and a half in Singapore to complete my national service, this time as an army doctor, I came back to England four years ago to do my specialization in gastric-abdominal surgery.

I love my work. Yes, absolutely. When you are operating, it's a different world. You are always trying to do your best, and you forget the rest of the world. It is the challenge that gives you a buzz. If you do something well, there is a sense of accomplishment. I just enjoy it immensely, like people enjoy hobbies. I have always felt that it's a shame that one needs to rely on medicine for income because that changes one's perspective about practicing. Right now while I am still a junior I get paid a salary. It does not matter how many patients I see. I am sure when I become a senior and have to pay my bills according to the number of people I see, then it's going to be different.

My goal is to become a consultant in a decent hospital. I would like to be a professor of surgery in a major teaching hospital, in this country. So far I have done all the right things, like working for the right people. My aims are quite clear to everyone that I want to head up a more academic track rather than just settling to be any surgeon. That's going to be quite difficult even if I were white. As I'm not, that makes it even more difficult.

Being British

I am a British citizen. I studied here on a student visa. Then I applied to stay as a permanent resident, and they granted me that. After a few years I applied for citizenship. I wrote a few letters saying please let me stay. Hong Kong was going back to China—I had a Hong Kong passport—and I had no intention of going back to live in Hong Kong. I had grown up here. So I managed to get British citizenship.

I enjoy living here: London, the west end, being close to Europe. I know that I am not English. I know I am not white. On the other hand, I feel that because I came when I was so young and have lived here for so long that I have integrated as best as I can. Most of my friends are English; I have few Chinese friends here. I like to live here partly because of the greater job opportunities and partly because of the lifestyle.

I think that once people get to know me they realize that they can deal with me on a professional and a social level. When they are looking for people to be their fellow consultants, they want people they can work with, they can socialize with, not just someone that is academically the best. So this may come across as racism. I think there is a lot more racism against the blacks and the Indians (South Asians). To a certain extent that's because the Chinese in England don't make much noise. We are known to be hardworking, conscientious and intelligent. The Chinese are not protesting or marching for rights or whatever. We more or less know our place. I don't think that's a bad thing. I look at it this way that it is someone else's country, we migrated here, and it is not for me — certainly not my generation anyway — to stand up and say, I want that right. If I can stay here, that's great, because if I don't like it, I'll leave.

Being Chinese

In what ways am I Chinese? It's something I must say I don't like to think about very much, because when I think about it too hard, I find so many conflicting things and so many different things pulling me in one way or another.

After the second stint of army service in Singapore, when I came back here to work, within a few days, I thought this is what I enjoy; there was no need to get used to anything. There's a bit of guilt, actually. My parents want me back in Singapore. I don't particularly want to. That's one of the conflicts. What do I do? So much is expected of me being an only child. I still think that I should look after them, respect them, and all that. But I am still climbing up the ladder here. The door to go home is not shut yet partly because of my parents. I am willing to consider going back there to work on a trial basis in the future, when I have made it to what I feel is the top of my profession, to be a senior, to be a consultant. When I get there I'll think about what the offers are from Singapore, if there are any. If there aren't, I am quite happy to stay. At this moment, I am not quite willing to give up my career and happiness to go back for something that is uncertain.

I think that's a very Western way of thinking; sometimes I don't know whether I should feel that way. Certainly my friends who are Western have this idea that it's our life, this is how we live it, we live it how we want. If folks don't like it, tough. Maybe I feel a little differently from my English friends. I still feel that I can't just abandon my parents, my filial piety. And to a certain extent I would expect my children to think of how I feel. Having said that, I can actually see why kids rebel and want to get out of their shell. I don't know whether it's good or bad. I think it's just two different ways of doing things.

The other thing is that I suppose I know that I would get so far but I might not get right to the top. If I'm not happy here, I would not hesitate to go to Singapore forever.

I don't know what I want to do so far as marriage is concerned. If I marry someone from Singapore or Hong Kong, I don't think that they would necessarily feel comfortable living here. And I don't think that we'll be able to think on similar wavelengths. I think it will be hard work. Having said that, I think that I'll be looked after very well. Even now, I don't think that Chinese girls from Singapore or Hong Kong are so ambitious that they want to overshadow you. So I think that I'll have a stable relationship. Parents will be happy.

If I marry someone from here, then I think that while I'm living here I'll be quite happy. But my parents would be very upset. And the chances of my going home to Singapore, if that's home, will be very slim. So I haven't even begun to think about children. I don't even get very serious with girlfriends, which I think sometimes is not fair even to myself. I should just follow my heart wherever it drifts, just take the plunge whatever color she may be, whatever her background. I suppose the ideal would be a cross between the two, someone who still has Chinese values as much as I have, or as little as I have, and yet someone who has lived over here or lived in a Western culture, educated here, so that we can have something in common. Not easy to meet such a person. I must say I haven't consciously gone looking. The girls who are like that want to marry a white English boy, not a Chinese boy. So I haven't dared think about it too hard. I just concentrate on my career. I would just see what fate is going to bring.

That's the other thing. I suppose I believe very much in fate, which I don't think the English do. I believe that there is a lot of stuff which I don't understand, and I agree with the Chinese idea of fate, of how everything sort of falls into place. If you fail, it doesn't necessarily mean the end of the world, but there might be something else around the corner. That's the Chinese thing that I feel, which not many people share here. And I believe that things will fall into place. So maybe that's why I don't think about it too hard.

Something else I believe in is fengshui. I don't understand it. I don't know it very well, but I believe in it partly because it won't let anything bad happen, and partly because I just feel comfortable with most of it. Say, when I was buying my flat, I looked at all these places which were dark or drawn in a very funny way. I didn't feel comfortable. It's not just what people say, it's how you feel as well. I mean it's something that's been around for so many thousands of years. It can't be wrong.

Chinese medicine is something that I believe in too. Although I am a surgeon trained in Western medicine, I realize that there is so much that cannot be explained. I have always taken Chinese medicine as a child. And I still do. When I have a cold or when I feel it coming up, I would take my Yin Chiao tablets; I have got bottles of Yin Chiao at home. If I hurt myself or grazed an ankle or whatever, I have my herbal rubs. Yes, I do believe that there is a lot to Chinese medicine. There is also a lot that Chinese medicine can't cure, but I think Chinese medicine revitalizes you in ways that Western medicine cannot understand. Obviously some Chinese medicine has dubious value, but that's not what I take anyway. It's something I love to explore, not to be a practitioner, but just to understand it for myself later when I have time.

These are the Chinese things. I think in the Chinese culture these things and Chinese values are drilled into you, right or wrong, more so than in the Western society.

I was in Hong Kong for the handover in 1997 because the year before I spoke to my parents, "Look, this is a big occasion, once in a lifetime. There are no colonies in the world which will be going to a country. I think we should be there. I was born there." And I, like many Hong Kong people, have mixed feelings about it. My father was over the moon. He loved it. He thought that it was great, the best thing that had happened, because he felt the shame of being colonized. He thinks it doesn't matter who is in government; Hong Kong is now ours. He is very pro-China, although he came out of China. He feels that the regime in China is so different now that it's fine.

I thought that the whole ceremony was very dignified on the British side. There wasn't much China-bashing. It was a dignified withdrawal, whereas China's takeover was very loud and over-the-top celebration. It was to show the world, but the world looked and thought this was too much. You are proud, but it's one thing to be proud and it's another thing to irritate. I felt that it irritated me. It was a big event, but some of the things that people said, and the way they said it, were too condescending.

I understand that in the political world much happens behind the scenes. I am sure that some countries are trying to stop China becoming a power. But this politics which is behind the scenes should not come out into the open because there are so many Chinese who live outside. I think that, OK, you might feel that but still you don't need to say it. I felt that it undermined my position here in England. On a day-to-day living basis, for us the public, the masses, I don't think it's fair. It's like connecting the overseas Chinese with the Tiananmen Square incident of 1989. When people ask me about the politics of Tiananmen Square, the incident and all, I find it very difficult to say anything. I don't know all the facts. I just go by the Western media, which would be biased. I find it very difficult to say anything. Maybe it's because I don't want to create waves.

Now I can understand why some people think that parents shouldn't send kids abroad, because they don't come back. I am not saying that Singapore is bad or that Hong Kong is bad, or that I don't want to live there because it's awful. What I am saying is that I enjoy it here more. Little conflicting things pulling me. I want to stand up and say I am Chinese. But I don't think it's quite appropriate to do it here. I think that if you do it, yes, you might feel that you are very proud. But to others it smacks of racism, that you are against them. I think that very often what the English will say very nicely is: If you don't like it, don't complain. Just go back to where you came from.

18 Chinese Faces
Bernie Dun and Lee Dun (Canada, United States)

Bernie Dun (Father)

Having an Ethnicity

My mother and father were born in British Columbia. My mother graduated from high school, while my father, who was the first-born in a family of twelve children, left school when he was in his teens to work at his father's restaurant. I was always aware of being Chinese with all the Chinese faces of the large extended family around me, whether playing with my cousins or working at my grandfather's restaurant in Victoria. There was a great deal of eating and talking in Guangdong dialects. Being Chinese was always stressed as something good: the diversity of foods, various customs and traditions, and ideas of family. Every Saturday evening my brother and I would earn a dollar by scraping chewing gum from the underside or legs of tables and washing floors in the restaurant.

I went to fairly integrated elementary and junior high schools, which were not so common in those days. For example, in grade three, in a class of about thirty pupils, half were either Chinese or South Asian.

Growing up in Victoria Chinatown, I understood the meaning of having an ethnicity. One of my earliest recollections of race was in the 1950s when I was about eleven years old and read in the *Victoria Times* about a woman named Rosa Parks. She refused to go to the back of the bus because of her race. She was African American. This was quite perplexing because I always thought that race was just a game in which kids ran from the starting point to the finish. Then I understood that there was racism in countries where people of color form the minority.

Most of my Chinese classmates never went beyond high school. I noticed in high school and university that most of my classmates were European Canadians. So the focus of my world now shifted from being Chinese as a credible entity to an environment where being white and European was considered the more appropriate ethnicity. I also became aware of a conflict centered around being Chinese and being European Canadian, or being yellow and being white. I knew that in order to resolve the conflict, I had to find out more about China. As China studies, especially courses on modern China, were not readily available in Canada in the mid-1960s, I went to a graduate school in Ohio to learn about China and Asia. My objective was to reclaim my past, from which my extended family in Victoria came.

During university I was able to work as a dining room waiter at the famous Empress Hotel in Victoria. This was in the early 1960s, a period in which Chinese were never seen serving the public in a posh and high class place like the Empress. Chinese were usually mopping the floor, vacuuming the carpets, or washing dishes at the Empress. The fact that the English maitre d' hired me to be the first Chinese waiter in the dining room of the Empress Hotel said something about his tolerance and sensitivity. But even wearing a black tuxedo did not disguise the fact that I looked Chinese. I encountered many, many racial slurs, subtle or not so subtle. One time when I approached this old white couple — remember now this was the fashionable and prestigious Empress in Victoria — the man looked at me and said, "Will you ask the waiter to come over and take my order." When I replied that I was the waiter, he said, "Things have certainly changed at the Empress."

Another incident of blatant racism was when I worked as a television reporter for the Canadian Broadcasting Corporation (CBC) during the 1980s. I was on an affirmative action program that the CBC had devised to make the corporation reflect the diversity of Canada. But many of the European Canadians resented this because they felt that we were jumping the queue and not paying our dues. At CBC Edmonton, one of the anchors used to leave notes in my typewriter saying, "We'll get you yet, signed KKK." Another was: "Rots of Rock (for lots of luck), signed Charlie Chan." I worked at three other stations for the CBC: Regina, Saskatoon, and Calgary. I then moved

Bernie Dun (second left last row) in Grade 5 class picture

on to produce and host my own public affairs show in Hong Kong at the Television Broadcasting Limited.

Chinese History and Culture

Even though I am a third-generation Chinese Canadian, I continue to study all things Chinese. I have a Ph.D. in modern Chinese history, for which I spent a year at the Beijing Language Institute learning Mandarin. Having studied Chinese society and traveled in China, and having also studied and worked in Canada and the U.S.A., I am able to have a sympathetic understanding of Chinese and North American cultures. Tourists in China are almost always aggravated by people never queuing but swarming all over the place while buying train tickets or getting on the bus, and the bad services in restaurants and other public places. I have heard North American tourists complaining that the salespeople in China should be able to speak English. Moreover, the Chinese in China or the Chinese overseas always seem to vie for social status and prestige. In North America, there is aggravation of another kind: road rage and the "me-first" attitude seem to surface every now and then. People also seem to brag about their accomplishments or possessions. But I look at things this way. These behaviors of *some* Chinese and *some* European North Americans, annoying as they are, cannot be taken to mean that all Chinese, or all European Canadians and Americans, behave like them. One tries to understand the circumstances under which they occur, and perhaps also the personal reasons behind them. For every Chinese, in China or in the diaspora, who seeks social prestige and status, there are nine others who are modest about their accomplishments despite the 120 percent of energy and efforts they have put into whatever work they undertake. I have noticed that the Chinese value system teaches the people ever to work harder and strive for higher goals. I like the modesty and dogged steadfastness in Chinese culture.

There are indeed certain kinds of conduct in China that I do not like, just as there are behaviors of people in North America that I loathe. There are such things in every culture, every society. Yet beyond the irksome behaviors in individuals, my assessment of Chinese culture is that it is incredibly rich. First, it is focused on people co-existing in this world, on this earth. The central question has always been how do we human beings relate to each other. Second, this overriding concern has been recorded through the ages. This is the amazing legacy of the Chinese writing system, which in essence is traceable to the oracle bones of almost four thousand years ago, such that the Chinese have the longest continuous civilization in the world today.

Stories told by my grandparents about historical figures and their heroic deeds of justice, loyalty, perseverance, filial piety, and courage have been recounted from generation to generation. They have also been recorded in official histories and in poetry, essays, and drama. The Chinese have pretty much done everything under the sun. This ancient people have accomplished astounding feats, and they have endured all manners of hardships. They have been through everything, from tremendous cultural flowering, technological breakthroughs, and prosperity, to humiliation at the hands of conquerors, betrayals by their own people, and abject poverty. Yet they have endured and bounced back. The endurance and resilience of the Chinese are probably the most edifying aspects of the Chinese heritage to me. I can always look upon the legacy of this people as a solace and an encouragement. It has always been deeply sustaining to me. I am proud to have that legacy, to be a part of that heritage, and to pass it on to others who come after me.

Western Media

Although my specialization is in Chinese history, I never taught Chinese history on a permanent basis. But having a Ph.D. along with my television experience gave me the opportunity to work academically in media studies. After working in Hong Kong I began my teaching career in mass communication at a state university in California.

The whole idea of being Chinese in this predominantly European and white North America is always being challenged, especially through the media. Living in Canada and now living in the U.S., I see the Western media portray China as merely a cog in the free enterprise system. In it the Chinese people and China itself are merely commodities to be bought and sold. If China provides easy opportunities for Western business to enter into its huge consumer market, then China, according to the media, is playing the game. When China protests that spy planes should not be hovering over its territory, then the U.S. media say that China is aggressive and not a fair player. Of course this means that the game is created and developed by Western media specialists who have absolutely no idea of the philosophical and cultural foundations of China.

The media portrayal of China, I think, makes it very difficult for people of Chinese descent anywhere in the world, and particularly in the U.S., to have any positive views about China. I think the media make us very suspicious about China, creating a distance between the people of Chinese descent and China. If it were not for my firm grounding in my extended family in my childhood, my knowledge of Chinese history, and my experience as a journalist, I think my views about China and attitudes towards my own ethnicity would have been influenced by the media. If I did not see through a lot of the media messages, I definitely would not be so positive about being Chinese.

Lee Dun (Daughter)

My ancestral origins are in both China and Canada, because my mother's family emigrated from China to Canada, and my father's family is rooted in Canada. I am a fourth-generation Canadian and a first-generation Canadian American. Because of my dual citizenship, I can work in Canada and the United States. I am a college student right now.

Heritage is a big concern to me. Without my heritage I would be a lost fish in the sea. I heard many stories about my heritage when I visited my grandparents in Victoria. One story was about my great-grandfather's restaurant. It was during the depression, and my great-grandfather, my grandfather, and my great uncles baked one thousand loaves of bread for an Indian (First Nations) potlatch celebration on Vancouver Island. The potlatch, which included a ceremony of gift giving, was banned by the government at that time because the gift giving was considered to be wasteful. Also, the ceremony would bring many Native Canadian bands together, which would pose a threat to public order, according to the government. But my great-grandfather felt that he should help the Indians. The Indians valued the potlatch just as he and the other Chinese Canadians treasured their own customs. It took my great-grandfather and his sons a whole week to bake a thousand loaves of bread. Four of my great uncles (sons of this great-grandfather and brothers of my grandfather) also served in the Canadian air force or army in World War II. When I sat there in my grandparents' living room listening to these stories, I realized that my family was very hardworking, would help others in times of need, and loved and served Canada. Others also appreciated my family for these reasons.

Throughout my junior high and high school years, I was a member of the Chinese community girls drill team, which had about seventy members. The team did the military drills while marching in parades, but for uniforms the members wore the costume of the women warriors in Chinese opera. Through the years I was on almost all of the positions in the team, from carrying an umbrella to being an officer. What I learned was that every member in the drill team was

Lee Dun (with long-feather headdress) as Chinese girls drill team officer commanding the banner girls in parade

important, no matter where they stood. Besides marching in parades, we were also in competition with other drill teams. The pace can be grueling with twice weekly practices.

The drill team was important to me in yet another way. My family lived in a mostly white suburb. Throughout my years of schooling there were never more than five Asian students in my class. So it was good to see Chinese faces and interact regularly with girls who all had something in common, our Chinese background. Many of the members were actually of bi-ethnic or multi-ethnic heritage. But all of us had at least some Chinese blood. I learned to value my Chinese ancestry.

Being both Chinese and Canadian, I can enjoy two cultures. I have family customs and traditions from both groups. The most important feature from my Chinese family traditions is that you must respect your elders. Greeting people shows this respect. If the person is an elder, I must address him or her as "uncle" or "aunt." When invited as a guest, you must bring something to the host's house, such as fruit, cookies, or candy. Upon arriving at the house of your host, remove your shoes. I also remove my shoes when entering my own house.

I still follow some Canadian customs. We celebrate the Canadian Thanksgiving in October. I always wait for the traffic signal before crossing the street. I also drink black tea with milk and sugar.

My heritage is illustrated in a beautiful three-panel silk embroidery wall decoration gift that was passed on to me after my paternal grandfather's death in November 1999. The three panels were a wedding gift to my grandparents when they got married in Victoria in 1932. Each panel is framed separately in mahogany. The middle and the larger panel of the three (three feet by four feet) shows a pair of peacocks embroidered on silk. The two small panels on each side bear inscriptions in Chinese, embroidered in black thread on silk, so the Chinese characters appear to have been written in ink. The gift was from my grandfather's maternal grandfather, my great-great-grandfather Koo, who lived in the New Territories of Hong Kong. The interesting thing about the inscriptions is that although the gift was meant for my grandparents, the bride and the groom, the congratulatory words were addressed to my grandfather's father, my great-grandfather Dun. This was to honor the groom's father, my great-grandfather Dun, for having raised a child to adulthood. This three-panel gift is the evidence that I am a fourth-generation Canadian of Chinese heritage. Now that the gift has been passed on to me, I see these three panels connecting five generations of my family. I have a deep sense of the family.

19

Working All My Life
Yeoh Ean Tin (Singapore)

I WAS BORN IN Singapore in 1936. Five generations of my family have lived here: my grandparents, my parents, myself, my children, and my grandchildren. My father was born in Chaozhou in 1913. He came with his parents in the 1920s, while he was in his early teens. He died in 1995. When the family first came, they had a tough time. There were few houses in Singapore then, and not very many people. There were just hills. My father cut bananas and farmed. There was no place to plant rice, but he grew potatoes, papayas, red peony, and durian. Afterwards he was a construction worker building houses for people.

My mother was born in Singapore. Her parents came from Hainan Island, although the family was originally from Chaozhou. Her father was a zhuzai and worked in the tin mines in Malaya first. Her mother came to Singapore later.

I was only five or six during the war when the Japanese occupied Singapore. I remember those days. I remember the air raids just before the invasion. At that time my mother had only me and another three-year-old daughter; the rest of the eleven children were not born yet. She would drag my sister and me to the air raid shelter. The underground shelter was at my grandmother's place, constructed by ourselves. Sometimes it was hard to find a shelter; we would run all over the place.

During the Japanese occupation I did not go to school because there was no school. After the war one or two teachers would come and teach a handful of students in some people's house. It was quite informal. In those days, the idea that girls should not be educated was still popular. My grandmother used to say: "Why study? There is no need for girls to study." So even though the classes were free, I did not get much education. I wanted to study but did not have the opportunity. Now I am angry and frustrated because I cannot read very well. I see that others can understand the newspaper while I can't. It makes me mad. My Mandarin is not good, can you understand me? It's not my native tongue; I learned it on my own.

Later there were formal schools, but my younger brothers still did not get much education. They had the opportunity but did not make use of it. They finished primary six and went to work. It was a difficult life for my father. He did not earn very much as a laborer, only five or six dollars a day. How could he support such a large family?

You see that I have to work till old age. I have worked since a kid. When I was small, I harvested bananas too. Then when I was fourteen, I went to work in a factory that made big sheets of plastic for wrapping. I worked in different kinds of industries. The last was a textile factory where I worked for thirteen years, until it closed down. It moved to China or Hong Kong; I was not too clear. The owner was from Hong Kong. I could not find work in factories because they did not want older workers, those reaching fifty-five years of age. I have been a janitor in this school since 1989.

I got married when I was nineteen, arranged by a matchmaker, as was the custom then. My wedding was quite simple. The matchmaker introduced us to each other. Then a wedding day was picked, and we were married. We have three daughters and four sons. My husband's family came from Fujian Province, but my mother-in-law was also from Chaozhou. She liked me and treated me very well. We lived together. She did not have many children, one son and one daughter. After her daughter was married and moved to her husband's house, there was only her son left. So she lived with us, and we got along very well. I went out to work every day, and my mother-in-law looked after all my children until they were grown up. You could say that all my children were raised by her. They loved their grandmother very much. She passed away in the early 1980s.

My husband retired in 1990. His health was not good. He also worked for a school as a custodian. Of our seven children, all are married except one son. The oldest son is in business. The second one fixes doors and windows in the construction and renovation business.

The third son is a truck driver. The youngest son works in a factory; he is married and is already a father. The youngest daughter also works in a factory. Two daughters stayed home to raise their children. But the oldest daughter is working again now that her children are older. I have over ten grandchildren. The married children all have households of their own. They come to see me every week so my house is always full every weekend. In Singapore we are all a short distance from each other, so it is easy to visit.

The second daughter had the biggest wedding: a banquet for over two hundred guests. That was because her father-in-law wanted to celebrate. His other children married Christians and had church weddings, whereas the son who married my daughter followed the old Chaozhou custom. He came to our house before dawn with four gifts of gold: a bracelet, a pair of earrings, a pendant, and a chain. He brought her to his parents' house, and together they paid respects to the spirits of the ancestors. Later they went to the botanical garden to have their pictures taken. It was too lavish, but the old man was obstinate.

Singapore is a very good and prosperous society now. You can eat all you want and buy whatever you wish. It's not like the old days when we could not buy the food we liked. All my children and grandchildren went to government schools. But you still need to pay some tuition; it varies whether it is primary or secondary school. That is why each family has only two or three children. It would be expensive to support more children to go to school. For example, my oldest daughter has three children. Her daughter is in senior secondary school, the younger son is in junior secondary school, and her elder son is in the army, doing his national service. When he gets out of the army, he will go to the university. The excellent students can win scholarships. Now I am not too concerned about my grandson in the national service. I know what it is all about since every boy has to get into the army at the age of eighteen, for two and half years. When my oldest son first went for military training, I was really afraid.

I went to China with my husband as tourists several years ago. There are many relatives on my father's side. But I don't know them, so I did not look them up. I just wanted to go to Chaozhou and have a look. I also went to Hong Kong, Macau, Guangzhou, Beijing, and even the Great Wall. I traveled all around. I never saw the old China, so I would not know how to compare. From what I saw on my tour, China compares favorably with Singapore. It is also very good. The places in China I visited were also very clean and safe; I don't know how it is in the countryside. What I saw was very good. They dressed better in China. The clothes I saw in Shanghai were prettier than what the Singaporeans wear.

My father lived to his eighties. I won't be able to live to that age. Those born in Singapore do not live long. They certainly have enough to eat; they can eat all they want. But people born in Singapore do not have long lives because the climate is not good. In China, there are hot days and cold days, four seasons in a year. The people there live long. It's different in Singapore. It is always hot here. No cold weather. It is considered a long life if Singaporeans live to their sixties or seventies.

The most important thing in life is xiao. You remember your parents and ancestors for giving you life and for bringing you up. I still wish that my parents were alive so that I could look after them. I would like to give my mother the good food and comforts that she never had; she died early. My parents had a hard life raising so many children. Now my children know too that rearing children brings headaches and heartaches. So they are attentive to my husband and me.

I don't aspire to high things; neither do I want much. As I live in this world, I just hope that I will not be burdened with too many cares. I'll work as long as I can.

20 Bow Wow! A Second Language
Florence Chan Chow de Canseco
(Mexico)

Translation and Languages

I started doing translations about ten years ago. The brother of a neighbor of mine, a Mexican working in the U.S., needed some translations of the minutes of a board meeting from Spanish to English. He was selling or privatizing companies and needed translations in order to sell them to foreigners. The translation he already had was very bad. I translated for him. It turned out to be fairly good. He took the minutes to the U.S. embassy and they certified them as a true translation. Then my neighbor asked me to translate some bank documents. That's how I began translation work, by chance. I do prospectuses for mergers and acquisitions. All my customers are investment banks and financial companies.

I did some work for the Asia Pacific Economic Cooperation Transportation Working Group a few of years ago. They held their semi-annual meeting in Mexico. The meetings were held in English, and all the documents had to be written in English. That's what I worked on. I was the gofer for the "head shepherd." I don't know why the leaders were called shepherds. Well, were we the lambs? Actually, it was Indonesia's turn to be the head shepherd, but because of the problems in Indonesia (1998), the Canadians had to take it over. They were so organized that by six o'clock on the last day, the documents were all done.

I am used to "fighting fire" — in Spanish it is called "people putting out fires" — so you are always doing things at the last minute. I usually work under pressure. A lot of my translation is, "Oh, I needed it yesterday." It's that kind of fun work. I usually choose jobs that don't take me more than half an hour to get to. That's one of my criteria. Mexico City is so big, something like forty kilometers in diameter, it takes you two hours to cross it by car. A lot of people who live in the suburbs take maybe two and half hours to work and another two and a half hours to get home because they cannot afford to live in the city. I can be selective about my work because my husband actually supports me. He is an architect and designs layouts for a chain of restaurants in Mexico. He has been doing this for 28 years. Doing translations, however, keeps my neurons working.

I was born and raised in Canada. I studied economics and psychology at university. I did some social work in Chiliwack, British Columbia, after graduation but did not like the policy there. I left after two years. Then I went to Toronto. The public schools were looking for teachers. I got hired even though I had no teaching certificate. I did two summer courses and I interned in one of the schools. I was paid the whole time. That's how I got into teaching. I taught grades five, seven, and eight for three years. Then another teacher and I went on holidays to Mexico. We met a tourist guide who happened to be my husband's best friend. That's how we met. I left and moved to Mexico the next year. I have been here since 1970.

The funny thing is that when my husband was growing up, he had this Chinese calendar, as he liked Chinese things. It's very strange for him to end up marrying a Chinese. He loves Chinese food, especially the crab, the salmon, and the steamed fish.

I actually took three years of Spanish at university. But I am afraid that when I got here, all I could say was yes or no, thank you, how are you, and things like that. At that time we did not have language labs. What I learned was from books, just memorizing. After I came, I took a course at the university but found it rather ridiculous. They changed the teacher six weeks into the course. Then for homework it was something like writing five sentences using I don't know what. And I thought, How could this be a university course? So I just took the one course and sort of taught myself Spanish.

Spanish was a little difficult to me. It's like French, very complicated for me. You have to learn all the genders. Then you get really lazy because in English we don't have to know if it's feminine or masculine. It's just "it." A good part about being Chinese is your ear is trained. You can pronounce other languages better. When I finally decided to learn Spanish properly, I learned it from a little girl. My neighbor had a little girl who was learning to talk. I thought I would take Spanish lessons with children learning how to speak. She would say certain phrases and I would repeat. Then I would go to the supermarket, and I would look at the vegetables and fruits to see what they were called. I would make up my own vocabulary list. And I would read the newspaper everyday. That's how I learned Spanish. I just read and taught myself. With the translation work you learn even better because you have to know the exact meaning of the words. You use words every day, and you think you know what they mean, but when you translate you have to know what they *really* mean. That goes for English too. I actually improved my English and my Spanish by doing translation.

Learning English is really big, especially now with the North American Free Trade Agreement and all these foreign companies coming in. So everybody wants to learn. I have taught English here privately. But teaching English as a second language is also very boring because after about five years, you are teaching the same irregular verbs, and people keep making the same mistakes. Then there is the ego trip, you know. The higher the position of the student, the less he is going to learn English because you can't correct him! And there is no way they are going to learn English. They don't want to regress to the level of three-year-olds, whereas someone who is not so educated will learn it much quicker. Now I tell people when they want English lessons to read children's books, like Dr. Seuss's books, take a basic course, and work on the pronunciation. Then go on holidays to Canada or the U.S. Save your money; just take a trip. Go by yourself and take an intensive course somewhere. They would learn a lot faster and won't have this problem with their ego thing in Mexico.

I heard a joke recently. There was a family of mice in a house. A cat appeared. So the mother mouse went, "Bow wow!" And the cat ran off. The mother mouse said to her family, "You see how important it is to have a second language!"

Cultural Cues

Mexicans are freer in their expressions. Laws are to be broken; nobody takes the law very seriously. Everybody jaywalks. Now driving is quite dangerous because people run red lights. But when they speak, you have to read between the lines. They are like the Chinese in that they say things so as not to offend you. You have to know what they mean. It took me a long time to catch on. I just took what they said at face value. But they did not mean any of that. Foreigners think that Mexicans are hypocrites, but actually it's just that we don't know what the code is. They will say, "I'll call you tomorrow." That doesn't mean that they'll call you tomorrow. It means sort of, well, nice talking to you. It's just a way of saying goodbye without offending the other person. I used to think that they were going to call me the next day. But they didn't, of course. So you think, What's wrong with these people? What don't they say what they mean? It's because we don't know their language; it's a very special language. A friend finally told me, "If somebody wants to phone you tomorrow, he or she will say, 'What time shall I phone you tomorrow?' not just, 'Okay, I'll call you tomorrow.' "

Another example is when you are a tourist walking along the street and you ask someone for directions. They would say, "You go down here, turn right, do this, do that." They may not know, but it's not polite to say you don't know. They will, therefore, tell you something anyway. It does not matter if it's right or wrong. And you say, Why did he give me the wrong directions? But they were trying to be nice, answer your question, say something. After a while you know enough to ask a number of people and then draw your own conclusion.

In many ways, they are like the Chinese. They remember their ancestors. On the day of the dead, they go and fix the graves. They put the favorite foods of the dead there. They have altars in their homes. There is the portrait of the deceased, and they would put special flowers like marigolds, the favorite foods, and candles. Mexicans make tamales, which are very much like the Chinese zong. Like the Chinese, as far as the family is concerned, they are very close. They may hate each other's guts, but they are very close. They have this extended family. You are expected to look after the grandmother. But if anything happens, the grandmother will look after the kids. They also do these adoptions like the Chinese. If a family does not have a daughter, some other family, often if it is very poor, will say, Do you want to adopt my daughter?

People in Mexico now are becoming interested in fengshui, rearranging their houses and things like that. This is the new gimmick. But it's funny, you know. I live in a complex with fourteen houses. These houses have very sharp, steep roofs, and they are triangular in shape. There is no harmony in this complex. There is so much fighting! We can't get along. It could be the fengshui, all these steep roofs and triangular shapes.

I don't hang around with Chinese in Mexico. There are not very many Chinese to begin with. Most of my friends are Americans or Mexicans. The Americans are translators. The Mexicans are my neighbors; I live amongst them. The people I work with are all Mexicans. There are Chinese down in Chinatown. Well, it's only a block long, so we call it China Block. That's way downtown, so I only go there maybe once every six months to get groceries. I can speak a little bit of Guangzhou dialect. That is not of any use to anybody except for shopping in the China Block. But I can ask for things in Spanish.

My being Chinese is not a really major factor in Mexico. They do treat me differently, but they treat all foreigners differently. They will always regard me as a foreigner. I did learn that in a northern state there were a lot of Chinese and they became quite prosperous. I don't know what kind of businesses they had. Apparently there was a massacre because they were too prosperous. They slaughtered many Chinese. It might have been in the 1930s, during the depression. I have got to confess that I don't know.[1]

Quite often people who do not know me take me to be a Japanese and think that I have got piles of money. Then I get all this good treatment. My Mexican friends see me as a mixture: She is Chinese, but she has never been to China. To them I am not the exotic Chinese from China but a Canadian who eats Chinese food. They like people from the First World because they can speak English.

I really didn't learn to cook Chinese food until I came to Mexico. There were some exchange students from China, and they were offering free cooking classes. So I went to one of these classes, met some Chinese from China, and learned how to cook a little. I did not learn it from my mother, who was also born and raised in British Columbia. My mother was strange in that she was the kind of person who could do everything but she didn't bother to teach us. She did it all. I only found out a couple of years ago why she did not teach us. It was because she learned everything by herself, so she expected us to learn everything by ourselves. She can tailor, she can sew, she can knit, she can cook, so she did everything. She had five daughters, but she never asked us to do anything. So I learned how to cook Chinese food in a cooking class in Mexico.

21

Chinese Words on Sleepless Nights
Diana Hong Hop-wo Hart (Canada)

Vancouver Island

I was born in 1942. I have lived on Vancouver Island all my life. My mom was born in Vancouver. According to her, when her father and mother came to Canada, he still had the pigtail. He had a tailor business in New Westminster (a suburb of Vancouver). He and his wife did not get along very well, so they split up. He lived in New Westminster with one son while my grandmother lived in Vancouver with a daughter and another son.

My paternal grandfather used to raise fish when he was back in China. My paternal grandmother was sold as a small girl. She was partly Burmese. That's why I am dark. My father is very dark and so are my brothers. Many people say that I look like the First Nations people. I have been asked to give my number lots of times.[1] I think I totally look Chinese.

My father was also born and raised on Vancouver Island. My family really has roots here. My paternal grandparents had a potato farm near Koksilah,[2] just outside the Indian reservation. They also had a laundry named Hop-wo. Our family name is Hong. People used to get the names mixed up. So they changed the family name to Hop-wo.

The Hop-wo family is quite well known because we are such a large family and we have been in Chemainus all these years. Take my eldest brother, he is in hockey and the president of the ice-skating club in Chemainus. He is in all the functions and knows a lot of people. Two other brothers and a sister live on the island, two sisters in Vancouver.

We lived in a neighborhood called Chinatown in Chemainus. We were picked on by the white kids and called chinks. I felt bad. There was not much we could do because I was only in grade two, and [the main boy who picked on me] was about fifteen. He badgered my dad too. Otherwise integration was easy, as it was just a tiny community.

Chinatown was right down by the boom where my dad worked for McMillan and Bloedel Company. We could actually see him sorting logs in the water according to species (hemlock, fir, et cetera), size, and grade. Then he would raft them using a boom pole. He used to wear cork boots that would grab on the logs for stabilization. After 1970 they did the sorting with boom boats. He was the only Chinese in that division. He worked there for forty years and retired when he was sixty.

We had to move out of Chinatown later because they were making the sawmill bigger. We built a house in a place called Scotchtown, a little bit north of Chemainus, but we went to school in Chemainus.

Sons and Daughters

As I was growing up, I hated being a girl, because in the Chinese family the boys always meant so much more. The daughters weren't as good; that was hard on us girls. The daughters couldn't go out with the boys, as they had to think about getting pregnant and all that in those days. My parents were strict about this. The boys could go out. They couldn't do much wrong and didn't do as much housework as the daughters. They could get away with murder. Probably this is still true in a regular European Canadian household.

Just before my mom passed away, she gave all her expensive jewelry to the sons. It was really hard on us girls. I tried to talk her out of giving it to the sons, but to the daughters so that we could pass on to our daughters. I thought that the sons would give the jewelry to their wives, and if they get divorced, there is no way the wife will give it back to the son. My mom was ill and turned it around, saying that I just wanted it for myself. Consequently, the jade bracelets and a beautiful Chinese gold bracelet all went to the sons' wives. It was a bad scene. I vowed that I would never do that. All my jewelry would go to my daughters.

Diana Hong Hart

Work

I am a counselor in a group home for psychiatric patients. I work twelve-hour shifts on weekends. I like working with people who have schizophrenia, manic-depression, or other behavior problems. They are a challenge. They can outsmart you. As counselors we talk to them, work out programs, and take them on outings. They have their own psychiatrists and general practice doctors that they visit. We give out medications, and we are just there. We do the cooking, but not the chores. They have specific jobs from a chore list that they have to do every day. The residents, men and women, are of all ages. Some have been here for a couple of years. We try to move them on, to another care facility or back home, when we can't do any more for them. We try to get them to be more independent so that they can be integrated back into the community. The work is quite rewarding.

Previously I had a greenhouse program at the college in Nanaimo. It was called therapeutic work program, growing plants as a way of therapy. I had clients from the home.

In my spare time I do fish prints, called *gyotaku*. The art of fish printing began in China and was later adopted by the Japanese. A real fish is first painted and a print is taken from it using rice paper. The imprint is then transferred onto aprons, t-shirts, shopping bags, or other sheets of rice paper. The aprons and t-shirts are fully washable.

Being Chinese

I am the only Chinese at work. I have always been the only Chinese person at any function, whereas in Vancouver there would likely be many Chinese. It doesn't make any difference to me. I forget that I am Chinese because all my friends are just friends; I think they forget that I am Chinese. Sometimes I do think about it. When Brian, my second husband, and I first got together, he never used to think that I was Chinese. But then we would get these looks. Like a couple of weeks ago, we were in Coronation Square. There was an old lady looking at a silver car. We were walking together on the sidewalk, hand in hand. She looked at us. I thought, Oh yeah, what is she thinking about? I am Chinese, and that's why she's probably thinking it's kind of weird. There are not many Chinese and white couples in Ladysmith.

You know what? I would like to say that I understand now how my mom and dad felt when I first got married to a white person. Not that I am not happily married to Brian. But in a way I wish that I had married into Chinese because then my kids would keep their heritage. Maybe that's the old-fashioned part of me.

My kids' father is white. I have three beautiful daughters and now also three lovely grandsons. I taught my daughters the regular values like being honest, telling the truth, not starting to eat at supper time until the mother sits down, helping with the dishes, and the other normal things. I taught them how to use chopsticks early, the right way to use them, and how you hold your bowl instead of eating hunched over without holding your bowl. I taught them the proper Chinese etiquette. I also taught my girls how to do Chinese cooking and how to do all the dim sum, like wrapping zong and other things my mom taught me. I taught them how to do all that so they have not lost the Chinese cooking part.

We have Chinese food at our house three or four times a week with chopsticks and bowls. Brian loves that. He usually likes all sorts of Chinese food. He won't eat chicken feet, but I love them. I love chewing them and spitting out the small bones.

My mom is buried in Duncan. We just take the flowers to the graveyard and we bow three times. That's pretty Chinese. I remember that when we were kids, we had to go down to see our grandma and grandpa in Koksilah. In their dining room they had Chinese joss sticks burning at the ancestral shrine. We had to bow three times. When we were kids, we would run into the room, do our bowing three times, then out we went. I know we had to do that. Bowing three times is just to give respect.

I am proud to be Chinese, to be of a race that is hardworking and respectful. I am hardworking because I'm Chinese. I had one resident who came up to me once and said, "Diana, do you take ginseng? You have so much energy." I said, "No, I don't take ginseng."

When we were small, my mom hired a tutor from Chemainus. He was called gou bak (tall uncle) because he was tall. He came every Tuesday to teach us Chinese. Then it was too difficult for him to come. So we learned a little bit, just elementary Chinese, such as how to write the figures and stuff. Only the three oldest children learned Chinese.

We spoke Chinese at home but kind of lost it when we went to school. I can speak Chinese in a pinch. When we were in Thailand, we were down in Chinatown, and I ordered food in Chinese. It comes back to you after a while, you know. You know how sometimes you lie in bed and you think Chinese. I can think the words, but it's hard to get the words out of my mouth. It's been a long time.

I have a Chinese name but I don't know how to write it. I have it at home. My mom told me to take it to somebody to see that it is right. I should send it to you. My Chinese name is Hong Muin Yee.

 Being Chinese in the Diaspora

22 Living in the Diaspora

Biography and History

In this book, ordinary Chinese overseas have spoken for themselves. Their vivid, moving, and sometimes humorous life stories reflect the history of the larger society or the world and reveal how these individuals make history (see Mills 1959). These narrators and their families embody the processes of global migration and the historical conditions in China and around the world in the century 1842–1949. The lives of these individuals and their ancestors were inextricably woven into the history of the immigrant societies and that of China, although it might not have been always under circumstances of their choosing. Miranda's grandmother was part of the great Chinese labor migration that took her to the heart of Peru. Mr. Wong-Kit went to Hawaii in the same labor exodus. This biography-history connection is shown in the Indo-Sino War of the early 1960s. Political leaders chose to make war, but the war affected ordinary people like Springgay's family. She and her family lived out in flesh and blood India's policy to deprive them of citizenship and citizen rights. The restrictions imposed on their movement and opportunities, and their eventual decision to leave India, are the bits and pieces that make up history. T.Y.'s father fought in another war and bore the hidden injuries for the rest of his life. J. Li's migratory experiences were precipitated by both the Chinese and the Cuban revolutions. Chow's agreement to an arranged marriage overseas was influenced by the chaotic conditions in China during the Cultural Revolution in the 1960s. S. Chinque's father and husband were both seamen at a time when hundreds of thousands of Chinese sailed the oceans and the seamen's union was a considerable political force in China, in the 1920s.

These individuals and their ancestors certainly made history by settling in distant lands and raising families. With everyday activities, they made and continue to make history. Chung helps create black majority rule in Zimbabwe; Huang performs surgery; Woo looks after his sons at home while his wife works as a seamstress outside the home; Quan sings in a gay choir; and so forth.

Wars and revolutions in China, and discriminatory laws against Chinese immigration in many immigrant societies, produced a well-known phenomenon in the Chinese diaspora: long years of separation between parents and children. We see this in the narratives by J. Li, Woo, and Louie. J. Li first set eyes on his father when he himself was already a parent. Louie did not see her mother for over forty years. The intersection of history and biography no doubt caused pain, but in their maturity the narrators did not dwell on it. There is no resentment because the extraordinary circumstances responsible for the separation were understood and accepted. Even though these three narrators were deprived of the parents' presence in childhood, once united with their long-separated parents, each attended to the needs of the parent right to the end.

Integration and Discrimination

Today most Chinese overseas narrators live very much like the general population of whatever their society of residence. As citizens of those countries, they have the corresponding rights and obligations. Although the issue of social class is not explored in depth in the narratives, the narrators occupy specific socio-economic statuses in their societies. Whatever these positions may be, the narrators are well integrated in the societies of residence, which probably cannot be said of the more recent immigrants from China, Hong Kong, or Taiwan.

Much as the narrators are integrated into their countries of citizenship, they have also borne prejudices and still must contend with discrimination. While individual prejudices and personal discrimination, such as being called ethnic slurs, are hurtful, narrators seem to be able to bear such abuse stoically. What the narrators are most fearful and resentful about is legal or institutional racism, such as that against the Chinese in colonial Rhodesia and in India after the 1962 war between India and China (Chung; Springgay). This kind of discrimination is written into law or routinized into the everyday assumptions and practices of a society. Australia, the United States, Canada, and New Zealand all passed laws in the nineteenth and early twentieth centuries forbidding the immigration of Chinese into those countries (Chan; Woo). Before this law was introduced in Canada in 1923, the government began in 1886 a head tax on all Chinese arriving in Canada (Louie), a practice to which no other group of immigrants was ever subjected. Countries, or states or provinces within these countries, also proscribed the ownership of land or entry into professions by Chinese (Chan 1982).

Although restrictions on Chinese immigration to some countries were repealed after World War II, legal discrimination against the Chinese overseas still exists in several countries. A notable case is Malaysia, where restrictions on Chinese entrance to public universities and on Chinese ownership of business are still in force (Tan). The Indonesian government imposed a ban on Chinese schools and the use of Chinese in signs and billboards in 1965 (D.T.). Most Chinese were also pressured into abandoning their Chinese family names and assuming Indonesian names instead. These legal and institutional discriminatory practices were imposed after horrific massacres of Chinese, and looting and burning of their businesses and houses in Indonesia in 1965, and in Malaysia in 1969. The environment of intolerance is still volatile, as shown again in the way the Chinese were killed and raped, and their properties burnt, in the late 1990s in Indonesia.

In the Netherlands, Chow and family enjoyed the benefits of the welfare state, such as excellent health care, and most of the citizen rights. However, in that country, there were quota restrictions on entry to the professions, such as medicine and dentistry, for citizens of non-Dutch ancestry. That was an important consideration in their decision to remigrate to the United States.

Memories of legal and institutional discrimination that their ancestors suffered may not be in the forefront of their consciousness every day, but neither are they forgotten. Past and present discrimination of this kind serves as a reminder for caution and vigilance. Personal prejudice, such as name-calling, paves the way for legal discrimination. Conversely, where discrimination is legal, personal prejudice and individual discrimination become more acceptable and prevalent in that society, as was the experience of Springgay after the 1962 war.

Marriage and Family

The family is a network of people who are related to one another by blood, adoption, or marriage. The family in the Chinese diaspora is varied: nuclear family (parents with unmarried children); three-generational family; divorce; second marriage; families with half brothers and sisters; families with adopted children and siblings; and, as mentioned above, families in which husband, wife, or parents were absent for long, long years. We see affection and caring in the family, but also conflict and resentment.

Endogamy (marrying within one's own group, meaning Chinese) is an ideal in Chinese culture. However, in reality, from the earliest time of emigration, exogamy (marrying outside one's group, anyone who is non-Chinese) is part of the Chinese diaspora. In Southeast Asia, Chinese married native partners, producing, for instance, the *peranakan* households in Malaysia and mestizo offspring in the Philippines. As mentioned in chapter 1, in 1885 the San Francisco–based Qing consul-general Huang Cunxian noted the high rates of Chinese men marrying local women in Cuba and Hawaii. Among the narrators, Hart's paternal grandmother was part Burmese. S. Chinque's immigrant Chinese father married her U.K.-born English-Irish mother in Liverpool in 1906. Miranda's grandmother, an immigrant in Peru, married an Italian immigrant.

On the other hand, T.Y., a fourth-generation Chinese American, made a conscious decision to marry a Chinese. She realized that living with a non-Chinese might pose some serious problems because she would have to explain so fundamental an aspect of Chinese culture as food habits. She alone among her siblings seemed to have made the deliberate choice to find a Chinese husband. The reason for doing so remains a most cherished feature of her marriage, namely, there are common cultural grounds that require no explanation, interpretation, or justification. T.Y. feels that her mother relates more easily to her husband than to other children-in-law for the same reason, the common cultural understanding. Furthermore, T.Y. claims that with two Chinese parents, her children are exposed to more Chinese heritage, such as language, *weiqi,* and *Qingming* festival.

It is cultural retention that leads Hart also to wonder if her children would be able to retain more Chinese heritage if she had married a Chinese. Not that she was in any way unhappy with her European Canadian husband, she quickly adds. Hart, Canseco, and Springgay are all married to non-Chinese. They eat Chinese food regularly in their households. And eating Chinese food more often than not involves the extended family. So their husbands are at least culturally Chinese in terms of food and probably also in the acceptance of extended kin.

Concepts about endogamy and exogamy are of course elastic, not to be defined solely in terms of marrying a Chinese or a non-Chinese. A phenomenon observed perhaps more in North America than elsewhere, again with no reliable figures, is that the Chinese overseas would marry exogamously, but the partner would be another Asian, for example, Japanese or Filipino. Is this really exogamy or in fact a form of endogamy insofar as the Asian North Americans are seen as one grouping, with many common historical immigration experiences and cultural traits? On the other hand, in Singapore, where the Chinese do constitute the majority, the definition of the desired endogamy would include the same village or city of origin, or some other similar criterion. The father-in-law of Yeoh's second daughter was pleased with his son's choice of a wife because his other children had married Christians, even if they are Chinese.

Perhaps the narratives about marriage, family, and life in the diaspora in general all lead to the argument that retention of Chinese cultural heritage is important. To some, marrying a Chinese provides the advantage of ensuring that heritage. But for those who have married exogamously, retention of culture is viable if the partners at least make some efforts at being culturally Chinese.

Real Life versus Stereotypes: Women

There is a crucial distinction between how people actually live (real culture) and how they ought to live (ideal culture). The lack of distinction between the two results in stereotypes that are caricatures imposed on a category of people. While many stereotypes need to be addressed, attention here is focused on those of Chinese women because nowhere is the confusion between ideal culture and the real culture more astounding than in depictions of Chinese women. In the popular global culture, distinction is seldom made between the women in China and those in the Chinese diaspora. Thus in this section the discussion of the latter is linked to the former.

Stereotypical images about Chinese women, in the diaspora or in China, are that they are submissive and passive and are helpless victims of patriarchy. These stereotypes are based on notions of how women ought to behave. In the patriarchal Chinese society, the traditional ideology was that a woman should follow the "three submissions and four virtues." The three submissions were supposedly admonitions from the mother of the sage Meng Zi that a woman should obey her father before marriage, her husband during marriage, and her son in widowhood. These ideas were recorded in the section about Mother Meng in the *Biographies of Eminent Women (Lienu Zhuan)*, written by Liu Xiang (79–8 BCE) of the Western Han dynasty (Liu 1993). The four virtues that a woman should cultivate were proposed by Ban Zhao[1] (born 45–51, died 114–120 CE). She was a historian, a counselor to Empress Dowager Deng, and a teacher to the imperial ladies as well as male scholars in the Eastern Han dynasty. In her *Seven Lessons for Women (Nujie Qipian)*, Ban (1968) listed the four virtues as womanly virtue (chastity), womanly words (careful speech), womanly deportment (manners and clean appearance), and womanly work (sewing, cooking and serving guests, and so forth). Since those words were written, they have certainly been quoted often in the education of girls in China and in defining how women *should* act.

The word "should" in the last sentence is important. Both Liu Xiang and Ban Zhao wrote in the period after Dong Zhongshu (179–104 BCE), the prime minister of Emperor Wu Di of the Western Han dynasty, entrenched Confucian philosophy as the state philosophy while relegating all other schools of thought to minor status. Confucian philosophy, with its emphasis on hierarchy and harmony, was much more supportive of a centralized empire, which at the time of Emperor Wu Di was in great need of stability. Before the triumph of Confucian philosophy under Dong, its chief rival was the Daoist philosophy, which with its laissez-faire naturalist orientation was more accepting of the equality and complementarity of the female (yin) and the male (yang). In fact, as Lee (1994) points out, the Confucian classic *Yi Jing* (*Book of Changes,* commonly spelt as *I Ching* in English), like the *Dao De Jing* of the Daoist school, sees yin and yang as "equally and mutually complementary opposites" (p. 13). However, Confucian philosophy underwent an important transformation into a state ideology in the Western Han period, from accepting more equality between men and women to advocating the subordination of women to men.

Both Liu Xiang and Ban Zhao were intent upon delineating how women ought to behave, but there were differences between the two. Liu Xiang's biographies were about exemplary women who were strong, chaste, prudent, and wise. The conduct of most of the women in his biographies was decisive, not at all self-effacing, and accepted as such by their male contemporaries, including their husbands. However, in Ban's *Seven Lessons for Women,* the prescriptive tone is unmistakably clear and heavy. She also went much further than Liu did in terms of the restrictions on a woman's words and actions. Yet the widowed mother of Meng Zi, who brought up the sage by herself; Ban Zhao, who was a historian and an official at court in her own right; and Ban Zhao's pupil, the Empress Dowager Deng, who as a regent ruled the Han empire for fifteen years were hardly retiring wallflowers by any stretch of imagination.

Not only was the discrepancy between the ideal and the real culture apparent in the lives of the Mother of Meng Zi, Ban Zhao, and other prominent women in ancient China, little attention was given to Ban's *Seven Lessons for Women* for fourteen hundred years. It was not until 1580 CE (Ming dynasty) that Ban Zhao's *Lessons* and works by others extolling the feminine virtue of submission became accepted canons of proper behavior for women in the ultraconserva-tive milieu of neo-Confucianist thought and ideology (Lee 1994:23). By the seventeenth century, this saying had also become popular: "A woman without ability or talent is virtuous." Thus the ideology of the submission of women was promoted more concertedly and defended more stridently in the later dynasties of Ming and Qing than in the earlier periods.

By the time mass Chinese emigration began in the late Qing dy-nasty, this ideology was well entrenched, and as part of the ideal culture would have been a piece of the cultural baggage brought by the Chinese venturing overseas. But can that ideology be taken as a description of how early overseas Chinese women lived or how the Chinese women in the diaspora live today? Obviously not. How the Chinese women — in China, immigrant, or born abroad — lived a cen-tury ago or live today is an *empirical question* that can only be an-swered by examining the historical facts. This is of course easier said than done. How the Chinese women actually lived in those long centuries before the present is now the subject of intense interest and study because, for the most part, the voices of Chinese women, whether in China or abroad, have not been heard beyond intimate circles. Before the last century, few literary works of the women of ancient China were read in their own right by a wider public. Through the different dynasties there were certainly many women writers, poets, artists, and even military leaders. But men wrote the official histories and other influential tomes. Until very recently, men have always interpreted and described the lives of women, especially for the foreigners, such as missionaries, scholars, and diplomats. Such discourses not surprisingly have been more accurate about how women *ought to live* rather than how they actually thought, felt, lived, or worked. But there would undoubtedly be a difference be-tween the ideal culture and the real culture for at least two reasons.

First, the ideology of the submissive woman from the Ming times to the twentieth century was predominantly aimed at the upper class gentry women. The gentry women were expected to remain in the inner space (home) and not to venture into the outer space (public affairs), nor come into contact with any men except those in the family and household, just as Ban Zhao admonished in her *Lessons*.

Such ideal norms for behavior could only be followed expeditiously by the gentry women, who would have few reasons to leave the confines of their chambers and home grounds. The gentry women were also expected to be virtuous and to be educated, but not beyond the rudiments of literacy. Even then, women of the Ming and Qing dynasties did not necessarily live like this. They often managed to circumvent and subvert such norms as they toured places and excelled in learning. The poems, dramas, and paintings created by some of them were well-known and admired even by men in their own lifetime (Ko 1994 and Lo 1988).

Second, some women were economically active. The farm women by necessity worked in and out of the house in order to help make a living for the family. They cultivated the land, gathered mulberry leaves for the silk worms, washed clothes at the village stream, bargained at the market, and so forth, thus meeting strangers outside the household. The circumstances would make it much harder for the farm women to practice the three submissions and the four virtues.

Women's bound feet in imperial China is often held up as the symbol of their submission and oppression, and indeed it was. However, a particularly notable phenomenon is the absence of foot-binding among the womenfolk of the *Kejia,* commonly romanized as the Hakka. Kejia is a sub-ethnic group of the Han who migrated from north China to the southern provinces in the Song dynasty (960–1279 CE) due to the political turmoil at that time. As latecomers they could only settle in the inaccessible and often scrubby hill country. They were regarded by the local people as intruders and therefore called Kejia, the guest people. While the origin of foot-binding is still subject to speculation, as a practice it most likely began in the Song dynasty and only became common in the Ming dynasty among the upper class women. After all, only the gentry women could be spared in various economic activities and be so sacrificed in the name of beauty and so inconvenienced as not to have a pair of natural feet to stand or walk on. The Kejia women prided themselves on the fact that they worked alongside their men and never bound their daughters' feet. Among the emigrants were Kejia people, such as the ancestors of D.T. in Indonesia, Quan's mother in Hawaii, and Louie in Canada.

While women did not emigrate at the same rate as the men, most of those who did came from rural backgrounds. The majority of women, like the men, came from the non-Kejia regions of Fujian and Guangdong Provinces. In the narrators' descriptions of their mothers and grandmothers, these women, whether of Kejia origin or not, hardly come close to the popular stereotypes of passivity and helplessness. It can be reasonably argued that both before and after emigration, many Chinese women were not likely to resemble the confined, retiring, and submissive female without a mind of her own. The "tradition" for the Chinese women overseas would, therefore, depart from the ideal culture, although some men and women in Chinese communities overseas undoubtedly could claim to have kept to the ideal culture.

It is true that in real culture as well as in the ideal, both in China and in the overseas communities, the treatment of women very often was and is not equal to the men in their own families or in the larger society. The present study affords a place for the contemporary women to speak for themselves, to describe in their own words how they live. The earlier generations of Chinese women overseas are also remembered in the accounts of interviewees to the extent these family histories are known. In the narratives presented in this book, there are certainly instances of preference for and preferential treatment of sons and grandsons. Sexist attitudes and practices come not only from men, but from women too. Hart's mother bequeathed her jewelry to her sons rather than daughters. Several fathers and grandparents did not see the value of education for a daughter. In all these cases, the ideal culture, or more specifically, the ideology of putting greater value on the male child is followed.

What is significant and noteworthy is that such sexist practices are by no means universal. The exceptions are important because they point to how people actually live. In an interview not included in this book, one father in poverty and in poor health encouraged and offered to support his oldest daughter's higher education in Singapore. In other families, we see one or both parents making sure that the daughters would receive the best education possible. This reflects the emphasis on education in Chinese culture. It also shows that men and women could be sexist or gender egalitarian. In this, the Chinese in the diaspora are probably similar to other ethnic groups. This point has to be stressed because of the facile manner in which Chinese women in China or outside of China are portrayed mostly and almost exclusively as victims of sexism, in movies produced in Hollywood as well as some produced in China. There are, therefore, rampant stereotypes of Chinese women, in the diaspora as well as in China (as stereotypes rarely distinguish between the two), that they are subservient and passive victims. Some no doubt are, or at least are such during some periods in their lives. But they are much more than simply being victims.

The popular global misconception about Chinese women wherever they are ignores a vital aspect of their lives: their agency, which includes the resolve, ingenuity, and action in taking control of their own circumstances. They are doers. They make things happen. There are some high achievers among the female narrators, from freedom fighter to business owner, from artist to mathematician, and from teacher to cafeteria manager. We see many examples of the women narrators or their mothers helping in the family business. Chung's grandmother took care of the bakery business while the grandfather cooked for the family in colonial Rhodesia. The illiterate widow Wong-Kit was the proprietor of a bar in Hawaii and ensured the financial security of her family by investing wisely. Springgay and Miranda, with admiration and affection, describe their grandmothers as very capable and resourceful. When Chow was a new mother and housebound in a new country, the Netherlands, it was her savings that tied the family over a very rough period. The talent and accomplishments of Ban Zhao herself, of Ming and Qing women described by Ko, and of valiant women in every generation most certainly have latter-day counterparts as told by the narrators.

The Chinese women overseas whom we have met in the narratives fulfill many different roles and have accomplished incredible things. Yet they are ordinary people. They are active, and they are agents of change. Is the achievement orientation of the female narrators a manifestation of their "modern" Westernized culture? Not according to the narrators. They did what they had to do, learning from their parents, imitating their mothers or grandmothers. They most often cite their own families as the important influence in their lives or the source of strength. Chung traced her participation in Zimbabwe's struggle for independence to her grandfather's political ideals and experience. Chow achieved her career and affluence because she feared the poverty of her parents. The narratives of Miranda, Spring-gay, and De la Cruz are testimonies to their awe-inspiring grand-mothers. T.Y. simply said that she found strength in Chinese culture. A glib explanation would have been that the Chinese women overseas are liberated due to Western influence, but that would be too gross an exaggeration. It is true that the structures of the societies in which the Chinese overseas live are different from those of China in previous centuries, just as the society in China has changed such that women there have less restrictions, limitations, and oppressive treatments imposed on them. However, what the women narrators are saying is that they are active, self-directing, and high achieving because they see models mostly in their elders and draw inspiration from their Chinese cultural traditions. Furthermore, there is an important char-acteristic of their agency not usually observed in the West: Their actions are not so much individualistic pursuits for personal fame, liberty, or happiness as they are steadfast, valiant, and unostentatious strivings for the survival, well-being, and dignity of their families or communities.

23 Being Chinese Overseas

Chinese Overseas: Dimensions of Identity

How are the Chinese overseas, the huayi, Chinese? The answers to this question are normally couched in terms of identity in contemporary Western social sciences.[1] However, some of the Chinese overseas whose thoughts, feelings, and experiences are recorded in this book have described how they are Chinese in the diaspora without using the term. In a sense, the term "identity" is adopted here with reluctance and reservation because it expresses both too much and too little: too much because it is an academic term connoting personality structures and coherence, which the narratives in part 2 do not claim to demonstrate, and too little because it fails to depict the emotional richness of being Chinese. In describing how they live, the narrators also verbalize how they are Chinese. "Being Chinese" is simply a way of seeing themselves, whether or not they think in terms of identity.

In the study of Chinese in Southeast Asia, Wang (1991) listed four common multiple identities as salient: the political, the cultural, the economic, and the ethnic. With his concepts as a guide in this study and as a springboard in the analysis of data, I interpret the narrators' views about how they are Chinese — that is, their identity as Chinese overseas, or the huayi identity — in terms of three dimensions of identity. The ethnic dimension is their views on their ancestral grouping among the world's ethno-cultural categories. It parallels while further explicating Wang's concept of ethnic identity. The political dimension refers to the recognition of their citizenship and political allegiance. The cultural dimension focuses on the awareness of their way of life, from the food they eat and the households they live in to their values and rules of behavior. There is certainly an economic dimension of identity, which consists of the perceptions of their socio-economic status, their occupations, and their general social position in their society. However, this dimension is subsumed in the other three in the analysis of the narratives in this book.

Dimensions of a person's identity are abstract ideas used by the observer or the social scientist; ordinarily a person does not partition his or her identity into dimensions. The three dimensions of Chinese overseas identity included in the conceptual framework here are not exhaustive because each person has other dimensions of identity (or other identities), such as being a mother, or a teacher, or a carpenter, and so forth. Nor are the dimensions used here mutually exclusive. The cultural dimension of being Chinese, for example, undoubtedly overlaps, to some degree, the ethnic and political dimension, and vice versa. In other words, in real life, the identity of each person is complex and defies neat classification. Dimensions of Chinese overseas identity are used here only to help us understand what is meant by "being Chinese" as told in the narratives.

Being Chinese: The Ethnic Dimension

Ethnicity is defined in sociology as a "shared cultural heritage" (Macionis 1997:321). The fact that members of an ethnic category are aware of having common ancestry, culture, language, or religion confers a distinctive social identity. In China the majority of Chinese belong to the Han nationality, and all the narrators in this book have Han ancestry. In China what characterizes a person as a Han Chinese depends less on similar physical features than on sharing the same cultural heritage, especially the Han Chinese language, which in English is simply called Chinese.

A few narrators point to facial features in describing their being Chinese. Brown eyes, straight black hair, relatively small nose, skin complexion, and so forth usually distinguish them from the majority of people in their countries of residence, even in Asian countries such as Indonesia and Malaysia. But physical appearance is not the only or even the most important basis of the ethnic dimension of their identity. Actually racial groupings do not exist in biology; they are socially defined. It is common knowledge that Han northerners and Han southerners of China have quite different physical features. Shades of Han people's skin color also vary from region to region in China. The prevailing anthropological knowledge among scholars is that the dominant Han nationality in China is the product of intermingling of many different ethnic categories over thousands of years, although many Han people accept the myths that they descended from common ancestors.[2] Some of the narrators would not have been ignorant of these ideas. But even if they were, biology is probably not on their mind as they describe how they are Chinese.

If there is anything physical to which they would peg their ethnicity, it is not so much genetics as geography. The narrators claim to be Chinese because China is where their ancestors came from, and they, therefore, have roots in China. Most of the narrators can point to the village from which their ancestors emigrated, sometimes in both their father's and mother's families. The hills and plains, rivers and lakes, and some islands on the eastern edge of the Eurasia land mass are important to them because that land is their origin.

Yet, if we listen to the narratives carefully, the geographical location by itself is not the key to their being Chinese. It is the land *and* what has happened in that land. It is geography and a feeling of history. Together the land and the history give them a sense of origin, an awareness of things passed down from one generation to another, and a feeling of belonging. B. Dun, who studied Chinese history, perhaps describes the ethnic dimension of Chinese overseas identity most explicitly and eloquently when he says:

> The Chinese have pretty much done everything under the sun. This ancient people have accomplished astounding feats, and they have endured all manners of hardships. They have been through everything, from tremendous cultural flowering, technological breakthroughs, and prosperity, to humiliation at the hands of conquerors, betrayals by their own people, and abject poverty. Yet they have endured and bounced back. The endurance and resilience of the Chinese are probably the most edifying aspects of the Chinese heritage to me. I can always look upon the

legacy of this people as a solace and an encouragement. It has always been deeply sustaining to me. I am proud to have that legacy, to be a part of that heritage, and to pass it on to others who come after me.

Clearly in his narrative Dun is very much referring to culture, the history and way of life of a people. But the interesting thing about the ethnic dimension is that most narrators claim that they are unfamiliar with Chinese culture and are generally ignorant about Chinese history beyond the briefest sketches. Similarly, many narrators are not able to speak any Chinese dialect beyond what they learned in childhood. Fewer still could read or write. Some of them point to specific values that they regard as Chinese and claim that they treasure them. Others mention bits and pieces of Chinese culture that have been handed down to them. However, as revealed in the narratives, there are no common values or practices, nor common knowledge of Chinese history, that can be seen as forming the basis of the ethnic dimension of identity. Being Chinese is simply the sense of whence they came. It appears that that simple acceptance of their origin is the foundation of who they are.

Beyond the awareness of being Chinese, many narrators seem to have gone through processes of questioning and even anguish in coming to terms with that reality. S. Chinque and D. Li are proud and happy being Chinese. Others such as Hart, Tan, D.T., and Springgay are also proud; they, nevertheless, remember other times when being Chinese meant or still means being the object of derision, discrimination, and even violence. Others, like T.Y., feel strong and confident in dealing with life because they are Chinese. The ethnicity nourishes and sustains them. It also links them to others who are like them in this way. But being Chinese can also be disturbing, as Huang describes: "It's something I must say I don't like to think about very much, because when I think about it too hard, so many conflicts and so many different things are pulling me in one way or another."

The sense of being Chinese was not inborn but acquired, the result of socialization. Somewhere in the narrators' social experiences, usually in childhood, family and friends instilled in them a consciousness of being Chinese. This development of a sense of being Chinese was usually coupled with elements of Chinese culture. But the narrators do not share common components of Chinese culture. So this ethnic dimension of Chinese overseas identity could be developed with little, or perhaps virtually no, Chinese culture. On the other hand, this sense of being Chinese and the positive feelings about it may be eroded by the negative media messages about China, the people in China, and people of Chinese ancestry in other parts of the world. Media, after all, like parents, relatives, friends, and teachers are also agents of socialization. They have a tremendous impact on the images and perceptions of people, even of themselves.

This sense of being Chinese is at the core of those who have spoken in this book. It is difficult to capture and describe this sense or quality that lies so deep within them and yet is so abstract. It is no wonder, then, that metaphors are evoked to express this ethnic dimension. A pejorative description of a Chinese who thinks and acts like a Westerner is the banana: yellow on the outside but white within. Quan sees that living in a Western society like Canada, it is impossible not to live according to Western culture. But he describes himself in terms of the Chinese fruit pomelo. His appearance is Chinese, yellow like the outer skin of the pomelo. His culture, that is, his way of life, is quite like the "big white pith" inside the yellow exterior of the pomelo because it is very much steeped in the dominant European Canadian culture of the larger society. But the pomelo has a core, the edible part, that is still yellow. The core of Quan's being, like the pomelo, is yellow, that is, Chinese. This metaphor can be applied to other Chinese overseas, with the "white pith" referring to the culture of whatever country of citizenship, be it the Philippines, the United Kingdom, Zimbabwe, or even Singapore.

So being Chinese is an awareness of history with a sense of belonging. It is a feeling and a sentiment. The narrators do not know how to think not being Chinese. This ethnic dimension of Chinese overseas identity is beyond the mere biological aspects of their existence. It is linked to the political and cultural dimensions of identity. Moreover, being Chinese does not preclude being other "things" as well, such as being Singaporean, Irish, Latino, Malaysian, Canadian,

Zimbabwean, American, or even more complex identities such as Chinese-Cuban American or Chinese-Indian Canadian.

All over the Chinese diaspora, there are probably some people in each society who would look upon the Chinese overseas in their midst as foreigners, as not belonging to that country, because they look different from the majority of the population (except in Singapore). It is, therefore, necessary and crucial for the Chinese overseas in each society to emphasize again and again that they are citizens of that society and should be treated like other citizens. The complexity of the situation is demonstrated by Quan's reaction to his instructor in the Chinese language course at the University of British Columbia in Canada. When the instructor said that all the ethnic Chinese in the class were Chinese, the comment could have fueled the kind of bigotry harbored by some Canadians that ethnic Chinese were indeed not Canadians. This sentiment could be repeated in other countries and with the same kind of prejudiced reaction. Hence the emphatic response from Quan was that whether he was Chinese or Canadian depended on who was in the classroom and what their state of mind was. In terms of citizenship, political allegiance, and culture, he was a Canadian and an American. But if the instructor was referring only to the ethnic dimension of identity, then Quan or any other Chinese Canadians in that class would have agreed with her that they were indeed all Chinese.

So the ethnic dimension of Chinese overseas identity as analyzed in this book modifies the sociological definition of ethnicity that appears at the beginning of this section. The shared heritage is not so much common culture, which includes language and religion, as common ancestry. Yet the ethnic dimension is not simply about biological heredity or physical appearance. It is an acknowledgement of ancestry. It is not necessarily "common ancestry" in the sense that all the Chinese had the same ancestors as the legends or the Han ideology would have it. It is rather a recognition of their place of origin. For the Chinese overseas it is being rooted in the knowledge that at least some of their ancestors came from the place called China, and that there is a long history connected with that place, which is always behind and before the people called Chinese.

Being Chinese: The Political Dimension

Loyal Citizens

The political dimension of identity is that aspect of self-definition regarding one's allegiance to the government and laws of a society. It is usually related to one's citizenship in a country that confers various political rights and responsibilities, such as the right to vote and the duty of service in the armed forces. None of the narrators is a citizen of People's Republic of China, or the Republic of China on Taiwan. The narrators are citizens of different countries. Many are citizens of the countries where they were born. Some have become citizens of countries to which they immigrated. Yet Woo was already a citizen of the United States even before he arrived there from China, his country of birth. Some have changed their citizenship, such as Chow, D. Li, and Springgay. Others have dual citizenship, such as Quan and L. Dun, who are citizens of both Canada and the United States.

This changing of citizenship points to multiple migrations either within one generation (Chow and J. Li), or over several generations (Springgay). Behind the multiple migrations are political and economic upheavals on the larger international scene. But in the face of Chinese ethnicity — and all the narrators are unequivocal about the ethnic dimension of their identity — and dual or changing citizenship, a question that can be legitimately asked is to which country do they pledge political loyalty?

Like identity itself, loyalty and allegiance are dynamic and can be multifaceted. Many national governments demand absolute and exclusive allegiance from their citizens. They do not recognize dual citizenship (for example, Malaysia and the United States) while others do (Canada). Yet for patriotism to be real, to the extent a citizen is ready to die for the country, there must be emotional underpinnings. Emotions, sentiments, and feelings, on the other hand, are utterly complex and often confusing even to the people themselves. Given the situation, most narrators are remarkably clear about the political or national dimension of their identity. They take their present citizenship seriously and feel loyal to their respective countries. Whatever economic and other utilitarian reasons they or their ancestors might have had as immigrants for moving to a particular place, there is no hypocrisy among the narrators in their bond to the country of their citizenship. The passport is not simply a convenient document for traveling.

It should be mentioned, nevertheless, that this book is not about the recent emigrants from Hong Kong, Taiwan, or China, whose ties to those places may still be very strong. In particular, there is the category of people from Hong Kong who migrated to various countries or territories around the world in the ten or fifteen years leading up to the return of Hong Kong by Great Britain to China in 1997. For some of them, once they have become legal residents of any country, one or both spouses would go back to Hong Kong, leaving their children in their new countries. They would stay in their adopted countries only for periods of time that were required by law for citizenship. These immigrants were referred to as "astronauts" because they spent a great deal of time in airspace. Not all emigrants from Hong Kong were like this. Nonetheless, among them were people who were only interested in acquiring a reliable and internationally respectable passport, with little political or emotional attachment to those countries that have granted them citizenship.

The situation before 1949 was quite different. China then was semi-colonized and divided up by the imperialist powers. There were insurrections, rebellions, and national salvation movements against the Qing government, the Western imperialists, and the Japanese invaders during the century 1842–1949. Within such a context, the ethnic and political dimensions of the Chinese overseas in many cases were close or even identical to each other (see, for example, Yung 1995). Many Chinese in the diaspora saw themselves as not only ethnically Chinese but also loyal Chinese nationalists. Some were actually members of the Nationalist party, or its predecessor, the *Tong Meng Hui*. In the Nanyang societies, most of which were colonies of Western powers, the Chinese overseas were generally regarded by the Nationalist government of China (1912–1949) as Chinese citizens (Pan 1998).

Today, the allegiance of our narrators to their countries of citizenship is likely due to the long years of residence and all kinds of involvement in those countries. Birth alone does not ensure that loyalty, as in the case of Louie's sisters, who, although born in Canada, were brought to Hong Kong by their parents at an early age, lived there all their lives, and have no desire to return to Canada. The narrators demonstrate that they have political loyalty to a country because they have developed some attachment to the place. This happens when they have become entangled in the social web of ties and activities there, whether it is their country of birth or adoption. Springgay feels a sense of belonging to Canada, the country of her choice. The political dimension of her identity is Canadian. In a similar way, Huang feels more comfortable in the United Kingdom, and he is much more approving of Britain and critical of China in the way Hong Kong was returned to the latter in 1997.

To the people of the Chinese diaspora, the issues of legal residency and citizenship were immensely important for which, for example, the Chinese immigrants to North America and their descendants fought fiercely to obtain. Between 1882 and 1943, when Chinese were legally banned from immigrating to the United States, there were at least 1,100 legal suits brought by the Chinese in the U.S. lower federal courts over these issues (Chan 1991:90). People of Chinese ancestry born in Canada were not recognized as Canadian citizens and were not granted the right to vote in federal, provincial, or municipal elections until 1947 (Chan 1982). To the Chinese Canadians and Chinese Americans, being citizens in those countries meant more than the passport. They also fought in the armed forces of these two countries in the two world wars (T.Y.; Louie; L. Dun). The right of Chinese immigrants to become naturalized citizens in both the United States and Canada after World War II was in large measure won by the Chinese Americans and Chinese Canadians who served their countries so valiantly on the battlefields.

The narrators are full participants in the political life of their countries of citizenship. They join political parties (Tan), and get involved in political action. They fulfill their national services as required in Singapore and the United States (Huang; T.Y.). They also serve in their governments as civil officials (Chung; Quan). When the narrators experience prejudice and discrimination on the individual level, they are able to endure the abuse and injury and remain loyal to their countries. However, as discussed in the last chapter, when discrimination is legal or institutionalized, then the caution toward the polity of the country in question may lead to a certain reticence or reservation. When the danger of loss of life and property is imminent, they leave for another country, if they can. They would want to remain loyal and law-abiding citizens in their countries of citizenship, but political changes and legal restrictions on their lives may lead them elsewhere.

Opinions about China

One interesting finding of this research is that the narrators have relatively few favorable comments about the People's Republic of China, yet their emotional bond to their Chinese ethnicity is loud and clear. Those who have visited PRC as tourists admire and cherish the historical sites and relics, but they also remember the frustrations of being unable to speak Chinese, the impolite and sometimes dishonest salespeople, the poor services in the tourist industry, and the lack of modern conveniences, especially the flush toilet. Personal experiences such as these and the attitudes of family members no doubt influence the views of the Chinese overseas about PRC. However, opinions about China are also shaped by powerful socialization agents, such as education and the mass media that present and interpret world events and trends. As has been pointed out in B. Dun's narrative, it is hard for the Chinese overseas to be positive about being Chinese given the negative portrayals of the PRC in the Western media. In fact, it is singularly remarkable to find in the present study that the ethnic and cultural dimensions of identity are so enduring in view of the powerful media content of antipathy toward PRC.

Feeling sympathetic or hostile toward PRC, finding its policies and actions repulsive or sensible, or being ashamed or proud of it, all enter into the identity of the Chinese overseas, because these opinions, attitudes, and sentiments are the positions by which they have chosen to define themselves. And the positions they claim through the opinions they hold have an immense influence on their other choices in life, for example, participation in certain activities, joining specific clubs, associating and interacting with particular friends and acquaintances, political action if any, other life experiences, and even the selection of a mate. Babbie (1994:39) puts it very succinctly thus: "Our identities get wrapped up in our opinions."

Holding negative opinions about PRC in itself is not detrimental to identity development. But if *all* opinions of a hypothetical Chinese overseas person about PRC are negative, he or she may suppress or renounce the ethnic dimension of identity. Whether or not these negative opinions would affect mental health is beyond the scope of this book. Ideally, a mature and informed individual's opinions about PRC are based on historical knowledge, after careful scrutiny and reflection. There is no blind faith in PRC. Nor is there unquestioning support for it. And one is not too obstinate to change one's opinions as new evidence comes to light or falsehoods are exposed. Uninformed opinions leading to a rejection of PRC is as pitiable a state of mind as blind acquiescence with everything PRC says or does. At the moment, on the continuum of opinions, there is greater likelihood for the Chinese overseas to stumble into the pitfall of the former type than the latter, given the preponderant power of communication of the Western media.

A brief examination of how China is portrayed in the Western media, news as well as entertainment, will demonstrate the kind of socialization to which the public — including the Chinese overseas — is subjected. Given the continual dominance of U.S. media content globally today, the discussion of the Western media here is mainly focused on the U.S. media.

CHINA IN THE NEWS. A public opinion poll was conducted by the U.S. television network ABC in July 2001, shortly after China was awarded the opportunity to host the 2008 Olympic Games. According to the poll, 35 percent of Americans singled out China as the greatest threat to world peace. This was 22 points ahead of the second most threatening country, Iraq, at 13 percent (ABCNEWS.com, July 24, 2001).[3] Given this kind of negative public opinion about China, one can with reason surmise that Chinese Americans, and perhaps the Chinese overseas elsewhere as well, will have some reservation about being ethnically Chinese.

The red scare of the 1950s has abated. Although China at the beginning of the twenty-first century is not in the U.S. State Department's list of "rogue nations," it is still treated with unmistakable suspicion, distrust, and hostility in the news media. The negative portrayal of China in the U.S. media can be seen in an example of a rather insignificant story in one of the most prestigious newspapers in the United States. In 2000, the U.S. Congress passed the Permanent Normalized Trade Relations Bill and extended to China the trading rights that the United States grants to other trading partners. It also paved the way for China to join the World Trade Organization, thus allowing the American corporations to enjoy lower tariff on American exports to China. On May 30, 2000, a week after the China trade bill was approved in the House of Representatives of the U.S. Congress, there was a news story about a commercial crime in China in the *New York Times* that began thus:

> China Jails Tycoon for Life for Fraud
> By Reuters
> Beijing (Reuters) — A central Chinese court on Tuesday sentenced Mou Qizhong, a flamboyant tycoon once billed as China's richest man, to life in prison in a celebrated case that underscored the perils facing private business in China. . . . (*New York Times* 2000)

The first part of the above quoted sentence is indeed reporting an incident. But the last part of the sentence is a comment, belonging to the editorial page because it expresses the writer's opinion. But the reader may wonder, What is the peril? Any honest company, Chinese or American, doing business anywhere in the world would want to see fraudulent business people punished and disallowed to conduct commerce. Whatever the intentions of the reporter might have been, the story left an unmistakable distaste for China in the mind of the reader.

The misconceptions about China and other post-colonial societies persist because, as Sklair (1995:159–162) points out, news reporting about the poor countries is very much controlled by the transnational corporations from the United States and western Europe. They could "dump" cheap news on the poor countries but restrict the flow of information in the reverse direction. As news from Chinese sources is regarded as biased and tainted, only stories of calamities and military buildup are presented in the Western press. However, few Western reporters or politicians, whose views and opinions are reported regularly in the media, bother to find out more about China.

If and when politicians and journalists, from the United States or elsewhere, do take the trouble to learn more about China, they may have to change their views or at least get a different impression about China. One journalist who made the effort to visit China found that no one asked him for his identity at a university campus. He was free to move about and "almost all the students were willing to talk. Their opinions tended to be different from Americans', and often from each other. They were nationalistic, but not robots." This reporter's conclusion was: "In China, they talk" (Ramsey 2000).

Earlier in the year 2000, with the vote on normalizing trade with China impending in the United States, the Clinton administration set up a trip to China for the representatives of Congress. Only two of the 435 representatives chose to go. One of the two who went, Representative Gregory Meek, Democrat, New York, spent time wandering through an apartment building and a migrant workers' camp with an interpreter. He said, "You do get a different feel once you have been there" (Ramsey 2000). It is difficult not to conclude that the volume and tone of the politicians' and journalists' persistent derision of China has something to do with their lack of knowledge about China and the Chinese, or their unwillingness to change their opinions. But then the globalization of culture, as it proceeds at the beginning of the twenty-first century and as it is fashioned by the transnational corporations, is not aimed at increasing knowledge of how people really live or how historical events and trends actually happen. It is aimed at promoting consumerism (Sklair 1995).

ENTERTAINMENT: PORTRAYAL OF CHINESE. An example from the entertainment industry will further demonstrate these assertions. The media transnational corporations are not unwilling or slow in taking cultural items from any local culture around the world, including China, and turning it into a marketable commodity for consumption around the world. One example is the 1997 Walt Disney production of *Mulan* in animation. The movie alters the theme and plot of the story of Hua Mulan. It trivializes a people's cultural heritage by forcing the elements of the story into a Hollywood formula. In the process, the plot of the folklore, cherished by the Chinese for over a thousand years, was distorted through embellishment and omission. More significantly, the very moral lessons of the folktale were totally debased and substituted with a theme straight from Hollywood.

In the traditional story, Hua Mulan joined the army in place of her father out of filial piety. She knew that it was out of the question for her old and infirm father to be mobilized, although he had served in the army with distinction. However, in the Disney production, her reason for enlisting in the guise of a man was the inability of the matchmaker to find her a husband because she was too much of a tomboy. In the folklore, Hua Mulan was instructed in the martial arts and military stratagems by her father, who obviously was one of those parents, albeit a minority, recurring in every generation that provided education to their daughters as well as their sons. She was not a hopeless female weakling who could hardly pass basic training as portrayed in the movie. In the traditional story, she rose in ranks quickly due to merit and with approbation from her superiors. Her fellow soldiers never found out her disguise until after demobilization. When they did, they admired her even more. In the Disney movie, the cruel Chinese, her male comrades-in-arms, left her to die on a snowy mountain after the doctor's examination of her battle wounds and discovery of her gender.

The values and attitudes the Disney movie promotes are not very different from those in many cowboy movies, with rugged individualism at the forefront. The moral lessons of filial piety, education of daughters, group efforts to accomplish common goals, and modesty are entirely missing. Mulan in the Disney movie is indeed a heroine, but the rest of the Chinese come out in a much less favorable light. Nevertheless, the Disney production is entertaining. When media content is entertaining, it sells, and it also sells other consumer products advertised with it.

The U.S.–dominated media portrayal of and reportage on China thus mold the opinions of the audience, including the Chinese overseas, wherever their programming is carried. The unfavorable opinions of the Chinese overseas about China are not surprising. But in their case, these opinions are also a part of their identity in the Chinese diaspora.

Being Chinese: The Cultural Dimension

The narratives in this book reveal that the Chinese overseas, with the exceptions of those in Southeast Asia perhaps, are not predominantly Chinese in their culture. To a greater or lesser degree, narrators all have Chinese culture in their lives, but the specific elements and components of Chinese culture retained vary from person to person, with no common cultural components that define the individuals as Chinese. The Chinese overseas have acquired components of Chinese culture in a different way from people in China. They have some traits or elements of Chinese culture that they have learned from family, friends, or schools. With every generation there is likely to be a reduction in the Chinese culture transmitted, while simultaneously the culture and subcultures in China undergo change. Culturally the Chinese overseas are more similar to the majority population of their societies than to the people in China. With the exception of Singapore, the culture of the majority group is not Chinese. However, whatever elements of Chinese culture the narrators have learned, to whatever degree, seem to help them develop a sense of a history, an awareness of where they came from, and a feeling of belonging to an ancient people. Their knowledge and practice of Chinese culture may be limited, but that sense of who they are seems to have given them roots in a world beset with uncertainties and rapid changes.

Chinese Language

Retention of heritage language is usually seen as aiding and supporting the development of any ethnic identity. The narratives, however, reveal some interesting aspects of this complex issue. The claim to being Chinese by all the narrators, their unmistakable ethnic dimension of personal identity, is most amazing when one realizes that the knowledge of Chinese language is limited if not entirely absent among most of the narrators. Many of them spoke Chinese in childhood; for example, Miranda was his grandmother's Chinese-Spanish interpreter in Peru but seemed to be less confident in speaking Chinese in adulthood. Some narrators even had lessons in oral and written Chinese language in their childhood, but with the exception of those who had studied Chinese in school in China, Taiwan, Hong Kong, or Southeast Asia, they do not speak Chinese today and fewer still know how to read and write Chinese characters. Moreover, in Indonesia, Chinese schools along with billboards and signs in Chinese were banned in 1965. Although the ban was partially lifted in 1999, two generations of Indonesian Chinese grew up without the opportunity to learn Chinese beyond what was provided at home (D.T.). Most narrators have Chinese names, but only about half of them know how to write them. Such is the bewildering mixture of proficiency levels in speaking, reading, and writing Chinese among the narrators. Yet many express a profound appreciation of the language.

How the narrators see themselves as being Chinese can certainly be augmented by language, especially the written language. Springgay, for example, still cherishes the few lessons in Chinese that she ever had. For those who acquired the knowledge of even a few Chinese words or phrases, such an experience has become part of their overall idea of self. Even when they are not consciously thinking of their ethnicity, these little "identity markers," so to speak, seem to have a way of surfacing gently on their mind unbidden. And they may not be unwelcome. Hart recounts how she may lie awake at night and go over the Chinese words that she apparently forgot but never quite entirely lost.

Those with even a little knowledge of the Chinese written language see the nuances in Chinese language as expressed by the large number of words for a wide variety of kin relationships. The writing system in China enabled generations of scholars, men and women, to pen historical events and their private thoughts for all posterity. B. Dun notes the overwhelming penchant of the Chinese to record everything through the ages. "This is the amazing legacy of the Chinese writing system, which in essence is traceable to the oracle bones of almost four thousand years ago, such that the Chinese have the longest continuous civilization in the world today."

There is, however, one category of Chinese overseas that I have come across from time to time and is not among the narrators in this book. They are those who know the oral and written Chinese language, some even competently, but appear to avoid the use of the language and, in a few cases, even the contact with anything or anyone Chinese. Two such persons were approached to be included in this project. They declined the invitation because they "did not feel very Chinese." Whatever reasons they had for their feelings, there appears to be a suggestion that knowledge of the Chinese language in itself may not be strongly related to developing a Chinese overseas identity. This phenomenon—the relationship between retention of heritage language and ethnic identity—needs to be examined in future research.

The narrators in this book seem to say that Chinese overseas can have a developed sense of being Chinese without knowing the Chinese language. Understanding some spoken words in Chinese, whatever the dialect and in however small portions, could deepen the sense of being culturally Chinese. The ability to read and write Chinese could further strengthen that sense. Thus it appears that knowledge of Chinese language can contribute to the development of Chinese overseas identity, but is not necessary to this identity.

Food

There is a popular Chinese saying: First of all people eat *(min yi shi wei xian)*. One may say that it is stating the obvious. It nevertheless reflects the overwhelming cultural significance that the Chinese people have attached to food.

While the sense of Chinese ethnicity may be developed independently from the knowledge of Chinese language, one cultural item seems to have contributed to almost every narrator's notion of "being Chinese"—the Chinese food. It is possibly the closest thing to being the common cultural item shared by all of them. When everything else in their daily life seems to be utterly non-Chinese or un-Chinese, there is Chinese food. In a few inter-ethnic marriages, Chinese food is consumed several times a week (Hart). Otherwise, one would not be too far off the mark to assume that it is the daily fare.

The incomparable tastes, flavors, textures, variety, salutary effects, and preparation techniques of Chinese foods have long been the subject of many television programs and books in a multitude of languages. There is no need to go into them here. But it is not food per se, however important and appetizing, that really matters to the people. It is food in the social context, the meal, that is of the utmost concern. Quan draws our attention to the important link between food and family. To him shopping for food, preparing it, and eating together make up the Chinese way of "manifesting kinship." Perhaps it is the partaking of food socially, with family and friends, that over the centuries has led to the excellent standards in Chinese cuisine. And perhaps it is the paramount importance of the family that has continually pushed the dietary and culinary endeavors to ever new heights. Or is it the other way around? Whatever the answer to these speculations, the narrators seem to concur that being Chinese and eating Chinese are inextricably intertwined.

Eating Chinese food requires knowing how to make Chinese food. The vegetables, cuisine, and styles of cooking used in the Chinese diaspora today are essentially the same as those of the Chinese in South China. Hart learned to make Chinese dim sum in Vancouver Island from her Vancouver-born mother. Springgay learned it from her grandmother in India. Both narrators have passed on their knowledge and skills to their children living in North America. Canseco is regarded in Mexico as a Canadian who eats Chinese food. But she learned how to cook Chinese food from Chinese graduate students attending universities in Mexico! Given the importance of food in Chinese traditions, the Chinese overseas, once socialized into eating Chinese food, seem to acquire the Chinese culinary arts in whatever way they can.

Food underlies the cultural dimension of identity in yet another way. The number of Chinese restaurants around the world is staggering. Several narrators worked in this business in various capacities.

None of the narrators mentioned ginger, but it is hard to imagine any Chinese meal without having some portion of it cooked with this condiment. I am ready to wager that the narrators all use ginger if they cook any Chinese food at all. In this tiny case of eating habit at least, facetiously speaking, the narrators would be following the example of Kong Fuzi. He once said that he never touched any meal that was not prepared with ginger (*Confucian Analects* 10:8).

Cultural Values and Philosophy

Beyond food, it is with regard to Chinese values that most narrators structure the cultural dimension of their identity. They perceive themselves to be culturally Chinese because they feel that certain Chinese values still influence their thinking or conduct, or are still meaningful to them. The values mentioned by the narrators are emphasized in other cultures as well, but the Chinese people seem to take them to a much higher level.

First and foremost is *xiao*. It is a Chinese concept that has no direct translation in English, requiring, therefore, two words to describe it: filial piety or filial devotion. It expresses the love, respect, obedience, solicitude, devotion, care, and utter sense of duty of the children toward the parents, with the implicit understanding that the children will look after the parents in their old age. It is the bond that ties the children to their parents, in return for the care, guidance, and devotion and, above all, life itself that the parents have bestowed on the children.

Xiao seems to be a fundamental value held by the narrators. Yeoh rates it as the essence of Chinese culture. Although many do not mention it by name, almost every narrator invariably speaks of his or her parents in ways expressing that filial devotion. Even if a child were treated unfairly, as in the case of Hart and her mother's jewelry, the child would still take care of the parents in their old age. The three narrators—Li, Woo, and Louie—mentioned in chapter 22 were still xiao to their parents even after decades of separation.

Xiao is also demanding. In coming out to their parents, Quan and his brother were mindful of the shock that their parents would undoubtedly experience. The inner struggles of being Chinese revealed by Huang are essentially related to xiao. He would like to follow his own heart, but he cannot be unmindful of the wishes of his parents. The Western way of viewing the situation is: Look, this is your life, so live it the way you want. But xiao demands something more. The respect and consideration he gives to his parents is what to a certain extent he would expect from his own children someday.

Xiao is extended to mean respect for all elders. This would certainly include parents-in-law. Here in the real culture is a different scene. Chow did not see eye-to-eye with her mother-in-law but she also took care not to sever relationships. In time the conflicts might not have been resolved completely, but both daughter- and mother-in-law adapted to accommodate tensions. It is the respect accorded to the elders that seems to have saved the day or, more precisely, saved faces and a functional harmony within the family.

Education is a second deeply ingrained value. Again it is not a uniquely Chinese value. As D. Li points out, it may not be in every Chinese family either. For example, Wong-Kit did not want to attend school despite the efforts of her adoptive parents. But parental attention to the offspring's education goes to great lengths according to several narrators. The Chow family remigrated from the Netherlands to the United States mainly for the education of the children. Huang's mother supervised his homework every day. D.T.'s parents sent their youngest child to Singapore at the age of nine so that he would learn Chinese. His and Hart's mothers arranged Chinese lessons for their children.

Other cultural values such as forbearance, perseverance, diligence, modesty, and frugality are the qualities the narrators see as the bedrock of Chinese culture. Together with xiao and love of education, they are from long-standing traditions. All of them require assiduous efforts of cultivation. They are perhaps most clearly observable in Chow's narrative: She spares no efforts in her work as a food services manager, in achieving financial security through frugality, and in nurturing her relationship with her spouse. Forbearance and perseverance are necessary for survival in the diaspora. The men and women, or their ancestors, were not too proud to do lowly jobs to sustain life. They worked hard, and some prospered while others made do. Several narrators persevered in learning. Some have excelled scholastically and become respectable experts in their fields. Some are ambitious. Others are not quite so driven.

Modesty is the lens that brings achievement and prosperity into a humanist perspective. B. Dun refers to it explicitly as something positive. Chung's achievement as a high-ranking official in Zimbabwe and at UNICEF is admirable and inspiring. Could it be that her modesty helped her navigate through the treacherous waters of officialdom, while her sails of personal ambition and integrity remained intact? The other narrators may not have Chung's high profile, although many have impressive accomplishments. Yet the impression they give out is that it is all in a day's work, nothing remarkable, even if it were something like baking one thousand loaves of bread for the banned potlatch, as when L. Dun's great-grandfather decided to help the First Nations people on Vancouver Island.

Can we say that any of these values is more traditional or more modern than the others? Where is the demarcation between traditional culture and modern culture? But these values are ridiculed as the traditional culture of the inscrutable Chinese in Hollywood movies and other media in the West. The label is often legitimized by the approval of some social scientists. The sage Kong Fuzi did extol the virtues of forbearance, learning, and so forth 2,500 years ago, but they are thoroughly contemporary and very serviceable in modern applications as we see these qualities put into practice in people's lives. There is no dichotomy between tradition and modernity, but there is unmistakable cultural continuity. Seeing their parents and elders emphasizing and sometimes modeling these values, the narrators internalized them, albeit not all of them by any single individual. Today their definition of being Chinese is expressed in terms of these cultural values. The narrators who treasure them reached their levels of attainment not in spite of their traditional values but rather because of them.

Although some narrators profess that they are not all that culturally Chinese, their behavior and the values they admire are in fact rooted in Chinese philosophy. It has sometimes appeared to the careful observer that the Chinese people, even before the officially atheist communist regime was established in 1949, have been less concerned with religion than other groups of people. According to the world-renowned Chinese philosopher of the twentieth century Fung Yu-lan, the place of philosophy in the Chinese civilization is similar to that of religion in others. Philosophy is "systematic, reflective thinking on life" (Fung 1964:2) while religion is philosophy with a superstructure, which consists of beliefs, dogmas, ritual ceremonies, and institutions (Fung 1964:3). The Chinese "are not religious because they are philosophical" (Fung 1964:4). The function of philosophy is to elevate the mind as the individual strives to identify with the universe. Therein lies the spirituality.

The Chinese as a people, generally speaking, are much more concerned with issues of this world, this life. The two most influential philosophical systems developed in China are the schools of *Ru* and *Dao*. The Ru school, commonly referred to as Confucianism in the West,[4] is traced to Kong Fuzi (551–479 BCE) and the second sage Meng Zi (Master Meng, popularly known in the West as Mencius, circa 371–289 BCE). The school of Dao is the philosophy that is traced to Lao Zi's *Dao De Jing* (*Book of Lao Zi* circa sixth century BCE) and the philosophy of Zhuang Zi (circa 369–286 BCE).

The school of Ru, as handed down by Kong Fuzi, Meng Zi, and all the other Confucian scholars through the ages, is concerned with harmonious social relationships and stable social order. This can be achieved by people in various relationships practicing the virtues of human-heartedness, righteousness, forbearance, loyalty, devotion to learning, modesty, and so forth. Of these, human-heartedness is the most important, the essential quality underlying all other virtues. In a ruler human-heartedness is benevolence and caring toward the subjects, while the same in the subject is loyalty to the ruler. Similarly, in a child it is filial devotion to the parents, while the parents bestow nurturance and guidance to the child.

The elevation of the mind to the universe is very pronounced in Daoist philosophy. According to the Daoist philosophy, dao (meaning path or way) is the basic principle in all the universe. It existed before the birth of the universe. It brought forth nature and everything in it. People follow the principles of the earth, the earth follows those of the heaven, the heaven follows those of dao, and dao follows itself naturally (*Dao De Jing* 25). While the human being is essentially linked to the universe through the dao, the book *Dao De Jing* is not a text of mysticism as is often the misconception today, especially in the West. Daoist philosophy, like other Chinese schools of thought, is mainly concerned with politics, governing a society, the inhumanity of war, and survival in the chaotic times of the Warring States period in Chinese history. It admonishes that in governing people and other human affairs, it is wise to follow the way or principles of nature and not do anything that is contrary to nature (Lau 1975).

The Daoist and Confucian philosophies, different as they are in outlook and emphasis, stem from the same root in ancient Chinese society. Both are related to agriculture, the way of life in ancient China as it is still of most people there today. The two differ by expressing different aspects of the agricultural way of life. Daoist philosophy focuses on the farmers' direct contact with nature, admiring its simplicity and wholeness but at the same time awestruck by its unrelenting force. Confucian philosophy dwells on the social requirements of the agricultural way of life: the paramount importance of the family rooted in the land, living and working together (Fung 1964:19).

From the common origin in agriculture, the two philosophies developed a common theory that argues that when anything, in nature or in human affairs, reaches one extreme, a reverse motion toward the other extreme will take place. The reverse movement of the dao is found in both the *Dao De Jing* and the Confucian text of *Yi Jing*. The endurance, hope, and perseverance of the Chinese in times of adversity, and the modesty and caution in times of success and prosperity are the result of self-cultivation in accordance with this theory of the reversal movement of the dao (Fung 1964:19–20).

In this conceptualization of Chinese civilization, it is not necessary for people to be religious, but it is necessary that they should be philosophical (Fung 1964:6). Philosophy eclipses religion. Kong Fuzi himself denied any knowledge of other-worldly philosophy (*Confucian Analects* 11:11). The few instances in the *Confucian Analects* where Kong Fuzi discusses forces beyond his control are in connection to *ming*, which is translated variously as fate, destiny, or will of heaven. In the teachings of later Confucian scholars, it has come to mean "the total existent conditions and forces of the whole universe" (Fung 1964:45). But Kong Fuzi's approach to ming is not pessimistic or passive. Rather the emphasis is always on effort, as in learning and self-cultivation. According to Kong Fuzi, people who have tried their best should then leave the final outcome, success or failure, to ming (*Confucian Analects* 14:38; 20:3). This attitude of putting in their best efforts while detached from the consequence of success or failure, far from leaving people gloomy, in fact frees them from anxiety and fear of failure (*Confucian Analects* 7:36; 9:28).

The key to conducting one's life is assiduous effort — keep on doing it, whatever it is. If one has truly put in the effort, even when the outcome is failure, it is neither permanent nor weakness, because "Reversing is the movement of dao, weakness is the means of dao" (*Dao De Jing* 40; see Huang). Failure, adversity, or calamity will not last forever; things will be better. On the other hand, neither will prosperity and good fortune remain permanently. So there is no room for arrogance.

Thus philosophy is not simply to be learned but it also demands to be lived. One reaches beyond the moral values of the present world, through self-cultivation, to the universe with human-heartedness, righteousness, loyalty, and forbearance (*Book of Mencius* 7A:1; 6A:16). As one practices these virtues, one eliminates selfishness to the point that there is no longer any distinction between oneself and others, nor between the universe and oneself. As Meng Zi describes the connection between every individual and the universe: "All things are complete within me" (*Book of Mencius* 7A:4). The virtues that an individual cultivates are nourished into a mighty and supreme *qi* that floods the space between heaven and earth (*Book of Mencius* 2A:2). The word qi literally means "gas" or "breath." It refers to the energy in the universe.

Is there then no place for religion in Chinese culture? Obviously there were many things that the ancient Chinese did not understand, for which the contemporary Chinese have no satisfactory explanations either. Based solely on their philosophies, they have no knowledge about "other-worldly" issues such as what lies beyond death, heaven and hell, reincarnation, god or gods. The only religion that can be said to be native to China is the Daoist religion, which, it must be emphatically pointed out, is different from Daoist philosophy (see Fung 1964). Daoist religion has disparate roots, combining animist and ancient shamanist beliefs and practices[5]; healing arts; a pantheon of gods and goddesses; the veneration of the philosopher Lao Zi and the legendary Yellow Emperor; and some ideas drawn from the Daoist philosophy. The founding of Daoist religion in the Eastern Han dynasty (25–220 CE) and its institutionalization were very much influenced by the influx and popularization of the Buddhist religion from India since the Western Han dynasty (202 BCE–9 CE). One specific characteristic of Daoist religion is the prominence given to women deities and the priestesses. This is reminiscent of the emphasis on the female principle in the *Dao De Jing*. Daoist religion is popular among the common folks, especially in the countryside.

Perhaps because the major schools of Chinese thought are all concerned with the human relationships and morals pertaining to this world and are generally silent about other-worldly things, the Chinese are eclectic and syncretic as far as the practice of religion is concerned, as shown in the Daoist religion itself. When it comes to beliefs—those ideas and assertions about other-worldly things that must be accepted on faith—the Chinese are wont to take them wherever they find them, from various religions, sects, and metaphysical doctrines. A case in point is the native Chinese tradition of paying respects and making food offerings to the deceased ancestors that has been kept for thousands of years till now, including by several narrators. Since the Chinese tradition itself offers only a hazy notion of where the ancestors go after death, elements from a wide range of religions, foreign and indigenous, are incorporated into funereal and memorial rites. The people presented in this book have affiliation to different religions—Buddhist, Daoist, Protestant, Catholic, and Islam—or are without any religions. Membership in specific religions, on the other hand, does not prevent them, or their family, from the eclectic and syncretic approach to other-worldly issues. The funeral of D. Li's grandmother, with ceremonies officiated by the Catholic priest, the Buddhist monks, and the Daoist priest, is a case in point. Tan's family can be said to be observing "Chinese religion" as a combination of Buddhist, Daioist, and ancestor veneration practices (see Pan 1998). In his household they make sure that vegetarian food is offered to the Buddha and bodhisattvas, but all kinds of delicacies, including meat, are given to the spirits of the ancestors.

One component of early Chinese cosmogony that has been transmitted through the centuries into the twenty-first century and become very popular in the Chinese diaspora is fengshui, literally meaning "wind and water." The central idea in fengshui is that since people are part of the universe, places where they live and where they are buried must be arranged in such a way as to harmonize with the forces of nature, that is, the wind and water. The location and direction of houses and graves can augment or block qi, the energy flow of the natural forces. Similarly, rooms within the house and even the furniture in a room should be so arranged as to allow the forces of the universe to articulate harmoniously with people's exertions in their relationships and affairs. To some observers, fengshui may appear to be mere superstitions, but to those who take it seriously, it is not so much unprovable as not yet fully understood by the uninitiated, because the ideas and locations on which fengshui is based refer to physical objects of this world. The fundamental idea is that people's activities and conduct are related to the energy in the universe.

Notions of fengshui are followed by a few narrators, while others maintain a generalized awareness of being connected to qi and to the universe (N. Chinque; Quan; Huang; Canseco).

In a similar way, Chinese medicine, with ideas of meridian points and energy flow, treats the whole person, encompassing the mental, emotional, and physical states of the patient. Again to the casual observer it may appear to be all in the imagination of the practitioner and the patient. Without rejecting Western medicine, especially surgery and its efficacy, some narrators, including a surgeon trained in Western medicine, are convinced of the salutary effects of some Chinese medicine (Quan; Huang). In the broader sense of health, Chinese medicine and exercises, such as taiji and qigong, are seen by many Chinese, in China and in the diaspora, as articulating qi and enhancing one's well-being. The entire Chinque family is faithful in doing the exercises.

It appears that many narrators indeed live by the various philosophical concepts and principles discussed in this chapter, without necessarily quoting the classics by chapter and verse. What is fascinating is the depth of the Chinese philosophical outlook revealed by the narrators, even when some of them claim that they do not know or live according to Chinese culture. The Confucian and Daoist philosophical texts are of course read only by the educated people. However, some philosophical ideas have spread through all layers and sectors of Chinese society. The narrators have somehow learned various aspects of Chinese philosophy. Most probably it was not through formal instruction in reading the classical texts, as in the case of the sinologist Adrian Chan. More likely it would be through grandparents recounting didactic stories of historical personages who lived the virtuous lives of righteousness, forbearance, filial devotion, loyalty, and so forth. Or it could be simply by watching how the older generations dealt with life and following their examples. Or on their own they may find spirituality in the *Yi Jing,* as N. Chinque is doing. It is within this philosophical tradition that certain cultural values discussed earlier have relevance for the narrators.

The narrators who express various versions of this kind of outlook are anchored in their own abilities and the support from the web of social relationships to carry on life. It is probably regarding this point that Chung expresses her penetrating insight into Chinese culture: "One of the strengths of Chinese culture is that . . . it has certain moral values which are not based on religion." Her view sums up the unique character and strength of Chinese culture as expressed not only by the content of its philosophical tradition but also by the place of philosophy in it. Chinese culture can embrace many different religions. Nevertheless, by and in itself, Chinese philosophy provides adequate and comprehensive systems of thought that can meet the intellectual and spiritual needs of those who learn and live by it. Chinese philosophy does not dispense spiritual strength as a pharmacy does with prescriptions. Yet for those who are socialized with Chinese culture, however sparsely or incompletely as some of the narrators may feel, the philosophical ideas and principles distilled from the culture can sustain and nourish their practitioners.

24 A New Conceptualization of Ethnic Identity

Toward a New Conceptualization

Being Chinese overseas has several salient features:

First, a common theme through all the narratives is that tracing their ancestry to China and an awareness of roots are meaningful and significant to the speakers. Some even find it as a source of strength. This ethnic dimension of the Chinese overseas identity is the edible yellow flesh in the core of the pomelo described by Quan. The sense of being rooted in one's ethnicity is not based on biological heredity. It arose out of life experiences, such as childhood socialization by a grandparent, reinforced by the treatment by a dominant group in the immigrant society. Moreover, the narrators answered the question about being Chinese very differently. To Chow, being Chinese is being frugal. The answers of many touch on filial piety and other Chinese values. Yeoh and J. Li describe their recent visits to China. Perhaps for de la Cruz, who recounted the story of Mrs. Wong-Kit, being Chinese is having her grandmother as an important part of her life. Chan's identity is revealed in his views on sinology. And D.T. simply replies, "We are good business people." None of these or others were flippant answers; they were given thoughtfully and reflectively. Being Chinese did not arise out of only one kind of experience but from a wide range of experiences. The task of this book has been to record and identify some of these experiences.

Second, the narrators have incorporated selective elements and varying amounts of Chinese culture into their lives, depending on the circumstances of necessity and opportunity. The identity of Chinese overseas is possibly strengthened by, but not necessarily dependent on, the retention of Chinese culture, especially Chinese language.

One can still feel "being Chinese," that is, develop a strong ethnic dimension of identity, without Chinese language or any other particular elements of Chinese culture. On the other hand, some narrators may think that they have little Chinese culture in their life yet in fact be living according to some Chinese values and philosophical principles without consciously knowing their source or origin.

Third, identity is a dynamic and multidimensional process. The narratives reveal a rich array of views and feelings about being Chinese in each individual. The discussion of the Chinese overseas identity in terms of ethnic, political, and cultural dimensions is merely an attempt to capture in words a process that is constantly evolving. It is an observer's way of analyzing a multifaceted and multilayered process. The classification scheme or a conceptual framework devised by an outside observer may or may not coincide with how the narrators see or feel about themselves. It will be, therefore, impossible to specify these dimensions in each narrative. Moreover, there could be other dimensions imposed on the narratives. Wang (1991) discusses an economic identity among the Chinese overseas. Another dimension that could be added, for example, is the one regarding the dialect or district origin of the ancestors who emigrated; this origin was mentioned by quite a few interviewees. It seemed to be quite significant to them. Conceptually there is no logical reason for limiting the dimensions to three, five, or whatever number.

How the narrators change their views about themselves and their feelings about being Chinese living in non-Chinese societies does not follow any set stages of development. We have seen pride in being Chinese, resentment for being Chinese, criticisms of China and Chinese culture, struggles with the demands of Chinese values, and conflicts arising from living biculturally or multiculturally. They can all be in the same person at the same time or they may appear at different points in the life of an individual. People change their self-concepts, most noticeably in a life cycle, say, from being a child to being also a parent. In a similar way, self-concepts regarding one's ethnicity also undergo modification, reinforced by experiences, positive or negative, or submerged when other life experiences are more demanding of one's attention.

Fourth, as identity is developed through socialization, the agents of socialization, such as parents, teachers, friends, and the media, are all important in shaping a person's identity. These agents of socialization passed on to the narrators a sense of history and a feeling of belonging as well as traits and items of Chinese material and non-material culture. The narratives also show the important role played by grandparents, especially the grandmother, in influencing the ethnic dimension of Chinese overseas identity.

Fifth, opinions form a part of identity. This statement is linked specifically to the media as agents of socialization. As opinions change, so does our identity. The examination of the portrayal of the People's Republic of China in the U.S.–dominated Western media suggests that persistent negative images and hostile comments about PRC will have an impact on the Chinese overseas and their views about being Chinese. How personal opinions about China itself develop, in agreement or in conflict with mass media content, will be a particularly intriguing area for further study.

Sixth, taken together, these findings offer a new conceptualization of the Chinese overseas identity or being Chinese in the diaspora. The Chinese overseas speakers in this book are accepting of their ethnicity, mostly happy about being Chinese, and proud of their heritage, even though they may know or practice very little Chinese culture. This is the most important analytical generalization from the study. It challenges the common view about Chinese identity in the diaspora, according to which a person is Chinese if he or she is culturally Han Chinese. What the narratives seem to show is that without, or with extremely limited, knowledge of Chinese language, and with only what appear to be bits and scraps of Chinese culture, the ethnic dimension of identity can still be strong. So the basis of ethnic identity is not so much heredity, or the cultural heritage that the people in China are expected to learn. The basis is the knowledge of where they came from, a sense of history, and some traits of Chinese culture. The cultural traits could be fragments of Chinese language, some values perhaps, and a few skills, such as cooking authentic Chinese food. The cultural bits could be as little as this: Those Chinese overseas who have developed an ethnic dimension of identity will regard others eating chicken feet with aplomb, as perfectly natural, even if they themselves do not take to that particular delicacy. Moreover, the narrators' traits or components of Chinese culture may be of the nineteenth-century vintage, as carried to the countries of immigration by their ancestors. The Chinese cultures in the diaspora, even in Singapore, are evolving differently from those in China. It will be interesting to see whether this conceptualization will be useful in studies of other ethnic diasporas.

Finally, each of the narratives is capable of generating some theoretical statements about the general phenomenon or more specific issues of diasporas for further research. For example, from the fourth-generation Chinese-American T.Y.'s narrative, there is a suggestion of the relationship between conscious choice and endogamy. She made an explicit decision to marry a Chinese, and she gave her reasons. A hypothesis that can be generated from this study is that endogamy is likely to take place for a member of a ethnic minority in a multiethnic society only if a conscious decision is made by the individual with clear understanding of the limitations on choices the decision entails. On the other hand, the opposite of what is said here about endogamy may or may not be true about exogamy. The narrators did not say much about exogamy, although quite a few have non-Chinese spouses.

Global Heritage

The global heritage of the Chinese overseas consists of the Chinese culture, material and nonmaterial, that was carried to the diaspora and that was retained, modified, and practiced in various Chinese communities around the world. Some of the components of Chinese material culture, such as methods of Chinese cooking and the Chinese cuisine itself, have become integral parts of those immigrant societies. Other less tangible components of Chinese culture, such as the virtues of filial devotion and perseverance, aesthetics as reflected in painting and calligraphy, and ways of looking at the universe, as in Chinese philosophy and fengshui, have also been extolled and emulated by non-Chinese populations. Collectively, these various items of Chinese culture are the legacy of the Chinese overseas to the world.

On a deeper level, the Chinese overseas, with their tenacity to hold on to their identity and components of their culture, and their resolve to overcome any adversity in their various new homelands, attest to the strength of the human spirit. In a real sense, they themselves are the global heritage for the world to witness and celebrate. Many Chinese emigrants and their children perished in their quest for a better place to live. They were killed by natural disasters or by insidious deeds of other human beings. The very survival of the Chinese overseas today, therefore, attests to their good luck[1] and their endurance, and those of their forebearers, in surmounting difficulties. The very existence of the Chinese overseas and their communities in different parts of the world, whether by chance, good fortune, or strenuous efforts, is the global heritage. It is refreshing and edifying to encounter, in a century when it has often been emotionally difficult for many to be Chinese, the men and women in this book who, with humor, affection, and pride, tell the world what it is like being Chinese.

Major Chronological Periods in Chinese History

Neolithic Cultures

Yanhshao culture	8,000–5,000 years ago
Longshan culture	7,000–4,000 years ago

Dynasties

Xia	21st–18th centuries BCE
Shang	18th–12th centuries
Zhou	~1122–256
Western Zhou	~1122–771
Eastern Zhou	771–256
Spring and Autumn period	770–476
Warring States period	475–221
Qin	221–207
Han	202 BCE–220 CE
Western Han	202 BCE–9 CE
Eastern Han	25–220 CE
Period of Disunity	220–589
Three Kingdoms	220–280
Western Jin	266–316
Eastern Jin	317–420
Southern Dynasties	420–589
Northern Dynasties	386–581
Sui	581–618
Tang	618–907
Five Dynasties Era	907–960
Song, Northern	960–1127
Liao	916–1125
Western Liao	1124–1211
Western Xia	1038–1227
Jin	1115–1234

Song, Southern	1127–1279
Yuan (Mongol)	1271–1368
Ming	1368–1644
Qing (Manchu)	1644–1911

Post-Dynastic Governments

Republic of China (Nationalist)	1911–1949
Taiwan	1945–present
People's Republic of China (Communist)	1949–present

Note: There were many kingdoms established by Han and non-Han nationalities in Chinese history. Thus some dynasties overlapped, and warlords and factious strife dominated other periods leading to years of disunity.

Notes

Chapter 1

1. The West generally refers to Western Europe (although the demarcation line across Europe may include Poland and Eastern Europe at times) and the immigrant countries settled predominantly by people of Western European ancestry, such as the United States of America, Canada, Australia and New Zealand. The term is traced culturally to the Greco-Roman and Judeo-Christian traditions. The difficulties of a precise geographical definition of the West are discussed by McNeill (2000).

2. For more about the Chinese overseas in Southeast Asia see Wang 2000.

3. Between 1600–1814, one tael *(liang)* of silver
= one Chinese, or 1.208 English, ounce of pure silver
= 1/2 pound sterling, or 6s. 8d. (six shillings and eight pence)
= US$1.63
= Spanish $1.57
In 1884 the value of one tael dropped to 3s. 2d., and in 1904 to 2s. 10d. (Hsu 1990: xxxi).

Chapter 2

1. It was not uncommon for immigration officials in the late nineteenth and early twentieth centuries, in both Canada and the United States, to put down the romanized last character in the Chinese name to be the family name, whereas in Chinese the family name is the first character.

2. Dr. Sun Yat-sen (Sun Yixian) is the courtesy name of Sun Wen, who was dedicated to the overthrow of the Qing dynasty. He studied and graduated in medicine from the University of Hong Kong, after spending part of his youth in Hawaii. He traveled extensively in the Chinese diaspora in the first decade of the twentieth century, raising funds for his political cause. The uprising in 1911 ushered in the republican period. He is also known as Sun Zhongshan. The name of his native town, Xiangshan, was later changed to Zhongshan in honor of him. T.Y.'s paternal grandparents were from the same town as Dr. Sun Wen.

3. Weiqi is a chess game that originated in ancient China. It is known in the West by the Japanese word *go*.

4. Qingming is the festival in the spring when people go to the cemetery to sweep clean the graves of ancestors; make offerings consisting of food, wine, and

burning of paper money and so forth for the dead; and pay respects to the ancestors. It falls on April 5 in the Western calendar every year. A lesser but similar festival occurring in autumn is *Chongyang,* the ninth day of the ninth month in the Chinese calendar.

Chapter 4

1. This is a novel about the heroes, their intrigue and strategies, of the period 220–280 CE, when China was divided into three kingdoms. The novel was written in the Ming dynasty.

2. See chapter 23 for more information about xiao.

Chapter 5

1. Dim sum is the pronunciation in Guangzhou dialect of *dianxin,* meaning a snack or light meal in lieu of lunch. It is served with many dishes, such as hakou (shrimp turnover), siumai (little meatball in rice wrapper), *cheungfun* (rice pastry), and barbecue pork bun. *Zong* is a large dumpling made of sticky rice wrapped in a palm leaf.

2. Taiji is a traditional Chinese exercise consisting of gentle movements intended to promote health. Qigong is a traditional Chinese system of therapeutic exercises involving disciplined breathing.

3. See discussion of fengshui in chapter 23.

Chapter 6

1. Bai sam is a colloquial term for veneration of the ancestors at their graves.

Chapter 7

1. ZANU stands for Zimbabwe African National Union, a political movement against colonial rule formed by a group of black intellectuals in 1963.

Chapter 8

1. Under the Manchu rule of the Qing dynasty (1644–1911), all Chinese males were required to grow a pigtail in accordance with the Manchu custom. That custom died with the dynasty.

2. White is the color of mourning, and red that of happiness in Chinese culture. The traditional bridal gown is red.

3. Bagua is the set of eight diagrams, each of which consists of three broken or whole lines. The eight diagrams are used for divination.

Chapter 9

1. See chapter 22 about the Hakka.

2. "Banana" is a derogatory term to describe Asian Canadians, Asian Americans, or even Asians in Asia who are yellow-skinned in appearance but thoroughly Western in their behavior, often with a repudiation of their Asian heritage. In recent years, there is a movement afoot among Asian North Americans to take back the term and infuse it with a positive connotation.

3. The pomelo is a fruit native to southern China and Southeast Asia. It belongs to the same family as the grapefruit but is bigger. It has a rough yellow exterior like the other citrus fruits. It has a layer of fluffy white pith, which is thicker than that in the grapefruit. The edible core consists of thick segments of yellow pulpy flesh.

4. A snack late in the evening.

Chapter 10

1. I was unable to find out the exact content or other details of this law.

2. The erhu is an instrument with two strings and played with a bow, which is clasped between the strings. The sound box is covered with snake skin. It is the most widely used bow-string instrument in China.

3. Pipa, the Chinese lute, is a four-stringed plucked instrument.

4. Sanxian, the Chinese long-necked lute, is a three-stringed plucked instrument with a skin membrane stretched over a resonator. It is rich in tone and has a wide range. It is used for accompaniment as well as in orchestral or solo performance. It has three sizes: large, medium, and small.

Chapter 11

1. According to Edward Said, Orientalism is a way of conceptualizing the peoples of the East (Orient) in the European West. It has "a history and a tradition of thought, imagery, and vocabulary that have given it reality and presence in and for the West" (Said 1979:3). An Orientalist, in this sense, refers to a scholar who is engaged in constructing the history and culture of a people other than his or her own, for ideological purposes, based more on preconceived notions, myth, and imagination than on reality.

2. Matteo Ricci (1552–1610) was an Italian belonging to the Society of Jesus (the Jesuits) of the Roman Catholic Church. He began Christian missionary activities in China in 1583, in Zhaoqing, Guangdong Province.

3. The mote and beam syndrome refers to the phenomenon when people only see the fault in others (the small mote in the eye of the other) and miss the similar problem in themselves (the big beam in their own eye). This was mentioned in the Gospel according to Luke, one of the four gospels in the Christian scriptures. Luke was reputed to have been a physician.

4. See Chan (1997).

5. Chen Duxiu (1880–1942) founded the *Aiguo Hui* (Patriotic Society) in

his native Anhui Province in 1902. He started the journal *Qingnian Zazhi* (Youth Magazine) in 1915. It was renamed *Xin Qingnian* (The New Youth) in 1917. Many leftist writers advocating political, social, and economic changes in China contributed to this journal. The journal was influential in shaping the thinking of the educated Chinese youth in the early part of the twentieth century. Chen was one of the founders of the Chinese Communist Party in 1921.

6. See Chan (1995).

Chapter 12

1. After the trans-Canada railway was completed, when Chinese labor was not so desperately needed, the government of Canada tried to stop the entry of Chinese workers into Canada by imposing on them a head tax in 1886. Every Chinese immigrant, with the exception of merchants, students, and diplomats, had to pay $10 per head. The tax was raised to $50 in 1896, $100 in 1900, and finally at $500 in 1904. The Chinese were the only ethnic group on whom the head tax was levied for coming to Canada (Chan 1983:11–12).

Chapter 20

1. The Chinese who first set foot in the Americas in historical times came with the Manila Galleon and landed in Acapulco in the early 1600s. This continued for the next two and a half centuries. Large numbers of Chinese went to Mexico after 1882, when the Chinese Exclusion Act was passed in the United States, and throughout the early decades of the twentieth century. They were particularly active as small store owners in the remote mining towns or agricultural settlements in the northern Mexican states. Anti-Chinese campaigns occurred sporadically from the 1880s to the 1930s (see Pan 1998).

Chapter 21

1. People of First Nations in Canada are often referred to as Indians or Native Canadians. Those who are registered as Indians have numbers, and when shopping they are exempted from paying sales tax if they can show their registration number.

2. The places mentioned in this narrative—Chemainus, Nanaimo, Koksilah, Ladysmith, and Duncan—are all on Vancouver Island, British Columbia.

Chapter 22

1. As mentioned in chapter 1, Ban Zhao completed the *Han Shu*. She wrote the section on astronomy and eight chronological tables. She possibly edited other parts of the book. For an informative discussion of Ban Zhao and her *Seven Lessons for Women*, see Lee (1994).

Chapter 23

1. Wheelis (1958) defines identity as "a coherent sense of self. It depends upon the awareness that one's endeavors and one's life make sense, that they are meaningful in the context in which life is lived. It depends also upon stable values, and upon the conviction that one's actions and values are harmoniously related. It is a sense of wholeness, of integration, of knowing what is right and what is wrong and of being able to choose" (19).

2. The early twentieth-century historian Gu Jiegang (1982) traces the notion of the common origin of all Han Chinese to the necessity of such an ideology by a unified China in the Qin and Han dynasties. According to this ideology, all the people inhabiting the Qin and Han domains belonged to the same tribe or ethnic category, thus suppressing the reality that there were different tribes or ethnic categories. The ideology thus promoted the notion that all the people within the domains, now regarded as the civilized Han people, descended from the same ancestors and originated in the same locale, the banks of the Yellow River. These notions were passed down through the millennia to the twentieth century.

3. In the same poll, Russia was picked as the greatest threat to world peace by 10 percent of the American public, United States by 8 percent, and Iran by 5 percent. The ABCNEWS.com survey was conducted by telephone July 18–22 among a random national sample of 1,022 adults. The results have an error margin of plus or minus three percentage points. The survey was done by TNS Intersearch of Horsham, Pennsylvania (ABCNEWS.com, July 24, 2001).

4. Chan (1998) points out that the term "Confucianism" has no Chinese equivalent. See also chapter 11.

5. Animism is the belief that elements of the natural world are imbued with living spirits. For example, plants, hills, and lakes all have spirits and may influence human life. Shamanist religions are characterized by a belief in gods, spirits, including ancestral spirits, and the power of the shamans, that is, priests and priestesses who can communicate with the spirits, cure the sick, divine the unknown, and thus influence human events.

Chapter 24

1. The notion of survival of the luckiest in relation to the Chinese and the Chinese overseas was emphasized by Mr. Louis Cha in a public lecture on immigration and tolerance at the International Conference on Immigrant Societies and Modern Education, September 2, 2000, Singapore. Mr. Cha is known to millions of Chinese readers since the 1950s by his pen name Jin Yong, the author of martial arts novels. He is universally popular in Hong Kong, where he wrote most of his works, and in the People's Republic of China, Republic of China on Taiwan, and the Chinese diaspora. He is currently the dean of the faculty of arts and humanities, University of Zhejiang, China, and senior research associate, Institute for Chinese Studies, Oxford University, England.

References

ABCNEWS.com. 2001. "Poll: China Tops List of Most Threatening Nations." July 24, 2001. Retrieved July 26, 2001 (http://more.abcnews.go.com/sections/world/dailynews/poll010724.html).

Anderson, Kay J. 1995. *Vancouver's Chinatown: Racial Discourse in Canada, 1875–1980*. Montreal: McGill-Queen's University Press.

Babbie, Earl. 1994. *The Sociological Spirit*. 2nd ed. Belmont, CA: Wadsworth Publishing Co.

Bai Shouyi, ed. 1982. *The Outline History of China*. Beijing: Foreign Languages Press.

Bailey, Paul. 1998. "Recruitment of Workers for Britain and France." Pp. 64–65 in *The Encyclopedia of the Chinese Overseas*, edited by Lynn Pan. Singapore: Archipelago Press.

Ban Zhao. 1968. *Seven Lessons for Women (Nujie Qipian)*. (Originally published during Eastern Han period.) Translated by Nancy Lee Swann. Pp. 82–90 in *Pan Chao: Foremost Woman Scholar of China, First Century A.D.*, Nancy Lee Swann. New York: Russell and Russell.

Book of Mencius (Meng Zi). Any edition or translation.

Book of Poetry. 1993. The Chinese-English Bilingual Series of Chinese Classics. Translated by Xu Yuanchong. Changsha: Hunan Publishing House.

Canada. Royal Commission on Chinese Immigration. 1885. *Report of the Royal Commission on Chinese Immigration*. Ottawa: Printed by Order of the Commission.

Chan, Adrian. 1995. "The Liberation of Marx in China." *Journal of Contemporary Asia* 25(1): 93–108.

———. 1997. "In Search of a Civil Society in China." *Journal of Contemporary Asia* 27(2): 242–251.

———. 1998. "A Stock-Taking on Chinese Culture: Beyond Orientalism." Presented at the Asian Cultures at the Crossroads: An East-West Dialogue in the New World Order, November 16–18, Hong Kong.

Chan, Anthony B. 1983. *Gold Mountain: The Chinese in the New World*. Vancouver, BC: New Star Books.

Chan, Sucheng. 1991. *Asian Americans: An Interpretive History*. Boston: Twayne Publishers.

Chen Bisheng. 1991. *Shijie Huaqiao Huaren Jianshi (A Brief History of Ethnic Chinese Overseas Around the World)*. Xiamen: Xiamen University Press.

Chen Guoqing and Zhang Keping, eds. 1994. *Zeng Guofan Quanji (Complete Works of Zeng Guofan)*. Xian: Xibei Daixue Chubanshe.

China Science & Technology Museum Preparatory Committee and the Ontario Science Centre. 1982. *China: 7000 Years of Discovery*. Toronto: Ontario Science Centre.

Chinese History: From Primitive Society Down Through the Qing Dynasty. 1988. Beijing: China Reconstructs Press.

Chung, Fay. 1996. *Memories of the Liberation Struggle*. Unpublished.

Confucian Analects (Lun Yu). Any edition or translation.

Dao De Jing (The Book of Lao Zi). Any edition.

Evans, Paul M. 1988. *John Fairbank and the American Understanding of Modern China*. New York: Basil Blackwell Inc.

Fan Wenlan. 1962. *Zhongguo Jindai Shi (Chinese Modern History)*. Vol. 1. Beijing: People's Press.

———. 1965. *Zhongguo Tongshi Jianpian (A Brief Chinese General History)*. Vol. 5, Part 2. Beijing: People's Publishing House.

Fung Yu-lan. 1964. *A Short History of Chinese Philosophy*. Edited by Derk Bodde. New York: The MacMillan Co.

Gould, J., and William L. Kolb, eds. 1964. *A Dictionary of the Social Sciences*. Compiled under the auspices of the United Nations Educational, Scientific and Cultural Organization. London: Tavistock.

Gu Jiegang. [1926] 1982. "Qin Han Tongyi de Youlai he Zhanguoren Dui Shijie de Xiangxiang" ("The Origin of the Qin and Han Unification of China and the Worldview of the Warring States Period.") Pp. 1–16 in *Gu Shi Bian (Discussions of Ancient Chinese History)*, Vol. 2, edited by Gu Jiegang. Shanghai: Guji Chubanshe.

Hall, Kenneth. 1988. "The Manila Galleon." Pp. 487–488 in *Encyclopedia of Asian History*, Vol. 2, edited by Ainslie T. Embree. New York: Scribner.

Hong, Lawrence K. 2001. "Chinese and Chinese Exclusion Act." Pp. 74–82 in *Encyclopedia of American Immigration*, Vol. 1, edited by James Ciment. Armonk: M.E. Sharpe, Inc.

Hsu, Immanuel C.Y. 2000. *The Rise of Modern China*. 6th ed. New York: Oxford University Press.

Hu Sheng. 1991. *From the Opium War to the May Fourth Movement*. Vols. 1 and 2. Beijing: Foreign Languages Press.

Ko, Dorothy. 1994. *Teachers of the Inner Chambers: Women and Culture in Seventeenth-Century China*. Stanford, CA: Stanford University Press.

Lai, Walton Look. 1998. "Emigration from China: Developments in the World At Large." Pp. 52–54 in *The Encyclopedia of the Chinese Overseas*, edited by Lynn Pan. Singapore: Archipelago Press.

Lau, D.C. 1975. "Introduction." Pp. 7–52 in *Lao Tzu: Tao Te Ching*, translated by D.C. Lau. London: Penguin Classics.

Lee, Lily Xiao Hong. 1994. *The Virtue of Yin: Studies on Chinese Women*. Broadway, Australia: Wild Peony Pty. Ltd.

Levathes, Louise. 1994. *When China Ruled the Seas: The Treasure Fleet of the Dragon Throne 1405–1433*. New York: Oxford University Press.

Liu Xiang. 1993. "Mother of Mencius," an excerpt from Liu Xiang's *Biographies of Eminent Women*. (Originally published during the Western Han period.) Pp. 72–74 in *Chinese Civilization: A Sourcebook*, 2nd ed., revised and expanded, edited by Patricia Buckley Ebrey. New York: The Free Press.

Liu Yuzun, Huang Chongyan, Gui Kuanhua and Wu Fengfu. 1979. *"Zhuzai" Huagong Fangwenlu (Interviews with "Zhuzai" Chinese Workers)*. Guangzhou: Zhongshan University, Southeast Asia History Research Institute.

Lo, Irving Yucheng. 1988. "Daughters of the Muses of China." Pp. 41–51 in *Views from Jade Terrace: Chinese Women Artists 1300–1912*. Indianapolis: Indianapolis Museum of Art.

Ma Yin, ed. 1989. *China's Minority Nationalities*. Beijing: Foreign Languages Press.

Macionis, John J. 1997. *Sociology*. 6th ed. Upper Saddle River, NJ: Prentice Hall.

McNeill, William H. 2000. "What We Mean by the West." *American Educator* 24(1): 10–15, 48–49.

Mills, C. Wright. 1959. *The Sociological Imagination*. New York: Oxford University Press.

The New York Times. 2000. "China Jails Tycoon for Life for Fraud." Reuters. May 30, 2000.

Pan, Lynn, ed. 1998. *The Encyclopedia of the Chinese Overseas*. Singapore: Archipelago Press.

Poston, Jr., Dudley L., Michael Xinxiang Mao, and Mei-Yu Yu. 1994. "The Global Distribution of the Overseas Chinese Around 1990." *Population and Development Review* 20(3): 631–645.

Ramsey, Bruce. 2000. "Editorial Notebook: Lessons in China." *Seattle Times*, May 3, 2000.

Said, Edward W. 1979. *Orientalism*. New York: Vintage Books.

Shen Fuwei. 1996. *Cultural Flow Between China and Outside World Throughout History*. Beijing: Foreign Languages Press.

Sima Qian. 1996. *Shiji (Historical Records)*. Beijing: Tuanji Chubanshe. (Originally published during Western Han period.)

Sklair, Leslie. 1995. *Sociology of the Global System*. 2nd ed. Baltimore: The Johns Hopkins University Press.

Spence, Jonathan D. 1990. *The Search for Modern China*. New York: W.W. Norton & Co.

Stanley, Timothy. 1996. "Chinamen, Wherever We Go: Chinese Nationalism and Guangdong Merchants in British Columbia 1871–1911." *Canadian Historical Review* 77(4): 475–503.

Su Kaiming. 1986. *Modern China: A Topical History 1840–1983*. Beijing: New World Press.

Sun Yu. 1982. "Introduction." Pp. 18–49 in *Li Po: A New Translation*, translated by Sun Yu. Hong Kong: The Commercial Press.

Takaki, Ronald. 1989. *Strangers from a Different Shore: A History of Asian Americans*. Boston: Little, Brown and Company.

Tan Tianxing. 1998. "Xiandai Zhongguo Shaoshu Minzu Renkou Jingwai

Qianyi Chutan" ("A Preliminary Investigation into the Migration of People Minority Nationalities in Modern China"). Pp. 447–461 in *The Last Half Century of Chinese Overseas*, edited by Elizabeth Sinn. Hong Kong: Hong Kong University Press.

Wang Gungwu. 1991. "The Study of Chinese Identities in Southeast Asia." Pp. 198–221 in *China and the Chinese Overseas*. Singapore: Times Academic Press.

———. 2000. *The Chinese Overseas: From Earthbound China to the Quest for Autonomy*. Cambridge, MA: Harvard University Press.

Wheelis, Allen. 1958. *The Quest for Identity*. New York: Norton.

Wolf, Eric. 1982. *Europe and the People Without History*. Berkeley, CA: University of California Press.

Yi Jing (The Book of Changes). Any edition or translation.

Yin, Robert K. 1984. *Case Study Research: Design and Methods*. Beverly Hills: Sage Publications.

Yung, Yuk-wai Li. 1995. *The Huaqiao Warriors: Chinese Resistance Movement in the Philippines 1942–45*. Hong Kong: Hong Kong University Press.

Zhou Shide. 1986. "Shipbuilding." Pp. 479–493 in *Ancient China's Technology and Science*. Compiled by the Institute of the History of Natural Sciences, Chinese Academy of Sciences. Beijing: Foreign Languages Press.

Zhu Guohong. 1994. *Zhongguo Haiqai Yimin: Yixiang Qianyi de Lizhi Yanjiu (Chinese Emigration: A Historical Study of the International Migration)*. Shanghai: Fudan University Press.

Zhu Xiuxia, ed. 1956. *Huaqiao Zhi Zongzhi (The Complete Record of the Overseas Chinese)*. Taipei: Haiwai Publishing Co.

Index

About the Author

Wei Djao is a tenured professor of global/Asian studies and sociology at North Seattle Community College.

Born in China, Dr. Djao grew up in Shanghai and Hong Kong. She has a Ph.D. in sociology from the University of Toronto, specializing in China. She was a tenured associate professor of sociology at the University of Saskatchewan and also taught in Alberta, Canada; Hong Kong; and California before coming to Seattle.

Wei has written two books: *Inequality and Social Policy: The Sociology of Welfare* (Toronto: John Wiley & Sons, 1983), and *Choices and Chances: Sociology for Everyday Life* (San Diego, CA: Harcourt Brace Jovanovich, 1990, co-author: Lorne Tepperman).

Her articles have appeared in scholarly journals, such as *Canadian Ethnic Studies, Journal of Contemporary Asia, Journal of Sociology and Social Welfare, Canadian Review of Social Policy, Service Social,* and *Social Praxis,* as well as in edited books published in Canada, China, and the United States.

Professor Djao's research and teaching interests include the global society, Chinese society, women of color, Pacific Rim studies, and the Chinese overseas. She is writing a book on the twelfth-century Song dynasty female poet Li Qingzhao.

She was the interviewer, narrator, writer, or researcher in the production of three television documentaries: *American Nurse* (an award-winning thirty-minute program about the experiences of New York–born Chinese American veteran of the Vietnam War Lily Lee Adams); *Another Day in America* (a documentary on Japanese American women artists in the San Francisco Bay area); and *Chinese Cafes in Rural Saskatchewan.* These documentaries are in the video collections of libraries in Canada, the United States, Hong Kong, and Singapore.

Professor Djao lives with her husband and daughter in Seattle. She enjoys hiking and cross-country skiing. She also does botanical illustration with Chinese brushes.